589240
Ship

D1634865

Southampton
SOLENT
University

WARSASH LIBRARY
Tel: 0148 955 6269

Please return this book no later than the date stamped.
Loans may usually be renewed - in person, by phone,
or via the web OPAC. Failure to renew or return on time
may result in an accumulation of penalty points.

Titles in the *Objekt* series explore a range of types – buildings, products, artefacts – that have captured the imagination of modernist designers, makers and theorists. The objects selected for the series are by no means all modern inventions, but they have in common the fact that they acquired a particular significance in the last 100 years.

Ship

Gregory Votolato

REAKTION BOOKS

For Phoebe

Published by Reaktion Books Ltd
33 Great Sutton Street
London EC1V 0DX, UK

www.reaktionbooks.co.uk

First published 2011

Printed and bound in China by Eurasia

British Library Cataloguing in Publication Data
Gregory Votolato.
    Ship. — (Objekt)
    1. Naval architecture—History.
    2. Ships—History.
    I. Title
    623.8'1-dc22
    ISBN: 978 1 86189 772 5

Contents

Introduction

Looking out from my window over one of the busiest sea lanes in the world, the English Channel, I strain to glimpse a ship. If I am vigilant, once or twice a day I may catch sight of a tanker delivering oil to the local Texaco terminal or a general cargo ship carrying Norwegian timber into the small but busy port of Shoreham a few miles along the coast. Occasionally, a little sailing yacht, a few jet skis or a flock of wind surfers will come into view. Otherwise, on a clear day the surface of the sea is an empty space ending in a crisp, unblemished horizon. From here on the shore, those cargo vessels that glide past appear large. Typically between 2,000 and 3,000 gross tons (the carrying capacity of a ship) with an overall length of around 90 m (300 ft), they travel long distances, from the Baltic and the Mediterranean, as well as plying British coastal routes. Yet size is relative, and these are minnows as compared with today's ultra-large ships with capacities as much as 550,000 tons.

From land, however, even such gigantic cargo vessels and the largest cruise liners quickly slip over the horizon to be lost from sight and from mind until they reappear along another coast or reach another port. And so, the largest moving objects on earth are invisible for most of their active lives, largely forgotten by the majority of the human population, many of whom depend on them for nearly

The 113,000-ton cruise liner *Crown Princess* moored in the harbour at Newport, Rhode Island, in 2009.

everything we consume. They are perceived like water in a pipeline, unnoticed until it flows from the kitchen tap into our kettle. Yet unlike water or air, another necessity we do not see and take for granted, they are astounding feats of human ingenuity and enterprise, although those who design and build them are almost entirely unknown to the general public. As the architect Le Corbusier wrote in 1923, when steamships were the only means of transport between continents and much more familiar objects than they are today,

> Engineers unknown to the world at large, mechanics, in shop and forge have conceived and constructed these formidable affairs that steamships are . . . our daring and masterly constructors of steamships produce palaces in comparison with which cathedrals are tiny things, and they throw them on to the sea![1]

Le Corbusier analyzed the proportions of ocean liners as models for his rationalist architecture of the 1920s. He studied their spatial configurations in terms of axes, volumes and vistas, and he noted, 'elements both vast and intimate, but on man's scale'.[2] Yet he never discussed the effect of their constantly shifting positions to our perception of them as objects or as spaces. Other modernist art theorists and practitioners, including Guillaume Apollinaire, Filippo Tommaso Marinetti and Alexander Calder, examined spatial relations between people and moving objects through the fine arts, while recent scholars of mechanized transport have expanded the investigation to include the car, train and aeroplane.[3] The ship, however, seldom enters the frame.

Ships look entirely different close up than from a distant shore or from a low flying airplane, while a voyager on board gets another, often confusing sense of the size and complexity of a large vessel. If experience is determined by your vantage point, then the ship is a designed object about which this phenomenon is most acutely apparent and ultimately significant. To find a rounded, multi-faceted view of the modern ship as a product of our age, this book presents a variety of different perspectives on the ways in which ships are understood, from those who design them, construct them, operate them, travel aboard them, regulate them, attack them, mythologize them or break them up.

Despite their mysterious existence at sea, ships generate power-ful feelings among those who live and work with them and even for some aficionados who simply observe them, perhaps only from pictures, written accounts and artists' representations. However, a real gap exists between the intimacy felt by mariners toward their ships and the incomprehension of many people who have no direct connection with the sea, for the vessels that bring them most of the goods they desire, possess and consume. Within the vast literature on ships, little of it aims specifically to involve the landlubber in an historical appreciation of what ships signify or how they have achieved their current roles and importance in our everyday lives. In this book I aim to do that by explaining the ship as an everyday object, like an aircraft or a factory, influencing the way we live even though it may rarely be seen and even less commonly be experi-enced at first hand.

Vessels are always unique, even those that have been mass-pro-duced. Their construction is tailored to specifications that distinguish them, if only slightly, from their siblings, and they are often altered subsequently. As with buildings, such distinctiveness of design im-parts to every ship a personality that may be either endearing or irritating in use. In addition to possessing personality, ships are also considered lucky or unlucky, a trait that results less from design than from the ship's history and performance in the testing condi-tions under which it operates. Thus, an aura of superstition hangs around all vessels that venture out into the ocean wilderness, adding to their mythic status.

In addition to the enigmatic condition of ships at sea, their changing purposes during the past two hundred years have left a confusing legacy. Their functions have evolved from moving people and goods to entertaining holidaymakers and from conveying a small percentage of the world's most expensive products and materials to carrying nine-tenths of the world's commonest commodities in our global economy. Since the 1950s the replacement of the passenger ship by the airplane as the primary vehicle of long-distance travel has made the ship seem remote and irrelevant despite a vast increase in the world's shipping tonnage, our continuing reliance on large long-distance ferries, and the heavy dependence of modern society on sea-borne cargoes. The military presence of the ship has also been transformed from a singularly imposing image of might and authority in the period of colonialism to that of a stealthy hybrid vessel of multiple capabilities in today's amorphous political climate of cold wars and terrorism. Except for publicity appearances and open days, secrecy is the rule for most military vessels, while even commercial container shipping is known as a 'stealth industry' because of its relative invisibility.

The twenty-first-century ship is still our largest and most expensive moving object; and modern cruise liners, supertankers or aircraft carriers continually push the boundaries of marine technology to their current limits. Yet they are replete with problems. When they fail, their failure is devastating to those on board and often to the natural environment as well. Their day-to-day functioning can be criticized for its profligate waste of natural resources and its contribution of pollutants to ecological imbalances and to global warming. The sea, their working domain, remains the most regularly hostile and unpredictable of environments. Danger is not only a result of the weather but also of actions by people who operate ships, both those working on board and others, who influence from land how ships behave at sea. And the negative effects of ships on the cultures and communities they visit can be slowly corrosive or instantly devastating.

Although the patterns of shipping at sea are to some extent regulated by charted lanes and channels physically marked by lighthouses and buoys, ships have little visible infrastructure except in port, where harbour walls, jetties, docks, cranes, warehouses, customs offices and intermodal links, such as rail heads and air-freight terminals, make the business of a ship material. The changing shape and nature of military, cargo or tourist ports provide hard evidence of what ships are and what they do, and these distinctive places serve as gateways to the maritime world. For those who enjoy leisure cruising, the port may be a desirable, exotic tourist destination, a place to view from an upper deck and then to explore briefly while shopping and dining. Yet the extravagance and innovative design of the cruise liner can overshadow the attractions of the places they visit for some voyagers, who might prefer rock climbing on the lido deck to rock climbing on a natural cliff.

Finally, my main aim in writing this book is to uncover how our images, experiences and impressions of the ship relate to the physical reality of these designed objects, extraordinary feats of human ingenuity, capital investment, folly and hubris. For those writing the history of an object type, the German historian Siegfried Giedion advised: 'What is essential is the panoramic and simultaneous view . . . for only through simultaneous perception of various periods and of various fields within a period can there be insight into the inner growth.'[4] I hope that this panoramic and simultaneous view will offer some fresh insight into the inner growth of the ship.

WHITE STAR LINE
TRIPLE SCREW STEAMER
882½ FT.
LONG
"OLYMPIC"
46,359
TONS

1 Voyager

Stormy Weather

Lying face up in my bunk, the uppermost one, I thought about my family and about the voyage we would have to make before reaching Cartagena. I couldn't sleep. With my head resting in my hands, I listened to the soft splash of water against the pier and the calm breathing of forty sailors sleeping in their quarters. Just below my bunk, Seaman First Class Luis Rengifo snored like a trombone. I don't know what he was dreaming about, but he certainly wouldn't have slept so soundly had he known that eight days later he would be dead at the bottom of the sea.[1]

In *The Story of a Shipwrecked Sailor*, Luis Alejandro Velasco, a seaman in the Colombian Navy, recalled hearing the alarming command, 'All hands to the Starboard side!', issued to stabilize a dangerously listing ship, the destroyer *Caldas*, during a fierce storm in the Gulf of Mexico in 1955. Worrying in his bunk a week before the voyage, Velasco was yet to learn that all those who live together aboard any ship may also, in a catastrophe, die together, although such shared sleeping quarters of ordinary naval seamen may intimate through their very communality that all their occupants are subject to the same forces of nature and chance.

The inveterate world cyclist Josie Dew offered a less foreboding account of her apprehension regarding the decrepit cargo vessel on which she travelled as a passenger, also in stormy weather:

> men and women are destined always to make a small world in the midst of a big one . . . When I'm camping . . . I make a little nest around me . . . because it makes me feel better . . . [And] here we are, on this insignificant lump of rusty metal making a small world in the enormousness of a very watery one . . . We all go about our daily routines . . . Just like on land. And yet we are not on land! . . . Instead we're bobbing about on the most ancient place on earth – a malicious primal force that plays havoc with human lives.[2]

According to the philosopher Gaston Bachelard, storms demonstrate the strength of any shelter, while the robustness of that structure enables its occupant to appreciate the aesthetic drama and excitement of the storm. This idea of the protected interior, in relation to the dangerous immensity of the outside, is the single most inescapable

'Between the decks' of an ocean steamer in 1885 during a storm.

fact of the sea-going vessel and a central concern in both its design and interpretation.[3]

In the earliest days of the transatlantic steamship, Charles Dickens wrote bitingly of his first North Atlantic crossing in mid-winter aboard one of Samuel Cunard's new paddle-wheel liners, *Britannia*, launched in 1840. Dickens famously described his 'state-room' as a 'thoroughly hopeless, and profoundly preposterous box'. It failed in every way to live up to the promotional literature displayed at the Cunard offices in London. Dickens compared its two bunk beds to coffins, and he avoided the cabin as long as the weather allowed him to stay on deck or in the public saloons. The primitive design and construction of the wooden ship provided a poor defence against the effects of the storm raging outside. Even with the portholes closed and the hatches battened down, seawater washed freely through the passenger quarters. When seasickness finally took hold, the cabin and the bunk were his last and only resort. Dickens noted that several berths were full of water and all the cabins were leaky. He added that below decks the stuffiness of the air was worsened by a 'compound of strange smells, which is to be found nowhere but on board ship, and which is such a subtle perfume that it seems to enter at every pore of the skin, and whisper of the hold'.[4] Although the historian Stephen Fox has argued that Dickens exaggerated the effects of bad weather aboard *Britannia* to make a better story for his readers, it remains true that the cabin in a storm was always a dubious refuge for travellers.[5]

This was confirmed by a young seaman, who travelled through many a storm in the Roaring Forties (an area of infamously turbulent seas in the southern hemisphere between 40 and 50 degrees Latitude) during the early twentieth century. He described the discomfort of the sailor's wooden berth, the thin, soggy mattress built up at the outer edge by anything that came to hand, coiled rope,

clothing or canvas, to restrain the seaman's recumbent body. 'We fit down into a V between the mattress and the sidewalls and can't be rolled out. Even at that, we frequently have to brace ourselves against the upright stanchions to stay in. Frankly, the bunks are about the least inviting spots on the ship.'[6]

One hundred years later Josie Dew concurred. This outdoors woman, driven by foul weather to her passenger cabin aboard the container ship *Speybank*, recorded her attempts to find some peace and quiet in her cabin, where she found the cupboard drawers crashing in and out with each roll of the vessel. Adapting her cycling gear, ad hoc, to the cabin's built-in furniture, she endeavoured to establish a semblance of calm. She 'rigged up elaborate drawer-ramming devices involving heavy panniers, gaffer tape and tightly stretched bungees' and, like earlier sailors, wedged herself against the bunk's preventer board, trying to sleep, 'Not an easy thing to accomplish when your body is being jolted about your bunk from one shoulder blade to the other in time with the ship's violently

Cramped and leaky, but well upholstered: a first-class cabin aboard an early transatlantic steamship, SS *Great Britain*.

rowelling jerks and shudders. So instead I lay listening to the howling wind and the rhythmic banging of a nearby door.'[7]

When Bachelard compares the nooks or corners where we enjoy curling up in our homes to a snail in its shell, he reflects Dew's attempt to find security and comfort in her spartan bunk, just as Henry David Thoreau found sanctuary in the smallest and simplest of huts, his built on the edge of Walden Pond as a refuge from the nineteenth-century world. There, he extolled the virtues of 'economy' and, like Bachelard, the close fit between occupants and cabins, 'whose shells they are'.[8] Thoreau described his house as 'a sort of crystallisation' around him, and when the winter storm raged over the pond outside, he sat behind the securely closed door and enjoyed its protection.[9]

While Dew described a relatively chaste adventure at sea, the novelist Evelyn Waugh exploited the North Atlantic storm as a catalyst for romance aboard the largest, fastest and most popular liner of the 1930s, *Queen Mary*, bound for England from New York. In Waugh's

A sleek modern cabin aboard the fast ro-pax ferry *Stena Hollandica*, which can carry 300 cars and 900 cabin passengers in considerable comfort.

Brideshead Revisited (1945), the central character, Charles Ryder, falls in love with a woman who, like himself, resists the effects of sea-sickness while most other passengers, including Ryder's wife, are confined to their staterooms. Ryder describes his effort to sleep in the large bed of a palatial first-class suite:

> In a narrow bunk, on a hard mattress, there might have been rest, but here the beds were broad and buoyant; I collected what cushions I could find and tried to wedge myself firm, but through the night I turned with each swing and twist of the ship – she was rolling now as well as pitching – and my head rang with the creek and thud which now succeeded the hum of fine weather . . . And all night between dreaming and waking I thought of Julia; in my brief dreams she took a hundred fantastic and terrible and obscene forms.[10]

The cabin in a storm is portrayed here as a locus of erotic fantasy. The stateroom, like a bedroom in a large country house, connects by corridors and stairs with all the other rooms, public and private, where the object of desire may be found. Yet, aboard a tossing steamship the privacy and separateness of the cabins are made more poignant by the difficulty of negotiating those stairs and corridors. 'We were both weary; lack of sleep, the incessant din and the strain every movement required, wore us down.'[11] Yet the intimacy found during the storm in the ship's private cabins and grand, empty public rooms heightens the lovers' sense of isolation from the rest of the shipboard community:

> We dined that night high up in the ship, in the restaurant, and saw through the bow windows the stars come out and sweep across the sky . . . The stewards promised that to-morrow night the band would play again and the place would be full. We had better book now, they said,

if we wanted a good table. 'Oh dear', said Julia, 'where can we hide in fair weather, we orphans of the storm?' I could not leave her that night, but early next morning, as once again, I made my way back along the corridor, I found I could walk without difficulty; the ship rode easily on a smooth sea, and I knew that our solitude was broken.[12]

Economy

While the 1840s had seen the development of the transatlantic steamship as a viable technical and commercial proposition, led by the engineering innovation of Isambard Kingdom Brunel and the entrepreneurial talent of Samuel Cunard, during the following fifty years the ocean liner evolved toward its mature form. And during those years steamships serviced the greatest voluntary migrations in human history, first from the ports of northern Europe and later from eastern Europe and the Mediterranean to the ports of North America, South America and Australia. During those five decades, when the North Atlantic passenger route was busiest, the ships that provided that shuttle service grew continuously in size, power and sophistication. These were the largest moving objects yet constructed and the most ambitious technical achievements of the Industrial Revolution.

Brunel's *Great Britain*, launched in 1843 and dubbed the world's first ocean liner, was a marvel of its age and by far the largest ship of the time at 98.15 m (322 ft) and 3,675 tons. Its first crossing to New York took just fourteen days and twenty-one hours at an average speed of 9 knots. The ship's innovative iron clinker-built hull was constructed with five watertight bulkheads for safety, and this was the first vessel with a balanced rudder for easy handling. Powered by a 1,000 horsepower engine turning a six-bladed propeller, the *Great Britain* was also rigged as a six-masted schooner (the first such) for additional speed, stability, security and economy. For comfort, the interiors were richly decorated, and all cabins were steam-heated. The *United Service Gazette* dramatized its size, calling it 'the largest vessel that has been constructed since the days of Noah'.[13]

The ship's transatlantic service between 1845 and 1847 demonstrated the potential of steam, iron and screw propulsion, but failed, due to a variety of unfortunate circumstances and significant navigational blunders, to achieve satisfactory financial returns for its owner, the Great Western Steamship Company, which became insolvent and sold the ship at auction in 1850. For the next twenty-five years *Great Britain* served the Australia route, carrying a generation of new emigrants to Melbourne from Britain in response to the Australian Gold Rush. For this purpose, the ship was converted to run as a steam-assisted sailing ship rather than a sail-assisted steamship, since it was not yet possible to bunker sufficient coal for a full run under engine power over such a great distance, a passage lasting around 60 days. Subsequently, the *Great Britain* made 32 trips to Melbourne, carrying up to 730 passengers in three classes.

On its first Australian voyage in 1852, the American Consul in Liverpool, the writer Nathaniel Hawthorne, rode the ship as far as Holyhead Light and reported 'immense enthusiasm amongst the English people about this ship, on account of her being the largest in the world. The shores were lined with people to see her sail.'[14] All this excitement over a ship that was already nine years old and converted from a radical design to a more conventional mode of propulsion!

The period of transition between sail and steam, between the 1830s and the 1860s, was characterized by an intense rivalry between the fast sailing ship, which was reaching its peak of perfection in terms of efficiency, speed and elegance, and the primitive new paddle-wheel steamship, which was experimental. During these years, Bostonian

Lauchlan McKay's treatise on marine architecture, *The Practical Shipbuilder* of 1839, explained the design of hulls and spars for the fastest sailing ships, while John Griffiths, also from Boston, defined the specifications of the mature clipper hull. The swift clipper ships designed and run by Donald and Lauchlan McKay dominated the lucrative tea trade during these years, when steamships could not yet carry enough fuel for voyages from Europe and North America to the Orient. And unlike the inefficient coal-burning steamships, clippers were cheap to run.

With such sophisticated and economical sailing vessels, Enoch Train and his cousin George Francis Train founded a shipping line that catered to the North Atlantic, Latin America and California trade routes. The McKays designed and built for them the 3,000-ton *Enoch*

The last word in grace and speed under sail, the clipper *Red Jacket* is pictured off Cape Horn in 1854 by Currier & Ives.

Train, the largest clipper of the day when launched in 1852, of which the *Boston Daily Atlas* wrote: 'In stowage capacity, strength of construction, and beauty of outline, she ranks the foremost of the clipper fleet. Never was there a ship to which the term beautiful was more appropriately applied.'[15] As a result of the Potato Famine in Ireland, annual immigration from Europe to the United States jumped from around 50,000 in 1846 to 300,000 in 1875; and in response these New England entrepreneurs answered this massive demand for cheap passage by outfitting the cargo holds of their economical sailing packets with as many as 400 closely stacked berths. They provided freshwater barrels in the hold plus a cooking shack on deck. Below-deck spaces were dark and badly ventilated. Sanitation was nil. In such conditions, which nearly equated in horror to those of slaving ships, their vessels carried the first generation of Irish emigrants to Boston and New York.[16]

This steerage-class dormitory aboard Brunel's technically innovative SS *Great Britain* (1,000 horsepower, iron hull, screw propeller) could easily be mistaken for that of a contemporary sailing ship of the 1840s.

In the 1840s and '50s even the fastest sailing ships still took around six weeks to sail, in a zigzag pattern, across the Atlantic, whereas a paddle-wheel steamer could make the crossing in ten to twelve days by travelling directly along the 'Great Circle', the shortest distance between the ports of the United Kingdom and those of the north-eastern United States. Yet the fare required to run such ships was far too high for the impoverished emigrants sailing to the United States. Thus, the first generation of fast transatlantic steamships was primarily designed for well-to-do passengers, including Charles Dickens. The wealthy steamed; most emigrants sailed.

The inevitable breakthrough in servicing the emigrant trade came from the innovative shipbuilding industry of the River Clyde near Glasgow in Scotland. In 1850 the company Tod & McGregor constructed the 1,600-ton, 72-m (237-ft) *City of Glasgow*, which could carry 52 passengers in first class, 38 in second class and 400 in steerage. Although the screw propeller was gradually becoming recognized as the superior driving mechanism for a steamship, inefficient single-expansion engines generated only enough steam pressure to propel a slow-turning paddle wheel. The *City of Glasgow*'s combination of a stiff iron hull to secure a long propeller shaft and a double-expansion engine to provide greater power made the propeller effective. With its advanced engineering and construction, including five watertight compartments, a long, narrow clipper hull and an efficient engine that consumed only a third of the amount of coal required by its paddle-wheel contemporaries, the *City of Glasgow* became the first Atlantic steamship capable of serving the fast-growing emigrant trade economically.

Originally designed as a passenger-cargo vessel, the *City of Glasgow* was converted by the Liverpool and Philadelphia Steamship Company, later re-branded as the Inman Line, to carry steerage passengers in the former cargo hold. Thus equipped, the Inman Line

eventually became the leading, low-cost specialist carrier of human cargo.[17] The ship's cabin-class accommodations (first and second class) were luxurious enough to appeal to wealthier travellers, and so Inman also became the first steamship line to offer both first-class comfort and large steerage capacity, an innovative and economically advantageous formula.

Founded by a partnership of Irish investors, Inman dominated the service from famine-stricken Ireland to the eastern ports of the United States between the 1850s and the mid-1880s. And it was during those decades that the major advances in safety and comfort for steerage passengers were instituted, largely due to the Quaker consciences of the line's founders, and primarily that of John Grubb Richardson, a benevolent capitalist and pioneer of model workers' housing at his industrial colony of Bessbrook near Belfast, a development in advance of W. H. Lever's Port Sunlight, George Cadbury's Bournville and Joseph Rowntree's New Eastwick.

An engraving depicting the horrors of steerage in an emigrant ship, c. 1875.

Although Inman liners accommodated their steerage passengers in open dormitories, housing around twenty in stacked rows of bunks and providing the cheapest food available, their layout was intended to offer increased security and comfort for all emigrants paying the 8-shilling fare typically charged in the mid-1850s. Single men and single women were housed at either end of steerage, separated by married couples and families, ensuring a degree of propriety previously unavailable to female travellers. Although the quality of food was reported to be variable, the quantities were sufficient and, to the poorest emigrants, may have been more plentiful than what they were accustomed to eating at home. They did not, however, benefit from the service of stewards and stewardesses, being left to air their mattresses and wash their own dishes on deck. Edward Steiner described the features that came to identify steerage from his personal emigrant experience in the 1880s:

The odor of strong disinfectants, mingling with that of various vegetables, the smell of sheep skin coats and of booted and unbooted feet, the cries of many children, the rough answers of sailors and stewards and the babel of guttural languages are all waymarks, if any are needed . . . When one has slid down two and sometimes three flights of iron stairs, located at the narrowest point of fore or aft, and sees a crowded space which may hold from sixty to six hundred passengers who are tucking themselves away on a series of narrow shelves – then he is in the steerage. It is his first business to find a vacant bunk, and having found it, stake it by placing his belongings there. On the way he will have bestowed upon him various tin utensils and a thin gray cotton blanket, so that the aforementioned shelf becomes his dining-room, dressing-room, parlour and sleeping room: unless the Fates are kind and the Atlantic is quiet enough to leave a dry spot somewhere on the narrow margin of the deck. The faster the boat, the less likely he is to find this dry spot, for the prow digs itself into the sea and is almost inundated, while the stern is so taken up by machinery and hatchways that even in a moderate sea it affords no comfort.[18]

Most important to steerage passengers travelling by steamship, the uncomfortable time spent aboard was now reduced from six weeks to two, and the risk of on-board epidemics, a serious threat to emigrants on sailing ships, was dramatically reduced.

Danger was never far away, however. Inman ships were typical of liners of the time in carrying only enough lifeboats for cabin passengers and crew. It was in this respect that steerage passengers truly became cargo, which was seen as expendable in the event of a catastrophe. William Inman, the line's owner, had travelled to Philadelphia on the *City of Glasgow* freighted with 400 emigrants to appraise the dangers they might present. He was afraid of fire beginning below

Emigrants taking the air en route to America, c. 1902. Steerage quarters were notoriously malodorous.

decks, a cause of some of the worst ocean disasters, but upon landing declared of the steerage passengers that he had 'learned to look upon them as the safest cargo . . . fire could not break out without some living person on board immediately knowing about it'.[19] Yet fire was only one of several causes of deaths at sea. Icebergs in the North Atlantic, navigational errors, collisions between ships and unexplained disappearances were all reported in the press on a regular basis. The disappearance of the *City of Glasgow* in 1854, after four years of reliable service and with the loss of an estimated 480 lives, became the worst ocean disaster to that date and remained so for another twenty years.

Luxury, economy, size and speed allied uneasily throughout the history of the ocean liner. When launched in 1850, the American-owned Collins Line's *Baltic*, *Atlantic*, *Pacific* and *Arctic* became the fastest and most luxurious liners on the Atlantic. They were designed by the prominent New York naval architect George Steers

White Star's *Atlantic* was wrecked on the Nova Scotia coast in 1873 killing 562 people, the worst civilian death toll at sea for the next 30 years, a statistic aggravated by the loss of nearly all the women and children while most crewmen survived.

and engineered by John Faron. Edward Knight Collins was subsidised by the US Post Office to run a bi-weekly North Atlantic mail service, and his wooden-hulled paddle steamers of 2,700 tons and 86 m (283 ft) achieved a top speed of 12 knots, which enabled them to make the westward crossing in under ten days, Collins is credited with bringing speed and glamour to the transatlantic steamship at a time when his chief competitor, Cunard, was trading on a reputation for safety with rather spartan ships. Alongside the mail, Collins touted for the custom of the rich American traveller, who was typically in a hurry.

To woo them his ships offered lavishly furnished public rooms, carpeted, steam-heated cabins, each with a commode and running water, a dedicated men's smoking parlour, a barbershop and hairdresser, and the most extensive bathing facilities of the time. Referring to the Collins ships, historian John A. Butler wrote: 'Bathing facilities were practically nil until the advent of the American steamships. Fresh water was not plentiful. Cologne, cigars, heavy outer clothing, and reduced nasal sensitivity helped to defer the task that most faced before the eventual landfall' – passengers and crew cleaning themselves and the clothing in which they would go ashore.[20] To reassure many justifiably nervous passengers, Collins advertised a doctor as part of the ship's crew. His ships served four elaborate meals per day and offered a popular soda fountain for snacks. Yet all this speed and luxury came at a price: Collins's ships burned approximately twice the amount of coal used by the more carefully operated Cunarders. The company always ran in the red and was wound up after losing its mail contract in 1858.

Yet during the early 1850s Collins Line's *Pacific* and *Baltic* vied with Cunard's steamers for the Blue Riband, winning in 1850, 1851 and 1854 partly because Collins's ships were pushed to their technical limits, in order to achieve speed well beyond the cautious

safety restrictions Cunard imposed on its captains. The result was the shocking loss of a number of ships, including the line's flagship *Arctic* with a prestigious roster of passengers, among them relatives of its captain, company executives and Edward Collins's own wife and children. The *Arctic* sank near Cape Race, Newfoundland, following a full-speed collision in fog with the French steamship *Vesta* and causing the deaths of an estimated 350 people. The *Arctic* catastrophe prompted not only the consideration of crew conduct in the event of accident, since in this case the crew saved themselves without regard for the passengers, but also highlighted the need for new navigational rules. US naval officer Matthew Fontaine Maury's *Steam Lanes Across the Atlantic*, published the year after the sinking, called for separate east- and west-bound shipping lanes 100 miles apart to avoid collisions and to keep shipping clear of the worst icefields. His recommendations were soon accepted and implemented.

Collins Line's flagship, *Arctic*, the most splendid ocean liner of its day, also became the most notorious when it sank after a collision with a French steamer in 1854. Accusations of recklessness and cowardice sullied the Collins Line's reputation.

In the following decades progress in passenger ship construction was relentless. Iron and later steel replaced wooden hulls. Double and triple expansion engines driving twin propellers made paddle wheels obsolete, while the reliability and power of the new engines rendered rigging for sails unnecessary. Straight stems supplanted clipper bows, and eventually all vestiges of the sailing ship disappeared from steamship design. Internal layouts also evolved with increased size. The number of decks multiplied, those higher up in the ship, away from the engines, becoming the most comfortable and desirable. With the disappearance of paddle wheels and the removal of propulsion machinery to the stern, the amidships area became the quietest and most stable position for dining rooms, which could span the breadth of the ship. White Star Line's flagship, *Oceanic*, launched in 1870 and considered to be the first modern ocean liner, was 143 m (470 ft) long and 3,700 tons. Its successor, White Star's *Oceanic* of 1899, was 214.5 m (704 ft) long and 17,274 tons. Horsepower leapt from the *Baltic*'s 814 to 28,000 for the second *Oceanic*. By 1900 the record for a westward journey was five days and fifteen hours at 22.5 knots, reduced from nearly fifteen days for the *Great Britain*.

The continual enlargement of vessels had several purposes, of which economy was first in importance to the steamship lines, and especially those running the so-called greyhounds, the fastest international mail-carrying ships. The more passengers, mail and cargo on board, the better the profit. The more coal on board, the longer the possible journey. Enlargement was also a response to the expansion of international business and the commerce in manufactured goods, as ships combined passenger and freight haulage. Greater size increased speed, a significant attraction for business passengers and eventually too for those who had to endure the less salubrious conditions of steerage. Size also suggested stability and safety, although it did not deliver either consistently.

Community and Privacy

In naval vessels, where interior space is severely cramped, berths have historically been occupied by two or three different sailors in a round-the-clock rota, providing no private space for any individual in what might be a very long tour of duty. The de-personalizing effect of such a living situation is, of course, congruent with life in the military, where individual needs are, de facto, subordinated to the regime of discipline and to the purpose of the group. Passenger ships, however, traditionally set a high premium on privacy and provided designers with the challenge of offering a semblance of insulation from the society of fellow passengers.

In 1835 the American traveller Richard Ingraham described the escape offered within the open-plan cabin of an early Mississippi River steamboat by his sleeping berth, 'where I could draw the rich crimsoned curtains around me, and with a book or pen pass the time somewhat removed from the bustle, and undisturbed by the constant passing of the restless passengers'.[21] Thus, a private space afforded by curtaining allowed the nineteenth-century passenger to retreat from the society of the ship by the very simplest of physical barriers, one that would also become commonplace in later nineteenth-century Pullman sleeping cars.

Aboard today's enormous single-class cruise ships the size and position of a cabin or stateroom determine the fare as well as con-firming the status of its occupant. Similarly, in the spartan cabins of military and cargo vessels, the quality and position of a cabin or bunk are as much a signifier of rank as the uniform one wears. David Stevenson recalled with satisfaction his first private cabin as a newly promoted officer aboard a worn-out twenty-year-old British oil tanker in the early 1940s: 'My cabin . . . was in the forward star-board corner of the bridge house. The usual fitments. Two ports, the

bunk running under. Settee on forward bulkhead with the wardrobe at one end. After bulkhead with desk and wash basin. Still, she was comfortable.'[22] Such homely comfort, derived from an appreciation of the bare necessities, was enhanced by the privilege of privacy.

Inspired by his transatlantic voyage of 1867 on Brunel's *Great Eastern*, Jules Verne, in his novel *Propeller Island* (1895), portrayed a self-contained society living on a fantastically huge vessel, a haven for the very rich and an insulator against other strata of society, slowly roaming the Pacific seeking perfect weather and pausing occasionally at beauty spots. This immense floating structure, *Standard Island*, was designed to appear indistinguishable from a natural island. Its rich 10,000 denizens included Goulds, Vanderbilts, Rockefellers; even the service workers living on board were endowed with at least a million dollars, eliminating any economic class division within the community. At 4.5 by 3 miles, the vessel featured two ports, farmland, pasture and parkland and its own city, Milliard. Electric tramways and carriage drives connected the mansions, hotels, shops and public buildings, all built of aluminium, artificial stone and

With barely 46 cm (18 in.) between mattresses, a sailor's bunk is no place for the claustrophobic.

glass for lightness, like the ocean greyhounds of the period. Supported by 270,000 steel watertight compartments, the vessel was electrically powered by two power stations, comparable to the electric engine layouts of today's largest construction ships, such as those that build offshore wind farms. Verne asked: 'what was the island but an immense ship?', also anticipating by a century the immense floating theme parks that are the twenty-first century's single-class cruise ships.

By contrast with *Standard Island*, no clearer stratification of rich, middle class and poor could be imagined than that designed into the ocean liners of the late nineteenth and early twentieth centuries. In 1967 Michel Foucault wrote: 'the ship is a piece of floating space, a placeless place, that lives by its own devices, that is self-enclosed and, at the same time, delivered over to the boundless expanse of

Like Verne's Standard Island, *The World* is a 21st-century, seagoing residential community for the super-rich slowly cruising the world's oceans in pursuit of entertainment and perfect weather.

the ocean, [it] . . . is the heterotopia par excellence'.[23] Despite the
rigid class barriers imposed by steamship companies during an
age of violent class struggle and the constant threat of revolution,
enterprising lower-class passengers found ways to enjoy the lavish
pleasures of the upper decks, while upper-class passengers occasionally seized the opportunity for relatively safe 'slumming'
available within the microcosmic society of the ocean liner. Such a
scenario was dramatized famously in James Cameron's film *Titanic*
(1997), in which a young emigrant from steerage is offered a taste of
indulgence and insults over a stuffy dinner in first class. Later, he
takes a young woman he has met in first class to what he calls a
'real party' held by exuberant passengers in steerage. The couple
then make love in the luxurious and illicit back seat of a limousine
stored under an obscuring tarpaulin on the ship's socially neutral

Departing first-class passengers were duly photographed for the family album or for the
press. The upper deck of a liner was always a congenial setting, c. 1910.

freight deck, all scandalous examples of class transgression and exciting escapes from the suffocating formality and exclusivity of segregated shipboard life. The placement of a vehicle within a vessel also demonstrates Foucault's definition of heterotopia, the 'juxtaposing in a single real place of several spaces, several sites that are in themselves incompatible.'[24] This can be seen as a portent of the diverse 'places' – casino, lecture theatre, shopping mall – juxtaposed aboard today's cruise liners.

Class and sexual transgression, set in the extraordinary bowels of a great ship, were exploited similarly in Jack Fritscher's homoerotic short story *Titanic*, in which two young gentlemen slip from their first-class stateroom down to the cargo area of the fatal liner to dally with the stokers. Fritcher writes:

> Promptly at 11, the steward led us down five flights of back stairs to the hold . . . The maze of catwalks was lined at both rails with sailors, coalmen, cooks, mechanics and . . . masseurs from the Turkish steam room. The hot red tips of the crewmen's rolled cigarettes and the gentlemen's cigars blinked with each drag in the dark like stars signalling in the night. We threaded our way through the silent, standing men, taking our bearings.[25]

For Fritscher the hold is an epic, Piranesian cruising ground where the classes mingle intimately.

Despite such glamorization of the mechanical bowels of steamships, the lives of the mechanics working in the din of those hot and airless spaces were hard. Feeding the multiple furnaces of a coal-powered steamship was the job of an army of stokers, who shovelled fuel onto the fire, and their trimmers, who tended the fire by raking the coals and removing clinker to keep the fire roaring. Skin blackened and hair singed, they laboured in the infernal conditions of a poorly ventilated and constantly vibrating iron container, where they would be burnt by any metal surface they touched and sometimes collapse from heat exhaustion or asphyxia. Even when they were not at work, they were kept within a crew's ghetto, well hidden from the privileged passengers far above them in the ship and from superior classes of crew.

Even after the transition, following World War One, from coal to fuel oil, which reduced the number of engine-room crew and eliminated some of the worst jobs, the life of any seafarer could be hard and the accommodation basic. A crewman who worked on the *Queen Mary* in its early years described as 'mediocre' the 'glory hole' he shared with 24 other boys. This vibrating, cockroach-infested dormitory was low in the ship's aft end near the propeller machinery. By contrast, the French Line touted its crew quarters aboard the *Queen*'s competitor, *Normandie*, declaring that it 'strikes a new high with bunks of steel frame construction, enamelled and designed for genuine comfort . . . the same perfect ventilation that serves the passengers is carried out in the crew quarters'.[26] According to former employees, the food was good, except that pressure of work meant eating it on the run. Although all ships' crews worked hard and long, their accommodation would vary according to the specific ship on which they served; and their wages (particularly those earning tips) were higher than for comparable jobs on land.[27] In today's cruise industry the accommodation and working conditions for ordinary seafarers has hardly changed: they 'sign on' with no contractual security or benefits; their wages are low for a working week as long as 120 hours; and yet individuals from around the world still choose to go to sea rather than stay at home labouring for even less or working in unadventurous jobs.

A 24-hour regime of invisible toil below decks has always been necessary to support the high life above. In the later 1930s the major

North Atlantic liners all catered famously to celebrities, political leaders and royalty. Discussing class issues involving ocean-liner crew, a *Queen Mary*, stewardess Edith Sowerbutts, described meeting countless celebrities during her years working in first class. Her list included the movie stars Douglas Fairbanks, Marlene Dietrich and Gary Cooper.[28] Thus, it is not surprising that the Cunard historian James Steele described the promenade deck of that ship as

> a sheltered, glass-enclosed enclave of privilege . . . crowded with strollers who were fond of its sunny warmth and protection from wind and weather. Lined with deckchairs on its inboard side, it was the place to see and be seen, and to meet the most prestigious guests on the passenger list; it was the maritime equivalent of the Via Veneto.[29]

Such interiors herald the ocean liner's conversion from practical transportation to the exotic and escapist – the significant characteristics of the modern cruise liner. Social rituals, such as the promenade, inspired by the design of *Queen Mary* and other grand ships of the period, were both products of and influences on the desires and expectations of the modern world for more than half a century, and they left a legacy of myths and images that have affected both the design of today's cruise ships and the expectations of those passengers who now holiday aboard them.[30]

However, the luxury and glamour associated with the liner's 'Golden Age' was far from the experience of most ocean travellers at the time. The reality was more like that described by novelist Katherine Anne Porter in *Ship of Fools*, set during 1931 on a fictitious North German Lloyd passenger/freight liner, *Vera*. Aboard was a group of mainly middle-class characters, 'from modestly comfortable to uncomfortably poor', crossing the Atlantic for emigration, study or business. Those travelling alone shared cramped cabins with one or more strangers, most of whose personal habits, conversation and physical presence were odious to their cabin-mates. These relatively well-to-do passengers were the lucky ones, looking down from cabin-class decks into the steerage hold, where passengers of the humblest means were crowded at more than treble the officially sanctioned number, most of them accommodated only in hammocks or in bedrolls on deck. There, they performed publicly all the rituals of daily life.

Porter's characters met their ship in very different circumstances from the departing celebrities regularly photographed by the press on the decks of the *Mauretania* or the *Ile de France*. Boarding the *Vera*,

> passengers, investigating the cramped, airless quarters with their old-fashioned double tiers of bunks and a narrow hard couch along the opposite wall for the unlucky third comer, read the names on the door plates – most of them German – eyed with suspicion and quick distaste strange luggage piled beside their own in their cabins . . . [they] washed their faces and combed their hair, put themselves to rights and wandered out again to locate the ladies' (or gentlemen's) toilets; the bar and smoking room; the barber and hairdresser; the bathrooms, very few.[31]

The *Vera* was modelled on a common type of cargo liner that carried a large amount of mixed freight along with several hundred passengers. Typically, many freighters and tankers also offered a few cabins to passengers willing to endure a slow and unpredictable passage. In 1946 David Stevenson was an officer aboard *San Felix*, a large, ageing British tanker with five passenger cabins on the boat deck amidships. He wrote:

> During the several voyages I made on *Felix*, she carried passengers each time. We had a crusty old colonel, his wife and daughter, whose

opinion of the National Coal Board, which had taken over his mine in the North East, was blistering. A wartime 'boffin' whose tales of poisoned cigarettes and wrist watch A/P bombs were fascinating if gruesome. His wife, a handsome lady of fifty, went nowhere on the ship, without clutching a large handbag, in which we swore were the family jewels. We carried women and children, wives of employees in the oilfields of Venezuela and Trinidad. We carried hard bitten Oilmen, who had drilled for oil in the mountains of Persia and the rich black lands of Texas and Oklahoma. These fellows drank pints of whisky and played poker, morning, noon and night.[32]

Aboard a similarly decrepit and potentially dangerous cargo ship, the 19,943-ton 174-m (570-ft) British-registered container vessel *Speybank*, Josie Dew made her voyage from Britain to New Zealand in 2005. Along with six other passengers, she experienced 55 days of vicious storms, engine breakdown, the failed rescue of a

Dinner service, SS *Great Britain*, 1843. From the beginning of the steamship era, fine dining was a standard first-class amenity.

distressed yacht, lengthy delays in various ports and one memorably obnoxious fellow passenger. Her purpose was less transportation than travel, experience and adventure since she had the option to fly, but chose to sail, noting that the only way to cross the ocean now aboard a commercial vessel 'is either by taking a cruise on one of those massively cushy floating five-star hotels . . . or as a fare-paying passenger on one of the few freighters that allocates a handful of cabins to people who like the idea of getting nowhere fast on board an oily greasy working ship'.[33] Yet it could be argued that Dew was in fact cruising, since the ship was as much her destination as was the port of Auckland. Socially, her relations with the other passengers were formed in a manner typical of shipboard life, and she benefited from a private cabin throughout the voyage.

On board a pre-war ocean liner such privacy was rare, except in the first-class sections of the best ships. Privacy, however, was not then an expectation among the great majority of passengers. Before the ubiquity of private automobile space and the reduction of long-distance travel time from weeks to hours by airliners, people in the developed world still tolerated each other's company while travelling for extended periods. By the later twentieth century this was no longer the case.

However, a major focus for the shipboard community has always been mealtimes. Food is arguably the most important part of a passenger's experience at sea, while meals form a great theme running through accounts by ocean travellers; and for anyone who has lived on board a passenger ship for any length of time, those meals may remain their most vivid memories of a particular voyage. Jules Verne recalled dining aboard Brunel's last and greatest steamship, the *Great Eastern*, during his crossing to New York in 1867. 'Four times a day, to the great satisfaction of the passengers, this shrill horn sounded: at half-past eight for breakfast, half-past twelve for lunch, four o'clock for dinner, and at seven for tea . . . one could have fancied oneself at a restaurant in the middle of Paris instead of the open sea.'[34]

Before the development of reliable shipboard refrigeration late in the nineteenth century, the necessity to feed several hundred people for extended periods at sea required the accommodation on board of large numbers of live animals, which were slaughtered en route. P&O historians D. and S. Howarth described how their presence

At Port Said, Egypt, cattle were delivered aboard steamships to feed passengers and crew en route to the Far East, c. 1900.

aboard gave the decks of early liners the pleasant, rustic atmosphere of a farmyard with cocks crowing in the morning. Yet the smells of the ship's abattoir could not have been enjoyed by anyone. A menu published aboard the P&O steamer *Simla*, travelling from Suez to Ceylon in 1862, indicates the quantity of meat consumed at a typical meal aboard a British ship of that time. The starter was mutton broth, followed by the main course of eight roasted meats, plus boiled leg of mutton, boiled fowls, kidney pudding, braised sheep's head, fowl and ham pies, stewed pigs' feet, chicken sauté and corned beef.[35]

Although grand dining was quickly established as a feature of first-class life aboard transoceanic passenger steamships, their instability in rough seas remained an impediment to the enjoyment of food throughout the steamship era. Sister Mary Mulquin, an Irish nun aboard the *Great Britain*, recorded a sanguine account of such discomforts that could equally have been written one hundred

The elegance of *Great Britain*'s dining salon could not mask the ship's discomforts, its peculiar odours or its vulnerability to the ferocious North Atlantic weather.

years later. 'Stomach in a fearful state, discharging every few minutes, and a breaking headache. If those at home could get a "coup d'oeil" of our state they would both laugh and cry; no description would suffice.'[36]

While in fair weather the ritual of meals provided a structure to the day and the obligation to chat, drink always lubricated the conversation, except between 1919 and 1933 aboard US-flagged ships that were 'dry' in accordance with America's Prohibition law. Indeed, for the first thirty years of steamship travel unlimited drink, including morning claret, celebratory champagne at every excuse, and brandy at bedtime, was included in the fare by most shipping lines. Therefore, it is not surprising that many passengers remained drunk from the moment of boarding to the moment of landing. This behaviour has not changed fundamentally in the past two hundred years. The travel writer Charlie Connelly's account of an overnight ferry crossing between Norway and Denmark in 2003 confirms that ships and strong drink still share a bond. 'Two men were prevented from boarding on the grounds that they were drunk. Given that the entire passenger list . . . was breathing enough proof to fuel the ferry itself, I can only assume that this was a token gesture.'[37]

The dining room was the most important communal space in all classes, and in first class seating positions at meals were always of great importance. If it were not a priority to sit near the door for an unobtrusive exit during bad weather, a coveted seat at the captain's table brought the greatest cachet. The lady seated at the captain's right was the confirmed social queen of the voyage. Typically, a young, pretty Bostonian, Fanny Appleton, sailing to Liverpool on *Columbia* in 1841, was taken under the wing of the ship's captain, Charles Judkins, 'who walked with her on the upper deck, showed her the machinery below, had her sit at his table and eat the choicest food'.[38]

For passengers of all classes, a voyage usually meant an enforced interruption of work. However, history records certain exceptions. The novelist Anthony Trollope, travelling from Britain to Australia in 1871, recalled:

> When making long journeys, I have always succeeded in getting a desk put up in my cabin, and this was done for me in the *Great Britain*, so that I could go to work the day after we left Liverpool . . . Before I reached Melbourne I had finished a story called *Lady Anna*. Every word of it was written at sea, and was done by me day by day – with the intervention of one day's illness – for eight weeks.[39]

Although ubiquitous internet and laptop provisions today blur the distinction between work and play, the passenger ship more typically remains a cocoon from the world of enterprise and industry, and it demands a relaxation of the productive urge in favour of time spent on pleasant and diverting activities. Thus, from the earliest steamships to today's floating theme parks, games have had a particular importance at sea. In addition to gambling, be it organized gaming such as roulette, or simple card games, whist or poker, the wager has always been a compelling shipboard pastime. The ship's pool on the exact time of arrival, average speed, or even the foot, left or right, with which the harbour pilot would alight onto the deck of the ship, were all the subjects of a bet – to the delight of some passengers and to the ruin of others.

Style and Design

As Mark Twain wrote of Mississippi River steamers in the 1870s, 'to the entire populations spread over both banks between Baton Rouge and St Louis, they were palaces; they tallied with the citizen's dream of what magnificence was, and satisfied it'.[40] Such was the significance of ship decoration. As a promotional tool in the selling of passenger tickets, the decoration of ships was meant both to reflect the ambitions of the ne'er-do-well and to satisfy the tastes of the refined passenger. Decor was also intended to promote a sense of security. Among travellers accustomed to elaborately furnished houses, first-class hotels or music halls and gin palaces, the appearance of a ship's interiors could serve as a link with life on dry land even while wallowing over a choppy sea in mid-ocean. Although each successive generation of premier liners outdid its predecessors for the scale and ornamentation of its interiors, certain ships stand out as milestones of design or as markers of changing taste.

As Brunel's *Great Britain* had boasted the most elaborate and spacious interiors afloat in the 1840s, Collins Line ships claimed the introduction of genuine luxury at sea during the 1850s. Yet for size, space and grandeur nothing in that decade or for many years after came close to Brunel's fantastic swan song, the *Great Eastern*,

Like the gin palace and the music hall, the lavish interior of a 19th-century American river steamer, used by the entire population, was a genuine people's palace.

launched in 1858. Unsurpassed in size for forty years, the 18,915-ton ship of 211 m (692 ft) was designed by Brunel and the shipbuilding firm of John Scott Russell, with engines by James Watt. This was an extraordinary transitional vessel with a double hull of iron construction, twelve watertight compartments, both screw propulsion and paddle wheels for manoeuvrability, five funnels, six masts rigged for sail assistance and a maximum speed of 12 knots.

Everything about the ship was radical, including the industrialized method of its construction,[41] and although it was a commercial flop in its transatlantic passenger service, it was distinguished for laying the first Atlantic telegraph cable in 1865. Capable of accommodating 4,000 passengers and bunkering 15,000 tons of coal, the ship was designed to travel non-stop to Asia or Australia via the Cape of Good Hope, although it never did. The ship's construction and launch were exceptionally well documented with highly detailed hand-coloured orthographic construction drawings by Scott Russell & Co. also intended for exhibition, and numerous photographs by

Brunel's SS *Great Eastern*, launched in 1858, remained the largest steamship to be built for the next 40 years and featured the grandest interiors afloat. It was far ahead of its time in every way.

Joseph Cundall and Robert Howlett that provided imagery for engravings published widely in magazines during the 1850s and '60s.[42]

Over the years tens of thousands of visitors toured the ship to experience its astounding size, its spectacular engineering and its luxurious Victorian interiors, executed by the plasterers Jackson & Sons of London and other prominent decorating firms. Public rooms with ceilings up to 4.2 m (14 ft) high were dramatically larger than anything previously seen afloat, and the sharp contrast between the ship's massive machinery and its ornate decor and furnishings excited the crowds, who were familiar with such amazing juxtapositions of technology and style from displays in London's Great Exhibition of 1851 and from railway design, both exemplars of modern industrial taste in the mid-nineteenth century. Along with powerful new express trains, steamships became the supreme symbols of iron-and-coal technology, and therefore Germany and Britain, as the world's leading industrial and naval powers, led in their development. From the late 1890s until the outbreak of war in 1914, Britain and Germany engaged in a relentless competition to build the fastest and most opulent first-class ships on the Atlantic.

In 1897 the German Norddeutscher Lloyd (NDL) launched a new flagship, *Kaiser Wilhelm der Grosse*, which became the first German ship to capture the Blue Riband, for fastest eastbound and westbound North Atlantic crossings. The *Kaiser Wilhelm*'s 33,000 horse-power triple expansion engines, driving twin propellers, could push the huge ship along at 22.5 knots with more than 1,500 passengers and 500 crew. At 14,349 tons and 200 m (655 ft) this was the largest liner afloat. Externally, its four funnels, arranged in two pairs, established an image of power that led steamship design for fifteen years. Following the example of the Orient Line, which in 1877 first employed an architect, the Arts and Crafts advocate J. J. Stevenson, to design a coordinated set of interiors for its flagship *Orient*, NDL

appointed Johannes Poppe as its architect to plan all the interiors of the *Kaiser Wilhelm*. Poppe would remain in charge of NDL interior design for their subsequent three ships, encrusting them with his trademark neo-Baroque style of decoration reminiscent of mad King Ludwig's Bavarian castles.

Poppe's deeply carved panelling, writhing plasterwork and sumptuous gilding attracted passengers' affection but critical disapproval, typically from a British observer, the architect Arthur Davis, who derided the German's tendency 'to overcrowd a room with heavy ornament and meretricious decoration . . . where refinement of detail has been often sacrificed to tawdry magnificence and over-elaboration'.[43] Nevertheless, Poppe's work would define the style for the next generation of German liners. The ship's furniture was made by A. Bembe of Mainz, a company that also furnished villas for a number of leading German industrialists. Only with the ascendancy

With grandiose public rooms designed by Norddeutscher Lloyd's architect, Johannes Poppe, the express liner *Kaiser Wilhelm der Grosse* (1897) represented Germany's challenge to Britain's dominance of the North Atlantic.

of the geometric Jugendstil, a simpler style promoted by the younger generation of innovators associated with the Deutscher Werkstätten and Wiener Sezession after 1900, would Poppe's elaborate historicist style be superseded aboard German ships.

The model of the hotel de luxe, rather than the palace or castle, became the standard among the newer British ships that eventually fought off the German competition to dominate the North Atlantic in the years leading up to the outbreak of war in 1914. Two new Cunard liners, *Lusitania* and *Mauritania*, recaptured the Blue Riband speed trophy from the Germans in 1907 and held it until 1929. Although they were structurally alike, *Lusitania* was built by John Brown & Co. of Clydebank, Scotland, while *Mauretania* was constructed in Tyne and Wear by Swan Hunter. To distinguish the sister ships, Cunard chose different architects to oversee their interior design, James Miller and Harold Peto respectively. Peto's designs for *Mauritania* were the more expensive and luxurious, but both referred to French and British domestic architectural styles such as *Louis XIV*, Adam and Queen Anne, which were popular in Britain and America at the time. While first- and second-class passengers enjoyed distinctive period-style rooms, the third-class sections of both ships were too plain to be distinguished by such references, they were characterized instead by the simplicity of their polished ash and teak panelling, bare timber floors and whitewashed ceilings. Furniture was similarly functional, as in the dining rooms with their long wooden refectory tables and shapely balloon-back chairs on rotating pedestals – comfortable, hygienic, unpretentious and without historical references.

The third ship Cunard built for its transatlantic shuttle service before the Great War was the *Aquitania*, launched in 1914. Designed by naval architect Leonard Peskett and built by John Brown, the ship was the largest of the three Cunard express liners at 45,647 tons and 275 m (900 ft), originally carrying 3,230 passengers and 920 crew. Its steam turbine engines, linked to four propellers, produced 59,000 horsepower to drive the ship at a maximum 24 knots. Like the *Kaiser Wilhelm der Grosse* and other pre-war liners, whose construction was supported by government subsidies, the *Aquitania* was expressly designed for conversion to military use, and indeed the ship served in both World Wars as an armed merchant cruiser and a troopship. Peskett reinforced the ship's structure for the potential installation of armaments, yet he also designed a light, glassy superstructure that enabled the architect Arthur Davis, of the firm Mewes & Davis, to create bright public rooms similar to his designs for the Ritz hotels in Paris and London. Elegant staterooms and public spaces, decorated in *Louis XVI*, Palladian, Adam and other relatively restrained historical styles were hung with reproductions of masterpieces by Holbein, Rembrandt, Gainsborough and other great European painters, earning the *Aquitania* its nickname 'Ship Beautiful'.

In its heyday during the early twentieth century, the ocean liner's interiors clearly reflected the economic status of its passengers: grand interior decor for the rich, bourgeois comfort for the middle class and stark, efficient accommodation for the majority of bread-and-butter passengers. Although progressive architects of the 1920s rejected such differences, they were influenced by ocean liner design when devising the imagery for the buildings they proposed to satisfy the rigorous economic demands and the social restructuring of the modern, post-war world. Therefore, it was the third-class sections, the open decks and the superstructures of liners that the Swiss architect and theorist Le Corbusier admired in his 1923 manifesto, *Towards a New Architecture* (*Vers une Architecture*), as models for a revolutionary architectural aesthetic. This effectively reversed the conventional influence of architectural style over the decoration of ships. He described the sun decks and promenades of the *Aqui-tania* as embodying 'the same aesthetic as that of a briar pipe, an office desk or a limousine'. The rectilinear white superstructures, cabin houses and bridges of such ships provided the forms for Le Corbusier's expensive private villas of the 1920s and for his two houses at the Weissenhof Siedlung, a model estate of workers' housing built in Stuttgart in 1927. Of the *Aquitania*'s promenade lounge, an uninterrupted linear space with a ribbon of unglazed 'windows' overlooking the sea, he wrote:

> For architects: a wall all windows, a saloon full of light. What a contrast with the windows in our houses making holes in the walls and forming a patch of shade on either side. The result is a dismal room, and the light seems so hard and unsympathetic that curtains are indispensable in order to soften it.[44]

He went on to suggest:

> Architects note: the value of a 'long gallery' or promenade – satisfying and interesting volume; unity in materials; a fine grouping of the constructional elements, sanely exhibited and rationally assembled . . . contrast this with our carpets, cushions, canopies, wall-papers, carved and gilt furniture, faded or 'arty' colours; the dismalness of our western bazaars.[45]

In *The Decorative Arts of Today* (1925), Le Corbusier illustrated a ship's third-class cabin, shown for the simplicity and 'honesty' of its design revealed through its exposed rivets, bare beams, ventilation ducts, metal-framed wicker-seated chair, linoleum flooring and clean white walls. The cabin is presented as a symbol of the modern world's response to technical and social need and to the conditions of economy and hygiene. Like other radical modernists of the 1920s, Le Corbusier imitated in all his buildings the appearance of spare efficiency that he found so impressive in the decks and third-class interiors of contemporary liners. And so it is not surprising that the fourth meeting of the International Congress of Modern Architecture (CIAM), organized in 1933 by Le Corbusier, was held in the Mediterranean on a liner, the 3,902-ton SS *Patris*.

Despite such radical attitudes, the tried and tested formula of technical innovation masked by historical interior design prevailed through the 1920s. Typically, Peninsular and Oriental Steam Navigation Company (P&O), serving routes extending from England to Asia and Australia, launched a new flagship for their Bombay service in 1929, the *Viceroy of India*, a ground-breaking ship in its novel use of steam turbines powering smooth, quiet and economical electric motors generating 17,000 horsepower to push the 19,645-ton ship at a brisk 19 knots. The ship's interiors were also novel for they were designed by a woman, the socialite, actress and daring aviator Elsie Mackay, daughter of the P&O chairman, Lord Inchcape. Unlike her radically modern lifestyle, however, Mackay's interior designs provided conventional images of luxury for both first- and tourist-class passengers of this two-class ship. The first-class smoking room was copied from the Great Hall of an Early Renaissance English palace, with an elaborate hammer-beam ceiling, carved mantelpiece featuring heraldic beasts, crossed swords flanking the fireplace and lashings of plaster strapwork.[46] Waring & Gillow produced its heavy James I furniture, a style popular in stockbrokers' living rooms at the time, often concealing radios and cocktail paraphernalia. Mackay also designed P&O's first indoor swimming pool in a simplified Pompeian style. Staterooms featured an updated version of period decor, with marquetry inlays in light-coloured timber, shallow plaster mouldings and geometrical light fixtures, a conservative version of Art Deco also found aboard luxury trains such as the *Orient Express.*

The ship that first demonstrated the full-blown Art Deco style, inspired by the Paris International Exhibition of Decorative and Industrial Arts of 1925, was the French Line's (Compagnie Générale Transatlantique) *Ile de France*, launched in 1927. Many of the same artists and craftspeople who decorated the 1925 exhibition pavilions produced interiors for the *Ile*; they included the glass artist René Lalique, metalworker Edgar Brandt and the couturier Paul Poiret, who covered the walls of the first-class dining room in fine straw reeds, arranged in patterns of palm trees. And like the exhibition, the *Ile de France* represented France's determination to assert its international leadership in contemporary taste. Regardless of the embarkation port, once on board the *Ile de France* a passenger was effectively in Paris, and rooms like its Terrace Café were nautical versions of the great Parisian cafés, such as Le Dôme and La Coupole. This ship's chic interiors signalled the beginning of the end for the architectural historicism of its Edwardian predecessors.[47]

A more technically and stylistically advanced ship was the NDL Turbine Steamer *Bremen*, of 51,656 tons and 286 m (940 ft), launched in 1928. This was the first passenger ship to feature a Taylor bulbous bow for speed and stability, and like the *Ile de France*, it was fitted with a catapult to launch a small seaplane near the end of the voyage for fast delivery of express mail and to land a few wealthy passengers a few hours ahead of everyone else. The ship's cutting-edge technology resulted in it winning the Blue Riband both westbound and eastbound on its maiden voyage. In 1930 *Bremen* and its sister ship *Europa* were the two fastest and most modern passenger ships in the world. This status was conveyed by the *Bremen*'s modernist interiors, designed by Fritz August Breuhaus (de Groot) in a sleek luxurious style that led the way for designers such as Brian O'Rorke and Raymond Loewy, who made similar use of contemporary elements, including indirect lighting, horizontal parallel lines running into radius curves and flush surfaces. In its synthesis of advanced technology and modernist style, *Bremen* antici- pated the great superliners of the mid-1930s, although aesthetically it may have been more sophisticated and unified than those ships that followed. The Weimar president, Paul von Hindenburg, launched *Bremen*, but after 1933 the ship became an important symbol of German pride for Hitler's National Socialitsts, who also purloined *Europa* and the two astounding airships, *Graf Zeppelin* and *Hinden- burg*, the latter with modernist interiors also by Fritz Breuhaus. This represents a notable exemption for the decoration of trans- port vehicles from the Nazi Party's general ban on avant-garde art, architecture and design.

Alongside the development of new hull shapes and technological advances in propulsion, including the very important shift from coal to fuel oil, in the 1930s a number of new ships employed distinctive versions of Modernism in the decoration of their interiors and in the architecture of their superstructures. The French flagship *Normandie* (1935) and Cunard's *Queen Mary* (1936) have been discussed exten- sively because of their positions as national flag bearers, their size and their speed, both winning the Blue Riband. Of the two, *Normandie* was the style leader, employing many of the same talents who fitted out the *Ile de France* but applying their work on a more grandiose scale. The ship's advanced architecture was the work of a Russian émigré naval engineer, Vladimir Yourkevitch, with interior design supervised by Richard Bouwens van der Boijen and Roger-Henri Expert. Together they created the supreme Art Deco grand hotel afloat. *Normandie* was destroyed by fire in 1942, while *Queen Mary* went on to a long and illustrious career, serving with distinction in World War Two, and becoming a dry-docked tourist attraction in its old age at Long Beach,

California. Its decor, initially criticized as the typically unsatisfactory work of a committee, today appears a quaint relic of faded Anglo-Hollywood glamour.

More representative of the active debates surrounding ship design in the 1930s were vessels such as the P&O Line's five *Straths*, launched between 1931 and 1938, and the Orient Line's *Orion* of 1935, all built by Vickers Armstrong Ltd at Barrow-in-Furness, Cumbria, and all serving British Empire mail routes carrying civil servants and their families from Britain to India and Australia. The design of these ships was intended to create an impression of comfortable modernity and to make the most of their warm water routes by opening up their interiors to sea views and fresh air.

In the heyday of ocean shuttle services, the Art Deco pomp of the French flagship *Normandie*, launched in 1935, set a standard for glamorous transport design.

The New Zealand-born architect Brian O'Rorke was solely responsible for the *Orion*'s interiors, establishing stylistic continuity throughout the ship. The Orient Line director, Colin Anderson, personally promoted the ship's modern styling as a landmark in the evolution of ocean travel and as a means of distinguishing Orient Line's contribution to progress in the field. O'Rorke also undertook other transport projects in the 1930s, including interiors for the Short C-class Empire flying boats. Yet it was his understanding of the tropical climate of the southern oceans, where *Orion* would be sailing, that led him to the use of folding partitions and sliding glass walls to impart an open-air feeling to *Orion*'s public spaces. The transparency of the superstructure also reinforced a flow of space from the interiors to the open decks, where games and social activities formed an important part of the passenger's experience. His palette of durable and unpretentious industrial materials included linoleum, Bakelite and chromium, arranged in simple geometric patterns that responded sympathetically to the lines of the hull and superstructure, creating an aesthetic unity between the ship's architecture and its decoration. *Orion*'s brand of modernity was warm and appealing, as exemplified by Marion Dorn's boldly coloured and geometrically patterned rugs that enlivened all the first-class rooms.

Following World War Two, there was a hiatus of several years before the most important post-war passenger ships were built, the first of these being the SS *United States*, launched in 1952. It was designed by William Francis Gibbs, and its construction cost was heavily supported by the US Navy to provide a big and very fast troop carrier capable of traversing the Suez and Panama canals. On completion the ship was passed to the United States Line and outfitted as an express ocean liner. At 57,300 tons and 302 m (990 ft), the ship was constructed with an aluminium superstructure to the Navy's specifications for fireproofing and also for weight saving. Its lightness combined with its four Westinghouse double-reduction geared steam turbines, producing 248,000 horsepower, drove the ship at a maximum speed of 38 knots, making it the fastest ocean liner ever built and holder of the Blue Riband throughout its seventeen years of North Atlantic service.

Architects Eggers & Higgins took overall charge of the interiors, but all cabins were designed by a firm of women interior designers, Smyth, Urquhart & Marckwald. Dorothy Marckwald had gained experience designing ship interiors in the 1930s when she decorated a fleet of vessels for the Grace Line using traditional styles derived from American country houses and country clubs. The choice of women to decorate ships was based on research concluding that women were the principal decision makers in the purchase of steamship tickets. In Marckwald's words, 'the majority of passengers are women, and no man could ever know as much about their comfort problems and taste reactions as another woman'.[48] Their appointment also reflected the new professionalism of women designers, a significant change from the familial engagement of the talented dilettante, Elsie Mackay, by the Orient Line. Marckwald's firm was highly skilled in design decisions that responded to the distinctive architecture of a ship, with its sheer and camber, and used the established professional tools of models and mock-ups in addition to drawings in the design process. They were also conversant in the range of modern materials including Lucite sheet, Marinite wallboard and fire-retardant paints that replaced the moulded woodwork of pre-war liners.

For the *United States* Marckwald and her partner Anne Urquhart created interiors with sleek modern lines finished in light colours to provide neutral backgrounds for contemporary furniture upholstered in bold blues, greens and reds. Marckwald wrote bluntly: 'We tried to use all clear colors because we think muddy colors

make people seasick.'[49] To meet Method One fireproofing standards, required of all US passenger ships, furniture and fixtures aboard the *United States* were constructed from aluminium and upholstered in new synthetics such as the durable, fireproof Dynel, which could mimic almost any natural material, from silk to fur ('It's Not Fake Anything, It's Real Dynel!') and which Marckwald wove with metal threads to give her textiles 'sparkle'. Marckwald's contemporary interiors represent a break from the Deco and Streamline imagery of pre-war ships, favouring the simple elegance of the International Style then becoming the architectural signature of corporate America.

Following the successful example of the *United States*, the remaining great liners of the 1950s and '60s adopted international modernism for their interiors, complementing the streamlining of

Designed by George G. Sharp to provide scheduled services between New York and the Canal Zone, SS *Panama* (1939) featured functional contemporary interiors by Raymond Loewy, the leading industrial designer of the day.

their hulls and superstructures. The most successful were those employing coordinated design teams including naval architects and interior designers to produce a unified work of seagoing architecture. The merged P&O–Orient Lines' 45,270-ton *Canberra*, launched in 1961, was the product of a well-knit design team led by the naval architect John West and the architect Sir Hugh Casson with Timothy Rendle (first-class public rooms), John Wright (tourist-class public rooms) and Barbara Oakley (cabin accommodation). The vessel's major structural innovation was the aft placement of engines, following the typical arrangement of tankers and cargo vessels, a layout leaving the most stable areas free for public rooms and cabins. It also eliminated circulation problems caused by the traditional placement of the engines amidships.

The fusion of form and space that resulted from *Canberra*'s co-ordinated design process was demonstrated in the first class ballroom, separated by a 9.1-m (30-ft) long, vertically retractable glass wall from the swimming pool, which was encircled by a series of games decks 'in gradually ascending contours, like a hill rising from a lake, terminated by the crest of the observation bridge surmounted by the radar mast which in shape and form would do justice to Reg Butler'.[50] Thus, the pool deck and dance floor became a single uninterrupted space to be enjoyed in the fine weather of the Indian and Pacific oceans. Art and furniture throughout the ship were from an international range of contemporary designers and artists including Harry Bertoia and David Hockney. Tourist-class accommodation for nearly 1,700 passengers, mainly emigrants travelling from the UK to Australia on the assisted passage scheme introduced to boost the Australian population, created a lively atmosphere reminiscent of fashionable coffee bars, hotels and restaurants. Details such as the swirling mosaics of the tourist-class swimming pool terrace, which echoed the floor treatment of the Alice Springs lounge overlooking it, was typical of the 'space stretching' design used throughout the vessel. *Canberra* was arguably the most beautiful and comfortable emigrant ship in history.

More conventional in its layout, Cunard's *Queen Elizabeth 2* was, nevertheless, a ship noted for its highly unified design; and it became the longest-serving ocean liner in history. Launched in 1967, the 70,327-ton, 294-m (962-ft) vessel was the last of the grand oil-fired steamships built for the North Atlantic shuttle service. Smaller than its Cunard predecessors, *QE2* was intended for easy conversion from a two-class liner to a one-class cruise ship for winter sailings on warm water routes. *QE2*, like the *United States*, was small enough to fit through the locks of the Panama Canal. Its steel hull and aluminium superstructure made the ship light and fast, originally capable of 32 knots, increasing to 35 knots when the engines were eventually replaced by diesel-electric units. *QE2* was also relatively economical, using only half the fuel of the earlier *Queen Mary* and *Queen Elizabeth*.

As *QE2* was intended to be used as a cruise liner for half the year, three-quarters of the cabins were positioned along the sides of the ship, providing views of the sea. With thirteen decks and an unusually tall superstructure, made possible by the use of aluminium in its construction, all restaurants and public rooms were located high up to offer excellent views of passing attractions and to minimize the effects of engine vibration. The consultant industrial designer John Gardner was responsible for the superstructure's sleek, yacht-like appearance. Its profile was dominated by the curving bridge flanked by swept-back signal decks from which sprang a series of concentrically arcing structures stepping down towards the bow and cascading aft towards the stern. This sculptural approach to form was also applied to the distinctive mast and to the scoop-shaped funnel, perfected in a wind tunnel. In addition to its internal layout, this ship's 1,828.8 m (6,000 ft) of open deck space confirmed it as a singularly luxurious cruise liner rather than an Atlantic super-ferry.[51]

The architect Dennis Lennon led a team of young designers that included Jon Bannenberg, Gaby Schreiber, David Hicks, Michael Inchbald and Theo Crosby to create public rooms and cabins that set a new benchmark for luxurious modern design afloat. Even those spaces unseen by most passengers, the hospital and crew accommodations, were carefully designed by Jo Patrick. Traditional pomp and opulence were replaced by flowing spaces delineated in stainless steel, glass and reinforced glassfibre (GRP), and characterized by dramatically contrasting areas of bold colour illuminated by state-of-the-art electronics. For younger passengers, the vessel included a coffee shop and the Juke Box, a gaming area designed by students from the Royal College of Art; while the London Gallery, operated by Marlborough Fine Art, featured painting and sculpture by contemporary British artists such as Francis Bacon, Barbara Hepworth and R. B. Kitaj, confirming the QE2 as a very hip ship.

Hip or not, the QE2, along with French Line's elegant France, was the last of its breed. Since the imposition of immigration quotas by the United States in 1920, the days of the big emigrant ship had been numbered. Some new ships, such as Canberra, were built as late as the 1960s to serve the continuing government-sponsored emigration from Britain to Australia, while older ships, such as the ornately decorated Italian liner Conte Grande, carried both wealthy business passengers and poor emigrants between Italy and Brazil from the late 1920s until its retirement in 1959. Yet despite substantial migration continuing from Europe and Africa to countries of the southern hemisphere, and the mass displacements of refugees by the two World Wars, ocean liners increasingly transported vacationers to their holiday destinations. When the Boeing 707 jet airliner entered commercial service in 1959, business travellers stopped sailing and

Dennis Lennon coordinated the interior design of Cunard's *QE2*, combining the best in contemporary fine art, furniture, innovative materials and new lighting technologies to create the greatest cruise liner of its time. Queens Room designed by Michael Inchbald.

started flying. The Boeing 747 jumbo jet of 1969 brought low inter-continental fares that finally killed the remaining ocean shuttle services. What then was left for the passenger liner?

Cruise Culture

Following the lead of the former Baptist preacher Thomas Cook, who began organizing temperance package tours from Britain to the Mediterranean and the Middle East in the mid-nineteenth century for the purpose of self-improvement, most steamship lines by 1900 offered warm-water cruises in the winter months to attract a new type of customer with modest disposable income and a desire to see the world. When US immigration quotas shrunk the North Atlantic steerage trade in the 1920s, steamship companies were forced to find new uses for their ships, and cruising was one answer. Through-out the inter-wars years budget cruises transported thousands of vacationers to exotic destinations for sightseeing, which used the shipping lines' spare capacity and extended the lives of many eld-erly vessels.

Following the accession to power of Adolf Hitler as German Chancellor in 1933, the cruise ship showed its full political potential. The director of Hitler's social engineering policies, known as 'Strength through Joy', was Dr Robert Ley, who exploited holiday travel as an instrument of political indoctrination and propaganda. Among his projects were the ingenious KdF-Wagen (Volkswagen), the massive Prora holiday camp and the Strength through Joy pleasure cruises, all for loyal Aryan workers of the Reich. To service Ley's cruises the German Labour Front commissioned the Blohm & Voss shipyard to construct two new single-class liners of 25,500 tons and 208.5 m (684 ft). The first, launched in 1937 and originally named MV *Adolf Hitler*, was eventually called *Wilhelm Gustloff* after a martyred Nazi mayor, and the second was named MV *Robert Ley*. Their historical significance is two fold; first they represent the politicization of pleasure cruising, and second their design innovations led the way for all subsequent cruise ships.

Unlike the conventional ocean liners of their time, they had no cargo hold and hence no large hatches or cranes on their foredecks. This liberated outdoor space for organized fresh-air activities, games and callisthenics. It also allowed for a longer superstructure accommodating bigger lounges, concert halls, lecture theatres and dining rooms where working people and Nazi officials could mingle for activities organized specifically to 'enlighten' and 'inform' passengers about the aims of fascism and the Nazi view of other lands and their peoples. Most cabins for passengers and crew alike were of identical dimensions, accommodating two berths; and every passenger had an exterior cabin with a view of the sea. With these two ships the cruise liner attained an unprecedented importance in the promotion of state ideology, and they presented 'a more acceptable image of the Third Reich' to the outside world.[52] Between their launches in 1937 and their requisition in late 1939 the two ships carried many thousands of Germans on ocean holidays. These voyagers included the Chancellor's mistress, Eva Braun, who filmed her jolly cruise holiday through the Norwegian fjords, Denmark and Lapland using the new Agfachrome 8mm colour film stock in the compact cine-camera given her as a present by Hitler.[53] Just six years later *Wilhelm Gustloff* was sunk by a Russian submarine while evacuating panicked civilian refugees from East Prussia, killing more than 9,000 passengers, the worst-ever loss of life on a ship at sea.

Employing a layout similar to those German ships, Cunard's luxurious *Caronia* of 1947 was the first purpose-designed cruise liner to be built for a major shipping line after the war, and by the 1960s similar vessels designed expressly for the cruise industry were finding a mature form. In countries bordering the Baltic Sea, innovative naval architects such as Knud E. Hansen and Tage Wandborg designed a generation of new vessels that offered pleasure cruising tailored to travellers in the world's largest archipelago, a highly competitive ferry market. Such vessels provided a combination of comfort, style and cruise-ship amenities along with high-capacity vehicle decks, satisfying the demands of Volvo- and Saab-owning Scandinavians. The Hansen firm also designed three groundbreaking Norwegian-Caribbean Line cruise ships, *Starward*, *Skyward* and *Southward*, launched in 1968, 1969 and 1971. These vessels were influential in several significant ways. They were built to American Method One specifications for fire safety and were therefore world-class. They were single-class vessels offering a high percentage of outside cabins. Their leisure amenities included a casino and a signature Skybar above the top deck, overlooking the swimming pool and providing panoramic views of passing scenery. Their fashionable modernity and emphasis on pleasure enticed many new converts to cruise holidays.

The success of these ships encouraged the design of other increasingly large cruise-ferries, serving long Baltic routes such as Helsinki to Stockholm. Typically, the *Silja Symphony* of 58,377 tons and 183 m (600 ft), launched in 1991, carried more than 2,000 passengers and 450 cars while offering all the amenities expected in a modern cruise liner as well as a full range of conference facilities, making it both a shuttle transporter and a primary destination for both tourists and business passengers. *Silja Symphony*'s internal layout was organized around an 8-m (26-ft) wide glass-roofed promenade running 140 m (450 ft) through the centre of the ship from bow to stern. All the ship's amenities were located off this tall, airy space and included restaurants, bars, shops and a children's playground that enabled

parents to enjoy the ship while increasing their freedom to shop and spend on board. The nightclub, accommodating 1,000 revellers, was adjacent to one of the largest casinos afloat. The gymnasium complex included pool, health club, beauty parlour and sauna. Conference rooms, audio-visual lecture theatres and offices accommodated business meetings and conventions, broadening the ship's earning potential.

Such new ships catered to an increasingly demanding clientele in the mass tourism market, also having to comply with tougher safety regulations and with the evolving economic parameters of the cruise industry. Hulls were designed with a shallow draft to enable ships to reach the maximum number of desirable ports. Like the largest cruise-ferries, newer liners such as the Norwegian-registered 90,090-ton *Jewel of the Seas*, launched in 2002, employed the spatial formula of a multi-deck atrium as the core of the interior. Similar to the atrium lobbies of contemporary hotels and shopping

After 40 years, Tage Wandborg and Knud E. Hansen's sleek 1971 design for the Norwegian Cruise Line's *Southward* (now Louis Hellenic Cruises' *Perla*) oozes period charm.

malls, these shipboard spaces induced a sensation of timelessness akin to that experienced by gamblers in Las Vegas casinos, an effect calculated to keep people spending without consideration for the passing hours.

The greatly increased demand for outside cabins led to the towering, boxy superstructure of such ships. These exterior cabins generated particular challenges, as illustrated in designs for the 49,400-ton, 241-m (790-ft) *Crystal Harmony* by the Italian naval architect, Vittorio Garroni Carbonara. To provide the most spectacular views from each outside cabin, the architect used a full-width glass sliding door assembly to divide the cabin from the veranda, with its own fully glazed bulwarks, enabling passengers to view sea

Jewel of the Seas. The multi-storey atrium became a standard feature of modern cruise ships, exhibiting extravagant design also typical of lobbies in Hyatt Hotels or Las Vegas casinos.

and scenery directly from the bed. Carbonara related his cabin design to the architectural nature of the superstructure.

> It's a structural matter. Most of the ships include the veranda within the structure and you face the sea through a big squared hole in the ship's side. The steel frame surrounding that hole reduces the visibility either in the horizontal or the vertical plane . . . In the *Crystal Harmony*, instead, the verandas are hinged out of the structure, are lighter and more transparent and allow an extraordinary visibility all around. Cabins are much brighter and, subsequently more cheerful and nicer for living. This kind of veranda is certainly more architectural and less naval than the recessed one, but this is a trend which will further develop in the future.[54]

Regarding the future of cruise ships, Carbonara saw two separate trends emerging in the twenty-first century. The first is what he called the 'classical typology of ships conceived to carry passengers along attractive routes, with interesting ports of call'. He suggested that these 'travelling cruisers' would not exceed 50,000 tons, especially for the Asian markets, in order to minimize environmental impact. The second trend he predicted was the 'recreational theme ship, a floating theme park where the major interest for the passenger is the ship itself, more or less independent of his itinerary'.[55] Current examples of this type include the Carnival cruise liners and the two 83,000-ton Disney cruisers, *Disney Magic* and *Disney Wonder*. He speculated that such new ships would be increasingly large, in excess of 100,000 tons, and asked in a manner reminiscent of Jules Verne: 'Will this kind of ship become an artificial island?'[56]

A small fleet of sail-assisted motor cruisers plying the oceans relatively unremarked since the late 1980s may also indicate the shape of some future cruise ships. Seattle-based Windstar Cruises, part of the Carnival Line, operated three vessels powered by computer-controlled sails and diesel-electric motors for a combination of reliability and romance. The largest of their ships, the 14,745-ton *Wind Surf*, was designed by the Finnish shipbuilder Wärtsilä and constructed in the French shipyard SNCH for the Club Med Cruise Line in 1990. Windstar ships aimed at the high end of the cruise market, advertising an intimate, adventuresome and informal voyage, stopping at unusual ports in the Caribbean and Mediterranean. *Wind Surf* accommodates 312 passengers in typical cruise liner comfort, but offers the distinctive atmosphere created by its hydraulically operated sails rigged from four masts.

Windstar liners were conceived to offer passengers closer contact with the elements by providing amenities such as their water sport platform, a large terrace that hinged down from the stern like the loading ramp of a car ferry to provide a launching pad for jet skis and other aquatic toys and an additional deck from which passengers can swim. Launched in a period of indulgent consumption, these ships were not designed primarily to make optimal advantage of their hybrid energy system. And although they reach or exceed current environmental standards, their diesel engines run constantly to power air conditioning and other creature comforts, and their marketing emphasizes luxury and recreation rather than the potential ecological advantages of sailing ships in an era of increased worry about fossil fuel consumption and CO_2 emissions. Nevertheless, they suggest the potential of hybrid wind- and engine-powered ships for providing a sporty cruise experience with the benefits of a less greedy motive power source.

In the last days of the transatlantic shuttle service E. B. White wrote: 'I heard the *Queen Mary* blow one midnight, and the sound carried the whole history of departure and longing and loss.'[57] For today's cruise passengers, aboard simply to enjoy an effortless holiday, these deeper emotions are less likely to be stirred than in the days when the passenger ship was the primary means of relocation, escape and adventure. In the twenty-first century the passenger ship is no longer a serious mass transporter, but a pleasure craft or a leisure resort afloat. Now, too, the passenger has been transformed from a scion of privilege or a piece of human cargo into a pleasure-seeking consumer, enjoying the ship as a giant playground at sea.[58]

In the twentieth century deck games such as shuffleboard became popular, while swimming in the ship's pool, a work-out in the gym, and callisthenics directed by an athletic deck steward all helped to fill time and stretch the limbs during a voyage, weather permitting. For less sporty passengers the ritual promenade was an opportunity to enjoy the scent of fresh air and to socialize while taking a bit of

Sun deck, *Rhapsody of the Seas*. The 21st-century cruise liner is less a floating city than a floating theme park devoted exclusively to leisure. Transportation is almost irrelevant.

exercise between heavy meals. Today, cruise ships' upper-deck rock-climbing walls and specially adapted surfing pools provide more varied physical activity. Shopping has joined musical entertainment, sport, dancing and persistent drinking as an important form of recreation aboard the modern cruise liner, which for the more cerebral passenger will also offer a well-stocked library and serious lectures on many subjects relevant to the ship or its route.

This tradition goes back at least as far as the 1900s when ships offered 'enrichment lectures' as part of their social activities for those in first class. At first captains would invite distinguished passengers such as academics, politicians and adventurers to deliver talks.

Despite its ascendancy as the reason to travel by sea, play has long been a feature of ocean voyages. Deck games aboard the fastest Edwardian passenger liner, RMS *Mauritania*. 1911.

Typically, during a voyage in 1929 the *Ile de France* hosted an illustrated lecture by Captain H. A. White vividly describing his year-long expedition to Abyssinia and Central Africa.[59] Eventually, shipping companies began the practice of hiring professional lecturers such as the art historian Suzanne Fagence-Cooper, who was engaged by Cunard to lecture on Victorian design to the passengers aboard the *Queen Mary 2* on its maiden eastbound voyage from New York. She commented on her status within the shipboard community, noting that, although there are no longer class divisions, there remain 'cost divisions'. Contrasting her experiences lecturing on the *QE2* and *QM2*, she felt more like a privileged passenger on the *QE2*, where she was 'upgraded to the poshest restaurant and poshest stateroom. We had access to a special bar/lounge for our afternoon tea and cocktails, which only certain passengers could enjoy.'[60] By contrast, aboard the *QM2* lecturing staff formed an intellectual subculture:

> We were berthed down in the bowels of the ship – still with a porthole, but much plainer, and ate at a table with all the other speakers in the Britannia restaurant. That was also great fun – to chat to A. C. Grayling and Simon Jenkins over dinner . . . it felt like Oxford High Table every night.[61]

Her scholarly talks were then delivered amid the extravagant decor of the ship's lecture theatre,

> like one enormous 30's cinema with translucent glass, elaborate wood panelling, chrome details . . . I felt quite dwarfed by my surroundings when I stood up on my first day at sea, to talk about Victorian interior design. I was lecturing in a theatre that doubled as a planetarium, flanked by allegorical figures of 'Cinema' and 'Electricity' that rather stole the show.[62]

This state-of-the-art multi-purpose room, the first planetarium on an ocean liner, regularly houses a 'College At Sea', offering tuition in subjects including celestial navigation, art or wine appreciation, oceanography and East–West relations, giving new meaning to the old adage, 'travel broadens the mind'.

2 | Myth and Image

Sanctuary

Whether one subscribes to a literal or an allegorical reading of scripture, the Ark of Noah is widely thought of as the archetypal ship of salvation, escape and rebirth. Throughout the histories of the world's major religions the story of the Ark has been interpreted and reinterpreted from its theological implications to the practical details of the technology it encompasses. Genesis (6:13-16) sets out the purpose of Noah's ship and then specifies its dimensions:

13. And God said to Noah, The end of all flesh has come before Me, for the earth is filled with violence through them; and behold, I will destroy them with the earth.
14. Make yourself an ark of gopher wood; make rooms in the ark, and cover it inside and outside with pitch.
15. And this is how you shall make it: The length of the ark shall be three hundred cubits, its width fifty cubits, and its height thirty cubits.
16. You shall make a window for the ark, and you shall finish it to a cubit from above; and set the door of the ark in its side. You shall make it with lower, second, and third decks.[1]

In the early Christian period St Augustine of Hippo (354–430) drew a parallel between the proportions of the Ark, as laid down in Genesis, and the proportions of the human body, seen as representing the body of Christ and used as the central planning device of the basilica and, later, the cathedral. Thus, the Ark has stood for the concept of salvation, both in what secularist society considers myth and in the symbolically charged proportions of real buildings throughout the past two thousand years.

St Hippolytus of Rome (*c.* 170–*c.* 236) left a detailed description of the Ark's structure and layout over three decks. At the bottom of the ship was a deck for animals of the wilderness. On the middle level were housed birds and domestic animals. The top deck was for the human cargo, Noah and his family. Within that 'passenger deck',

The most commonly reproduced image of Noah's *Ark* is that of a barn upon a barge. Such images reflect the specific culture in which they have been created, but the ship's dimensions and layout are based on Scripture. A Currier & Ives print of 1856.

males and females were separated by a barrier of sharpened stakes to prevent any sexual encounters that might lead to pregnancy during the enforced period of chastity lasting the duration of the Flood – the ship was intended to accommodate the same number of both animal and human occupants throughout its time at sea.

With the Renaissance came new interpretations of the Ark story, reflecting the growing scientific attitude of that age. In the fifteenth century the practical arrangements for waste disposal and ventilation aboard the Ark were discussed by Alfonso Tostado, while a hundred years later the geometrician Johannes Buteo offered detailed calculations of the Ark's displacement taking account of the space required for Noah's milling and baking during his six months aboard. These became influential models for later scholars in their portrayals of the Ark.

Early writers differed considerably, describing the Ark's form as cubic, pyramidal or, according to an early Islamic text, shaped like the belly of a bird. It was the seventeenth-century German Jesuit priest Athanasius Kircher who established the image of a rectangular Ark, which has remained the preferred shape among modern-day literal interpretations. Kircher's engravings show a barge-like, rectilinear hull, meant to ensure stability in relatively calm seas (scholars argue persistently about the extent and character of the Flood), three decks, a double-pitched roof, as on a low barn, and a large door in the side wall of the animal deck for entrance and egress. Kircher's design for the interior of the vessel employed a longitudinal passageway flanked by rows of cells on each deck. According to him, birds and humans were housed together on the top deck, while heavy animals were kept on the bottom deck to maintain a low centre of gravity, and food stores were on the middle deck.

There has also been constant debate about the Ark's size when converted to modern measures. Genesis gives specific dimensions in cubits, 300 long by 50 wide by 30 high; but what type of cubits? The cubit was based on a human scale, the distance measured from the elbow to the tip of the index finger. A Royal Egyptian Cubit derived from the specific length of the forearm and hand of the current ruling pharaoh, and thus was changeable. And so, depending on whether one uses the standard Egyptian Cubit, the Royal Egyptian Cubit, or other versions of the cubit to determine the size of the Ark in modern measures, the ship's overall length varies from 135 m (443 ft) to 157.5 m (516 ft). In any case, it would have been a huge vessel, considerably larger than any wooden ship ever built. Its capacity has been estimated at between 15,000 and 22,000 tons, as compared with the *Great Eastern*'s 18,961 tons in 1857 and the 151,687 tons of the *Emma Maersk*, today's biggest container ship. For all the efforts of religious scholars and archaeologists to find the Ark, to determine its form and size, and thereby to assess whether or not it could have performed the task set for it by God, the fact remains that this vessel has stood for thousands of years as one of the primary icons of salvation among Christians, Jews, Muslims and within secular society.

If the Ark represents a floating refuge from the wrath of God, then the *Nautilus* of Jules Verne stands equally for the adventurous individual's sanctuary from political tyranny. In *Twenty Thousand Leagues Under the Sea* (1870), Verne portrayed the depths of the world's oceans as the ultimate refuge for a political anarchist seeking a life of freedom and exploration. Yet the *Nautilus* is also a home, and an unusually stately one, that became a touchstone for the ambiguous relationship that has always existed between the interior design of ships and buildings on land, particularly the house. The significance of that relationship was the subject of an essay by Roland Barthes on the ship as a theme in stories by Jules Verne. Barthes suggested that the appeal of Verne's fiction for children had less to do with the 'mystique of adventure' than with his portrayal of closed places – the island, the balloon, the ship – and of his 'delight in the finite', similar to the child's love of huts and tents. In Verne's stories the ship's cabin provides such an enclosure, a place of apparent safety from the larger world outside in which 'the storm, that is, the infinite, rages in vain'. It is the quintessential space where the traveller can reinvent his or her own world and create a secure facsimile of home.

In 'The *Nautilus* and the Drunken Boat', Barthes portrays the ship as an ideal shelter from the enormity of the sea. He wrote:

An inclination for ships always means the joy of perfectly enclosing oneself, of having at hand the greatest possible number of objects, and having at one's disposal an absolutely finite space. To like ships is first and foremost to like a house, a superlative one since it is unremittingly closed, and not at all vague sailings into the unknown: a ship

An 1892 edition of Jules Verne's *Twenty Thousand Leagues Under the Sea* is displayed prominently aboard the world's first nuclear-powered submarine, USS *Nautilus*.

is a habitat before being a means of transport. And sure enough, all the ships in Jules Verne are perfect cubby-holes, and the vastness of their circumnavigation further increases the bliss of their closure, the perfection of their inner humanity.[2]

If Verne's stories were often 'an exploration of closure', then the *Nautilus* was to him the perfect vessel for domesticating the wild ocean depths. Its hull mediates with the elements of sea and weather

State rooms aboard Verne's *Nautilus* were modelled on elaborately decorated 19th-century imperial yachts, and finely sculpted classical ornaments ennobled even the vessel's fantastic engines.

to protect its lustrous interior, resembling the rich pearlescent lining of an oyster shell and filled with rare treasures like an oyster's pearl. The cabins of the boat were described as being furnished with the luxury of the finest first-class stateroom aboard an Atlantic greyhound of the 1870s. The main drawing room, which contained works of art by the greatest masters and a collection of rare natural marine specimens, also featured two large windows, hidden behind sliding panels that could be opened to reveal electrically floodlit views of the underwater seascapes through which the *Nautilus* passed, a morally neutral terrain, free from human interventions, except, of course, the ship's own.

The *Nautilus*, in this regard, is the most desirable of all caves: the enjoyment of being enclosed reaches its paroxysm when, from the

The image of the submarine is deeply entwined with the mythology of the sea monster – powerful, elusive, malevolent.

bosom of this unbroken inwardness, it is possible to watch, through a large windowpane, the outside vagueness of the waters, and thus define, in a single act, the inside by means of its opposite.[3]

Personality

The image of the *Nautilus*, as presented in films and in book illustrations, is that of a gigantic predatory sea creature capable of destroying even the largest naval vessel. And this is consistent with the narrative, in which mariners sighting the ship can explain such a phenomenon only in terms of ancient mythological monsters. Yet the vessel is also more intriguingly represented by Verne as an inverted mobile aquarium, the laboratory of a scientist whose extraordinary technological skills, responsible for the ship's fantastic capabilities, enable him to view the sub-aquatic world in a unique and penetrating manner. The vessel provides its master not only with a 'cherished seclusion', but also with eyes of magnificent power, eyes that can illuminate a mile of undersea terrain and all the creatures contained therein. It is designed as a roving observation chamber, capable of astounding speed and with a strength allowing it access to the deepest, most inaccessible and amazing of all ocean habitats. There, the *Nautilus* is at home, a creature of the deep fashioned by man to surpass the works of nature.

Another mythology of the sentient vessel can be found in the story of Jonah, retold in all the major religious texts with only minor variations. The whale or sea monster that saved Jonah from drowning was sent by divine writ to carry the reluctant prophet on a mission from God and to deliver him to a place where he could carry out God's instructions. This sea creature is kin to the sighted *Nautilus*, its 'belly' often depicted as a cave, a haven of safety and a place of contemplation, where Jonah comes to terms with his destiny. The whale may be the instrument of a miracle, but it also has its own eye and purpose, to serve as a benign vessel of salvation.

In these examples the ship becomes 'a travelling eye', also portrayed in Arthur Rimbaud's *The Drunken Boat* (1871), in which the boat, as narrator, is freed from the control of its captain and crew, wandering the oceans according to its own haphazard and tragic course.[4] This ship can be seen to resemble the depopulated cargo vessels of today's globalized maritime economy, the enormous supertankers and container ships ploughing across the seas with a vestigial care-taking crew of twenty, unseen in the vastness of the oceans, guided by satellite and roving over 70 per cent of the earth's surface according to their own automated steering devices and often in completely empty sea lanes, far from any other vessels.

In 1871 Rimbaud wrote from the perspective of the sentient boat, the boat that speaks in the first person, liberated from the authority of its murdered crew, and indeed from any practical purpose, such as the transport of passengers or haulage of cargo.

> As I was floating down unconcerned Rivers
> I no longer felt myself steered by the haulers:
> Gaudy Redskins had taken them for targets
> Nailing them naked to coloured stakes.
>
> I cared nothing for all my crews,
> Carrying Flemish wheat or English cottons.
> When, along with my haulers those uproars were done with
> The Rivers let me sail downstream where I pleased.

The chaotic, unreasoning vessel rambles the seas and tells of the wonders and horrors it encounters. And it suggests that, despite being shorn of rudder and anchor, it can go where it pleases, observing, absorbing sensation, transforming experience into art. The boat reports on the caprices of the sea and its effect on even the greatest of vessels, perhaps envisioning its own future. This boat is not only a personification of all ships, but also a representation of the poet, himself; this drunken boat sees not only the tumult of the aquatic world but also itself as the central character, the liberated hero, in an epic seafaring drama.

> I have seen the enormous swamps seething, traps
> Where a whole leviathan rots in the reeds!
> Downfalls of waters in the midst of the calm
> And distances cataracting down into abysses!

In the literature of seafaring, such a ship, out of control, drifting, is far from unique. The *Nautilus*, too, was sometimes free of Captain Nemo's control, when that titanic figure was emotionally indisposed. The book's narrator observed:

> that he was sad and irresolute I could see by the vessel . . . The *Nautilus* did not keep in its settled course; it floated about like a corpse at the will of the waves. It went at random . . . all supervision seemed abandoned.[5]

In this incident, the ship wanders for many days on and below the surface of the ocean, carried along by the Gulf Stream in company with a multitude of sea creatures that provide a spectacle for the passengers, who themselves become constituents of the ship's 'eyes', those two picture windows in the flank walls of the drawing room.

It is in such moments that the true melding of mariner and vessel becomes most intimate and most prophetic of the man-machine consciousness that arose in the early twentieth century, as developed in the writing of Marinetti or the paintings of Léger and Picabia.

Nemo is, unquestionably, the father of the *Nautilus*, but his captive passengers are also drawn into a symbiotic relationship with the ship, contributing their sentience and intellect to its optics.

All these vessels were portrayed as masculine, thanks at least in part to the gender conventions of the French language – the masculine *le bâteau*. Perhaps this is appropriate also because these ships represent in some degree their male authors, particularly in relation to their roles as observers. By contrast, in the English-speaking world ships traditionally have been described as female, at least until the later twentieth century, when the development of a feminist consciousness encouraged a less gender-specific language. The designation of a ship as female among English-speakers has traditionally had a poetic meaning for mariners, predominantly men, who may perceive a ship as womb, mother or mistress and express their admiration for a vessel in romantic terms. The figurehead adorning the bowsprit of important ships in the age of sail were, typically, female, and some captains, who may have owned their ships, might decorate them as

The naming ceremony for ammunition ship USS *Amelia Earhart* was celebrated in 2008 under a billboard linking Earhart, the heroine of early aviation, with her contemporary, Eleanor Roosevelt, heroine of social equality.

if dressing and bejewelling a beloved wife or fiancée. In his epic whaling novel *Moby-Dick* (1851), Herman Melville referred to the Nantucket whaler *Pequod*, as 'she', named after the doomed Pequot tribe of Native Americans who had lived around Long Island Sound.

Her ancient decks were worn and wrinkled . . . But to these her old antiquities, were added new and marvellous features, pertaining to the wild business that for more than half a century she had followed. Old Captain Peleg . . . had built upon her original grotesqueness, and inlaid it, all over, with a quaintness both of material and device, unmatched by anything . . . She was apparelled like any barbaric Ethiopian emperor. She was a thing of trophies. A cannibal of a craft, tricking herself forth in the chased bones of her enemies.[6]

In the waning days of the Cold War, MS *Mikhail Lermontov* represented Soviet culture around the world. Cossack dancing, all-day caviar and a library stocked with Tolstoy and back issues of *Pravda* were its hallmarks.

Katherine Anne Porter also followed the English convention of fem-
inizing the fictitious North German Lloyd cargo liner, *Vera*, on which
her cast of characters in *Ship of Fools* sail forth on a month-long
voyage from the Mexican port town of Veracruz to Bremerhaven,
Germany, in August 1931. She described the vessel as 'very steady
and broad-bottomed in her style, walloping from one remote port to
another, year in year out, honest, reliable and homely as a German
housewife'.[7] And the ship's name, *Vera*, signifying faith or truth, also
suits that description.

The personification of a ship through its given name is commonly
intended to ennoble the vessel, as in the case of the Russian battleship *Potemkin*, named after Prince Grigory Aleksanadrovich Potemkin,
who in the eighteenth century was field marshal to one of the most
important monarchs in Russian history, Empress Catherine II. He was
also her lover and, as such, exerted considerable influence over affairs
of state during her reign. His name gave the ship an instant cachet
of power and political significance, which was reflected through its
portrayal in the historical Soviet propaganda film *Battleship Potemkin*,

Government-sponsored passenger liners and naval vessels have long been designed as
cultural icons to represent national interests globally.

directed in 1925 by Sergei Eisenstein and a landmark in the evolution of cinematic art. In the film the ship's mutinous crew and the sympathetic proletariat of Odessa rebel against the myth of princely authority signified by the battleship's name, its powerful guns and the order of society it represents.

More recently Russian cruise liners were given the names of important Russian writers: Alexander Pushkin, considered the founder of modern Russian literature; Maxim Gorky, the force behind Russian Social Realist writing at the turn of the twentieth century; and Mikhail Lermontov, 'the poet of Caucasus'. The ocean liners named for the three in 1965, 1969 and 1972, respectively, were Cold War emissaries of Soviet culture around the world and carried the names of great artists as signifiers of their 'personality', instantly mediatized and understood by whole populations as quality.[8] Similarly, during the 1950s and

USS *Intrepid* is the fourth American warship named for those qualities of fearlessness and bravery expected of such a powerful and significant vessel.

'60s the Italian liners *Raphael*, *Leonardo da Vinci* and *Michelangelo*, all described as floating Uffizi Galleries, signified historic Italian cultural cachet through their names as well as their decoration. Thus the mythology of the hero has been transferred to passenger liners and to warships for a variety of nationalist, imperialist and commercial purposes during the past two hundred years.

More abstract concepts have also been employed in the interests of navies and shipping companies through the names of their vessels. Six British warships, launched since 1747 and including the Royal

Supernatural strength is the quality signified by the name *Olympic Hercules* given to this powerful and luxurious 4,477-ton multi-functional Norwegian tug and supply vessel for the offshore oil industry.

Navy's flagship aircraft carrier, were all named *Invincible*. Similarly, the fourth US Navy ship to be named *Intrepid*, an aircraft carrier commissioned in 1943, served in three wars and is now the iconic centrepiece of the Intrepid Sea, Air and Space Museum at Pier 86 in New York. Such heroic names communicate the qualities of strength, bravery and commitment intended to inspire pride among countrymen and fear in the enemy. Cargo vessels may also bear names signifying their purpose and design, such as the Japanese vehicle carrier *Hercules Highway* and Cunard's ill-fated roll-on, roll-off container ship *Atlantic Conveyor*, sunk by Exocet missiles while conscripted to serve in the Falklands War of 1982. Cruise ships, too, may be given myth-making names by their owners. The Carnival Cruise Line assigns names chosen to convey the image of fun in the sun: *Celebration*, *Ecstasy*, *Tropicale*, *Paradise*. Referring to its tradition of cinematic fantasy, the Disney Cruise Line named its first two liners *Disney Magic* and *Disney Wonder* and emblazoned their red funnels with a white Mickey Mouse silhouette floating over three black waves. Name and decoration assure prospective passengers that they will find a family-friendly entertainment experience on board these vessels.

Facsimile

The image of some modern cruise liners will have little relevance to the vessel's technical function – mobility – since such vessels are now conceived primarily as floating resort hotels where movement hardly matters. The imagery of passage may be suggested, as it is copiously aboard the *Queen Mary 2* (*QM2*) through ornamental references to historic ships of the Cunard Line, yet the reality of the ocean is kept as much as possible to the status of a picturesque background for a variety of activities performed in settings that are familiar and terrestrial: the shopping mall, casino, restaurant, café bar. The job of the cruise ship is to insulate selectively the holiday maker from the potentially uncomfortable realities of travel, allowing the otherness of both the sea and of ports visited to merge into the 'package' of a vacation that seldom extends to an immersion in another culture or to contact with the possible unpleasantness of troubled lands or their peoples, who may be found near to interesting tourist sites. Just as the mollusc's shell protects against predators, today's typical cruise liner protects its tourist passengers from the fetid odour of social or political problems in the exotic places it visits, treating those encounters instead as spectacles.

Sometimes just the image of a ship may be enough to trigger the sensation of a voyage in the imagination. Such an imaginary ship was given substance by Joris-Karl Huysmans, in his novel *A Rebours* (*Against the Grain*) of 1884, the story of a hyper-sensitive, nervous and exhausted French aristocrat, Des Essiente, who has grown increasingly disgusted with humanity and dreams of creating a 'hermitage combined with modern comforts, an ark on dry land', where he can find refuge from 'the incessant deluge of human folly'. Retreating from his Parisian life of excess and debauchery to a remote country house, Des Essiente constructed his personal ark within the existing walls of the old building, where his new dining room

> resembled a ship's cabin with its wooden ceiling of arched beams, its bulkheads and flooring of pitch-pine, its tiny window-opening cut through the woodwork as a porthole is in a vessel's side. Like those Japanese boxes that fit one inside the other, this room was inserted within a larger one – the real dining-room as designed by the architect . . . a large aquarium filling in the whole space intervening between the porthole and the real window in the real house-wall . . . This done, he could picture himself in the 'tween decks of a brig as he gazed curiously at a shoal of ingenious mechanical fishes that were wound up

and swam by clockwork past the porthole window and got entangled in artificial water weeds; at other times, he inhaled the strong smell of tar with which the room had been impregnated [and] would examine a series of coloured lithographs on the walls, of the sort one sees in packet-boat offices and shipping agencies, representing steamers at sea bound for Valparaiso or the River Plate, along side framed placards giving the itineraries of the Royal Mail Steam packet services and of the various ocean liners.[9]

Thus, the complete act of closure within a ship's cabin is synthesized as part of a conventional house set within the French landscape, and a long ocean voyage could be taken in the imagination without the 'traveller' stirring from his room. Like the cruise liners of the twenty-first century, Des Essiente's house offers its 'passenger' the

The extravagant Beaux-Arts façade of the New York Yacht Club repeats the theme of antique yacht transoms, romantic symbols of the club's *raison d'être*.

semblance of travel without any of the dangers or disagreeable side effects of an authentic sea voyage

The use of nautical imagery to decorate buildings of various types was a recurring theme in nineteenth-century architecture. In 1893 the Chinese dowager empress, Ci Xi, commissioned the construction of a summerhouse in the form of an American Mississippi river steamer for the garden of the Beijing Summer Palace, a warm weather retreat for the Qing emperor and his family. Similarly, the architects of the New York Yacht Club in Manhattan employed decorative motifs derived from ship design throughout the building, reflecting the nineteenth-century fondness for exotic symbolism in both exterior architectural ornamentation and the adornment of interior spaces. That highly romantic Beaux-Arts façade of the NYYC, designed in 1899 by Whitney Warren and Charles Wetmore, features three large bay windows framed in limestone to represent the sterns of seventeenth-century Dutch sailing 'jaghts', the name from which the English word yacht is derived. Both the convincingly detailed window frames and the glass curve out from the wall trailing their carved wakes behind them to create the impression that they are sailing through the plane of the façade and into the equally fanciful, nautically themed rooms of the clubhouse within. The main dining room, for example, takes the shape of an antique galleon's heavily timbered and curvaceous wardroom, hugely enlarged.

To achieve a similarly dramatic effect in more recent times, one of New York's most fashionable restaurants was fitted with an authentic ship's interior to provide its patrons with the simulation of a first-class voyage that lasted only as long as their cocktails and dinner. The Art Deco panelling, furniture and lighting of the first purpose-designed post-war cruise liner, Cunard's *Caronia* of 1947, known popularly as the 'Green Goddess', had been stripped out and auctioned when the ship was laid up in Manhattan before it was sent

to be scrapped. They were subsequently installed in the ground floor of a landmark Art Deco apartment building at One Fifth Avenue, also the name of the restaurant, where in the late 1970s Bobby Short sang and played the great American song book on the grand piano while diners enjoyed the sensation of a brief, faux Caribbean cruise in the heart of Manhattan.

Although lacking any such genuine maritime pedigree as One Fifth Avenue, the Coca-Cola Bottling Plant, built in Los Angeles in 1936 by the architect Robert V. Derrah, was designed with authentic detail to resemble closely a docked ocean liner. It was conceived in a theatrical, Hollywood-inspired streamlined modern style derived from Art Deco, which paid homage to the design of 1930s cruise ships such as the Matson liners *Mariposa* and *Lurline*, both designed

Coca-Cola Bottling Plant. Los Angeles, 1936. Ocean liner glamour enlivened even the most utilitarian buildings. A bridge, portholes, riveted wall panels and a nautical paint-job distinguish Robert Derrah's streamlined design.

Queen Mary, 1936: 'beauty of a more technical order', as Le Corbusier noted.

The bridge (below) provides a compelling image of authority over the mechanical titan: control relied heavily on visual reference in the pre-radar age of brass and class.

by William Francis Gibbs, the latter with a post-war interior refit by Raymond Loewy, who coincidentally styled the classic 6 oz. Coke bottle. The Coca-Cola building's design incorporated a bridge, hatches, porthole windows, ventilating funnels, promenade decks, riveted surfaces and ship's ladders as embellishments to its long, horizontal lines, radius curves and smooth white surfaces. Nearby on Sunset Boulevard Derrah also designed one of the world's first shopping malls, the Crossroads of the World, employing similar stylistic devices in that design to evoke the sensation among shoppers of being on a warm Pacific cruise.

While Hollywood's filmmakers exploited the image of the steamship for the purposes of mass entertainment, and the commercial architecture of Los Angeles followed suit, in Europe the form of the steamship was influencing an entirely more serious brand of modernist architectural innovation, that which became known as the

The design of the De la Warr Pavilion by International Style architects Erich Mendelsohn and Serge Chermayeff was inspired by the sleek lines of an ocean liner. Bexhill on Sea, Sussex, 1935.

International Style. Le Corbusier was the most vocal advocate of the lessons to be learned from marine architecture as well as from the design of other twentieth-century products including automobiles, locomotives and airplanes. But it was the passenger liner that became the primary influence both in his developing concept of modernist space and in the forms of the buildings he completed in the 1920s and '30s, arguably his most progressive period of work.

In *Towards a New Architecture*, Le Corbusier titled one of the book's three central chapters 'Liners'. Although he only discusses ships in the captions for his carefully chosen illustrations, they convey the principle points of his radical approach to the creation of space and form. From these images of the Edwardian liners in service during the early 1920s, he drew a set of architects' 'Notes' as a guide to what could be learned from ship design, and he established the ship as the primary exemplar of progress, rationalism and modernity itself. His selective representation of the steamship in that manifesto, which aims to change the world, exemplifies what Roland Barthes describes as 'Myth on the Left', referring to a kind of parable that is the opposite of myth as a dream world, which supports the status quo. In *Towards a New Architecture* the ship is employed as a political weapon in the architect's revolutionary arsenal. Le Corbusier writes as a creator who, as Barthes would argue, 'speaks in order to transform reality and no longer to preserve it as an image, wherever he links his language to the making of things . . . myth is impossible. This is why revolutionary language proper can never be mythical.'[10]

Icon

By contrast, the conventional mythology of liners between the World Wars typically served a commercial function, reaching a wide public through the medium of advertising, a field that grew exponentially during the boom years of the 1920s and continued its rise in the economic depression of the following decade. The United States led the development of the commercial arts in the Roaring Twenties, when a generation of young illustrators, theatre designers and commercial artists began turning their talents to the promotion of corporations and products under the newly invented rubric of Industrial Design. Among the leaders of this nascent profession, the French émigré to America, Raymond Loewy, was outstanding for his range of activities and for the elegance of his work.

His monochrome drawing for the White Star Line, used in an advertisement of 1928, presents the simplified silhouette of a liner's hull viewed from a snail's-eye view, a curving slice of superstructure and a towering pair of smokestacks. A ring of concentric circles draws the eye to the tiny figure of an officer on the bridge, a compelling image of command and security overseeing the great bulk of the ship. The modernist abstraction of the vessel's form creates the impression of high technology and ultimate sophistication, while the accompanying text strikes a particularly American, consumer-oriented chord by specifying the advertisement's inclusive target audience, the 'fashionables', signifying first-class passengers, 'confirmed travelers', those in second class, plus 'students, artists and economical vacationists' travelling in 'Tourist Third cabin accommodations' – a ticket for every budget.[11]

If Modernism was a key factor in advertising the inter-war steamship lines, then the most notable modernist illustrator of passenger steamships was the Ukranian-French Beaux-Arts-trained painter Adolphe Mouron Cassandre, whose posters for the Compagnie Général Transatlantique (the French line) became icons of the sophisticated, Cubist-derived Art Deco style. Cassandre's best-known poster image of the liner *Normandie* was a spare, elegant abstraction, its simple rectangular geometry and perfect symmetry emphasizing the immense size and stability of the vessel in addition to the flagship's celebrated

ARIJTOCRATJ OF THE JEA

With a background of fine traditions and
nautical lineage, and a foreground of
modern standards, White Star, Red Star
and Atlantic Transport ships traverse the
ocean lanes, the aristocrats of the sea.
. . . Chosen by the fashionables because
they are correct—by confirmed travelers
for their inimitable service and comfort
—by students, artists and economical
vacationists because of their delightful
TOURIST Third Cabin accommodations.

Ships for every purse and plan.

No. 1 Broadway, New York. Offices and agents
everywhere.

WHITE JTAR LINE
RED JTAR LINE · ATLANTIC TRANJPORT LINE
INTERNATIONAL MERCANTILE MARINE COMPANY

Parisian chic. Cassandre's style was, actually, more an adaptation
of Russian Suprematism, derived from Kasimir Malevich, than a
descendent of Braque or Picasso; but regardless of their stylistic ori-
gins, such images served throughout the second half of the 1930s
to proclaim French cultural supremacy, becoming symbols of the
country's excellence in all matters of contemporary taste and design.
Ultimately, Cassandre's image of the *Normandie* has become an
emblem for ocean travel itself.

Cassandre's contemporary, the self-taught British watercolour
painter Kenneth Shoesmith, had gone to sea as a young man and
worked on merchant navy vessels for more than a decade before

A ring of concentric circles draws attention to the tiny figure of an officer on the bridge,
a compelling image of command and security overseeing the great bulk of the ship.
Advertisement by Raymond Loewy for White Star Line, 1928.

becoming a full-time painter of ships. Unlike Cassandre's and Loewy's maritime abstractions, however, Shoesmith's naturalistic pictures showed a scrupulous concern for the factual representation of the ship's form and detail, a type of knowledge deemed essential by another important Cunard poster artist, the academic maritime painter Walter Thomas, who wrote: 'just as a man has his portrait, and is painted by the portrait painter, the marine painter aims at painting the portrait of his ship'.[12] Thomas's and Shoesmith's posters for Cunard and the Royal Mail Line were lyrical and descriptive, typically picturing huge steamers entering their ports of call around the world, often exotic locations where the liner is shown surrounded by welcoming tenders and celebratory fleets of small craft, with local figures in colourful costume placed in the foreground watching the ship's stately arrival. These images present a benign interpretation of the global British presence in the last days of Empire, its cultural

This 1957 US Navy recruitment poster by Joseph Binder echoes the formal symmetry and grand simplicity of Cassandre's famous posters of the 1930s for the French Line.

R.M.S. "ALCANTARA" LEAVING LISBON.

and economic authority signified by the impressive appearance of the grand mail steamer, a civilizing influence, under way. According to historians Lorraine Coons and Alexander Varias,

> the ocean liners were most astounding in their movement. It was beyond belief that such large objects, on a scale with the Giza pyramids or the largest buildings of the day, riveted together as industrial products, could move. Not only could they move, but they could cross the ocean at ever faster speeds in the process.[13]

And it was this aspect of the ship's image that Shoesmith and Thomas captured so convincingly.

By the end of the 1930s, when colour photography was beginning to appear in popular magazines such as the *National Geographic*, even more realistic but equally problematic images began to be produced

Kenneth Shoesmith's exotic portrayals of British Royal Mail steamers arriving and departing from their ports of call conveyed the great reach and power of empire in the last days of colonialism.

as incentives to sail abroad. In 1939 Matson Line, offering cruises from the west coast of the US to Hawaii, published an advertisement including a very small painted image of a sleek white liner beneath a large Kodacolor portrait of a white American female tourist, adorned in leis, watching a 'native' Hawaiian woman, dressed in a colourful floral print sarong, stitching together a curtain of banana leaves, an image as imperious in its way as the charmingly exotic natives of Kenneth Shoesmith's Royal Mail watercolours.

By the late 1950s, with the newly introduced Boeing 707 and Douglas DC8 jet airliners entering global commercial service, the portrayal of the ocean liner quickly underwent a reinvention through advertising. Less important were pictures of foreign ports, as the ship increasingly became the destination, and its revamped image became that of a party afloat. Although such pictures of

A Kodachrome snapshot of the cultural imperialism brought to Hawaii and the wider Pacific by the elegant white steamers of the California-based Matson Line, 1939.

In this 1958 advertisement for the French Line, sailing is portrayed as a calming alternative to the speed of jet air travel.

shipboard life were not altogether new, they became the norm in the Jet Age. Typically, the French Line used a Bernard Buffet-style painting of a moonlit deck party aboard a nameless liner in a 1958 ad, the image accompanied by the strap-line 'Greet Europe relaxed and refreshed by France-Afloat'. Here, the liner is shown as a 'gay French city on the sea' and the passenger is assumed to be on holiday. Gone now were the days of the commercial sea traveller; the cruise era had arrived. If Cassandre's image of the *Normandie* represented a distillation of all that was best in pre-war French style, this later image is essentially a Dior catwalk show, the evening gowns and fluttering scarves of the female passengers competing for attention with the portrait of the vessel, itself.

Although the ship as a setting for a fashionable party was well established in fine art, now it was simply being put to a new commercial use. The Frenchman James Tissot's popular painting *The Ball on Shipboard* of 1874 documented the fashionable society of Victorian England at play, and no setting provided a more suitable backdrop for the elaborate costumes and flirtatious manners of the young Victorian than the expansive deck of a large ship, draped with festive regalia. As in the French Line's advertisement, this vessel is simply decor, yet the moral ambiguity associated with ships and the increasing choice they brought to Victorian life is suggested. In another of Tissot's nautical works, *Portsmouth Dockyard* (1877), a handsome Royal Highlander is seated in a launch between two young beauties, both keen for his attention – the subject is once again the dilemma of choice. The destination of this trio is the imposing warship HMS *Calcutta*, looming in the background. John Ruskin complained that such pictures were merely 'colour photographs of vulgar society', and that they lacked any enriching social purpose or lesson. It is probably just as well that he did not live to see twentieth-century advertising. Yet Tissot was not a vacuous artist, and he cleverly included in his works many clues to the problems of bourgeois life and, particularly, its unstable romantic and emotional sides.

Other nineteenth-century British painters had exploited the ship as a symbol of the more serious social issues of their time in the world's leading maritime nation, which relied on gunboat diplomacy to preserve and expand its empire. Henry Nelson O'Neil's pair of paintings, *Eastward Ho! August 1857* (1857) and *Home Again* (1858), depict the departure and return of British soldiers dispatched to suppress an uprising, the Indian Mutiny, which threatened to disrupt the colonial order on which Britain's global domination and domestic prosperity relied. Thus, *Eastward Ho!* is a work of propaganda, which nevertheless touches the personal realities, the anxieties and the perils of a world bound together by international shipping. Its partner, *Home Again*, was painted in response to the popularity of the earlier work and appears as a confirmation of all the nationalist, patriotic values of *Eastward Ho!* Claire O'Mahony, in her catalogue to the exhibition *Brunel and the Art of Invention*, observed that in terms of the history of art, and like the steamship itself, these works 'helped to make modern experience a subject equally worthy and involving as Classical Antiquity or the Middle Ages'.[14] As such, they are a pictorial equivalent of the Dickensian novel, densely packed with personal incident and fevered emotion, all derived from present day events and the condition of modern life, represented forcefully by the image of the ship.

O'Mahony also draws attention to an 1864 painting by Edwin Aaron Penley depicting the dining saloon of the royal yacht *Victoria and Albert II*, as evidence of the domestic pleasures afforded to royalty in the Victorian era by their floating, steam-powered palaces, which were widely exposed to the general public through the rapidly expanding print media of the period. The most striking aspect of the room is its unpretentious cosiness, an image reinforced by the view

through a window toward Osborne House, Victoria's and Albert's summer home on the Isle of Wight, celebrated for its modern comfort. Both the ship and the house were designed under the close supervision of Prince Albert, whose taste was decidedly modern in terms of comfort and convenience, employing the latest technologies to achieve both. Thus, this royal yacht represented the ease and mobility of the Victorian nuclear family as emphatically as it demonstrated the power of the empire.

This was the second of three yachts named *Victoria and Albert*, a 360-foot steam-powered paddle-wheel schooner of 2,470 tons, capable of 15 knots. Launched in 1855, *Victoria and Albert II* normally carried a crew of 240, had two suites of staterooms for the royal family, twelve cabins for the queen's household and guests, a nursery, chapel, tea pavilion, and several reception rooms for meetings and formal receptions. The ship was used for royal relaxation and

The steam-powered paddle-wheel schooner *Victoria and Albert II*, used for royal relaxation and important affairs of state, was also a highly visible mobile symbol of British monarchy in the nineteenth century.

for important affairs of state; it was also loaned to visiting dignitaries on many occasions, making it a highly visible mobile symbol of the British monarchy until its replacement by *Victoria and Albert III* in 1899.

The appearance of great Victorian and Edwardian ships, be they warships, royal yachts or commercial passenger vessels, was of considerable public interest, and images of them were regularly published in magazines such as the *Illustrated London News*. While many of the pictures were black-and-white photographs, handsome monochrome lithographs by professional illustrators were featured, often in large-format double-page spreads. Typical among the latter was an imposing illustration of 1905, signed S. Begg, picturing Queen Alexandra descending stairs from the deck of *Victoria and Albert III*, moored in Portsmouth Harbour, and alighting on the deck of *Submarine 'A 3'*, one of the Royal Navy's first Connecticut-built Holland submarines, which had been brought alongside the royal yacht for the queen's inspection. Begg's interpretation of the scene

The heroic geometries of steamships were studied by avant-garde artists as they sailed the oceans between the two World Wars. *Queen Mary*, 1936.

emphasizes the immense size and power of the yacht while portraying the delicacy and the technological sophistication of the submarine. Although the image is nearly photographic in its detail and apparent realism, it nevertheless contains evidence of the artist's hand at work, making it something more than simple reportage – its draughtsman-like quality lends a sense of ceremonial importance and of timeless drama to the two ships as stage setting for the minor historic event it describes.[15]

The depiction of ships by fine artists continued to evolve in relation to the changing styles of painting during the 1920s and '30s, when the passenger liner was still the sole means of travelling the world. Le Corbusier referred to their 'beauty of a more technical order', and it was such opinion that informed their depiction in the work of modernist painters between World Wars One and Two.

The American Gerald Murphy had studied painting in Paris with the Russian émigré Natalia Goncharova, and through her connections he painted sets for the Ballet Russes. Amid his friendships with Picasso, Léger and other avant-gardists in the Paris art world of the 1920s, Murphy developed an original style of painting, which is now considered an antecedent to the Pop Art movement of the 1960s. This is because of Murphy's choice of commercially branded subject matter, his use of flat colour and his interest in the manipulation of scale, exploding the size of very small things and making large ones appear even more heroic.

Murphy selected objects from everyday modern life – the safety razor, matchbox, cocktail paraphernalia – yet he returned several times to the theme of the ocean liner, so central to the mythology of the machine in the years following World War One and essential to Murphy's own transatlantic lifestyle. His enormous stage backdrop for a Cole Porter musical, *Within the Quota*, presented at the Théâtre des Champs-Elysées in 1923, parodied the front page of a Hearst newspaper with the headline 'Unknown Banker Buys Atlantic' accompanied by a montage, typical of the period, comparing the length of an ocean liner, standing on end, with the height of New York's Woolworth Tower, then the world's tallest building. This comparative device was used frequently in promotional images by the leading shipping lines and was favoured in magazine and news articles about the largest liners of the time. Cunard, for example, depicted either the *Lusitania* or *Mauretania* (their profiles were virtually identical) leaning against the angled side of the Pyramid of Cheops with the ship's bow extending well above the tip of the great tomb, demonstrating its enormity.

In 1924 Murphy painted *Engine Room*, a composition of gears and cogs of indeterminate purpose suggesting the titanic machinery used to power the great transatlantic liners he so admired, but also reminiscent of the delicate mechanisms found inside a clock or watch – a provocative juxtaposition of speed and time. The geometric simplicity of the image is infused with drama by Murphy's use of light, which appears to be emerging from recesses within the composition, brightly highlighting some elements while casting other parts into deep shadow. This painting, like several others of Murphy's small output, mainly preserved in black-and-white photographs, has been long lost.

The largest and most ambitious of Murphy's ship paintings took as its subject the smokestacks and ventilators of an Atlantic greyhound. In this massive 5.5-m by 3.7-m (18-ft by 12-ft) canvas, titled *Boatdeck, Cunarder* (1923) because he used the Cunard colours for the smokestacks, Murphy began with forms that are large in reality and then made them appear colossal, an approach he had cited in a notebook relating to a domestic interior scene. 'Scene of house interior with all chairs and furnishings done in colossal (or heroic) scale. People dwarfed . . . climbing seriously into great chairs . . . struggling . . . Man's good-natured tussle with the giant material world'.[16]

As an American living in France, Murphy crossed the Atlantic frequently and photographed the superstructures and deck equipment of many ships. Therefore, *Boatdeck* represents a distillation of numerous stacks, vents, bridges, cabin houses, an abstraction based on cubic and circular shapes turned at various angles to the picture plane while generating a subtle balance of movement and stability, of complication and simplicity. Here, Murphy's heroic geometries closely foreshadow the poster art of A. M. Cassandre in the latter artist's depictions of ships such as the 40,000-ton French Line paquebot *L'Atlantique* (1931). In this image, like Murphy before him, Cassandre exaggerated the size of the ship and used the Russian Suprematist formula of overlapping squares, rectangles and circles to abstract the vessel's exterior forms and thereby to dramatize its power, grandeur and stability.

Murphy's *Boatdeck* was shown in the 1924 Independents exhibition and again at the Bernheim Jeune Gallery in 1936 but was lost during World War Two. Gerald Murphy's legacy as an original and intelligent painter was for many years overshadowed by his reputation as a famous American ex-patriot of the so-called Lost Generation and by his many friendships with leading figures in the Paris art world of the 1920s. A fictionalized portrait of Murphy appears as the central character in F. Scott Fitzgerald's novel *Tender is the Night*. Yet it is precisely his social position and transatlantic lifestyle that led him to create some of the period's most compelling and iconic images of the ocean liner as a symbol of transatlantic culture.

Like Murphy, his American contemporaries Charles Demuth, Charles Sheeler, Georgia O'Keeffe and Joseph Stella were all fascinated by the heroic architecture and engineering of the industrial age and took subjects from the commercial landscape growing up around them. They also shared an approach to representation that combined photographic influences, linear draughtsmanship derived from

Gerald Murphy's lost 18 x 12-foot painting, *Boatdeck, Cunarder* (1923), was a deadpan monument to a subject that the conventional art world would have seen as ugly and ordinary at the time.

engineering drawings and rigorous compositional formality that earned them a variety of titles including 'Cubo-Realist', 'New Classicist', and later, after World War Two, the title that stuck most firmly among art historians, 'Precisionist'. Although each artist developed a personal style of painting, their similar interest in the technologies of modernity and its geometries visible in factories, grain silos, railroads, bridges, skyscrapers and steamships linked them as a group.

Charles Sheeler wrote of the machine as 'the religious expression of today',[17] and when he photographed and painted the River Rouge factory, the largest industrial complex in the world, where the Model A automobile was being built, he was dubbed 'the Raphael of the Fords'.[18] Sheeler supported himself for many years as an architectural photographer, also producing photos for product advertisements as well as taking fashionable celebrity portraits for *Vanity Fair* and *Harper's Bazaar*. In 1928 he was commissioned by the White Star Line to photograph their Atlantic flagship, *Majestic*, which was then the largest and second-fastest ocean liner in the world. *Majestic* had been under construction in Germany at the start of World War One and was intended to become the HAPAG Lloyd flagship *Bizmark*. Left unfinished at the time of the Armistice, the ship was ceded to Britain and the White Star Line, which completed its construction and renamed the 56,551-ton ship, which made its maiden voyage from Southampton to New York in 1922.

Based on his photographs of the *Majestic*, Sheeler soon produced one of his best-known paintings, *Upper Deck*. In this picture the artist first successfully translated the qualities of his photographs into paint and achieved a composition of classic order akin to the contemporaneous buildings of International Style architects such as Walter Gropius, Richard Neutra and Le Corbusier. Most importantly for the subsequent history of painting, this work demonstrated clearly that its source was a photograph rather than a drawing or sketch, a lesson that would liberate painters from the accusation of 'cheating' (by using photographic sources) and that led to the development of later twentieth-century art movements such as Photorealism.

Although *Upper Deck* shares its subject with Murphy's *Boatdeck*, it is a painting with different aesthetic aims. Nevertheless, it too presents an image of the ocean liner that emphasizes the poetry of its geometric volumes, finding beauty in its mechanical nature. For those supporters of modern art who viewed either of these pictures when they were first shown, the lesson would have been obvious – to appreciate the elegance of modern machinery, such as the steamship, and to give it the status it deserved in the rapidly emerging twentieth-century culture, which was still struggling for recognition against traditional tastes. Here, the passenger ship, a product of the modern industrial and commercial world, is celebrated as a monumental aesthetic icon of its time, an inspiration for artists in a league with the pyramids of Egypt, the Gothic cathedrals or any great work of nature. Because Sheeler's portrayal of the *Majestic* is grand and solemn, lacking the latent irony and wit of Murphy's *Boatdeck*, it can be linked perhaps more firmly with earnest modernist theory than with the ironic Pop Art of the 1960s anticipated by the jaded sophisticate, Murphy.

Predictions

While the liner of the inter-wars generation was recognized as the pinnacle of maritime progress, its future form became a subject of speculation among ambitious inventors and the first generation of industrial designers, who established their profession during the later 1920s and published their concepts widely. Between the Armistice of 1918 and the outbreak of war in 1939, aircraft had not yet been perceived as a major threat to the future of passenger shipping, and so the futurologists of the day looked ahead to a generation of super-ships, faster and bigger than anything yet constructed, and they represented them in forms consistent with the most advanced industrial styling of the period, Streamlining.

The most outstanding example of this trend came from the drawing board of Norman Bel Geddes, an early leader of the industrial design profession in the US and arguably its most flamboyant proponent. Bel Geddes's background in theatre design and window display equipped him with the skills of representation and a dramatic flair for extravagant, sweeping forms that he applied to all modern products and building types, from large factories to gas stations, vacuum cleaners, refrigerators, automobiles and aircraft. Among the many futuristic designs he published in his 1932 manifesto, *Horizons*, his *Ocean Liner Number 1* remains one of the most radical ship designs of the twentieth century along with his visionary drawings of *Airliner Number 4*, nothing less than an ocean liner contained within the form of a flying-wing designed to take off and land on water.

While Le Corbusier was still admiring the airy, open promenades and the rectilinear superstructure of the Edwardian liner *Aquitania* and its generation of ships, Bel Geddes enclosed the decks of his 'ship of the future' within a streamlined carapace unifying the hull and superstructure, a teardrop shape distorted only by the two sweeping funnels and the cantilevered wings of the bridge. The fully glass-enclosed decks were intended to deliver a very low drag coefficient and simultaneously protect passengers from the high-velocity air currents that would be created by the unprecedented speed of the ship. Even the lifeboats would be enclosed within the vessel's organically shaped envelope. Only at the stern would a telescopically retractable glass roof over the tiered sun decks, sand beach and swimming pool provide passengers with an open-air experience in good weather. Like many of Bel Geddes's other visionary projects of the late 1920s and '30s, his ocean liner was forgotten for many years, yet today it appears prophetic in view of the current generation of cruise liners that incorporate many of its extraordinary features.

Although Bel Geddes presented his sketch for *Ocean Liner 1* as a serious proposal, its rhetorical value was recognized almost immediately in the popular arts, particularly in comic books and in set designs for the cinema. A big-budget Hollywood musical review, *The Big Broadcast of 1938*, was set almost entirely aboard a fictitious North Atlantic liner based very closely on Bel Geddes's ship design. This state-of-the-art vessel, *Gigantic*, racing against its more conventional rival – *Colossal* – for the Blue Riband, provided the settings of cabins, bars and lounges against which W. C. Fields, Martha Raye and Bob Hope sang, danced and clowned. The European émigré architects Hans Dreier and F. E. Freudeman designed and decorated the ship sets in the modernist style they and others brought to Hollywood between the wars, a style that was subsequently disseminated around the world through the medium of film. Although Bel Geddes's concept drawings did not extend to the ship's interior design, Dreier and Freudeman fleshed out the details in a convincing sequence of airy white spaces closely following the compound curves of the ship's external form. Dynamic rows of tall curving windows or dramatic horizontal ribbons of glass flooded the fluid interior spaces with light and provided magnificent views of sea and sky, while all interior details appeared to be products of the latest scientific thinking, as well as up-to-the-minute style.

Like the movies, magazines offered another outlet for the creative fantasies of visionary ship designers in the first half of the twentieth century. The cover of the American monthly, *Popular Mechanics*, March 1925, featured an illustration for its lead article, 'Wind Towers Drive Ship', in which an innovative cargo ship propelled by two tall cylindrical structures, surges past the ghosted image of a grand ocean liner. This fantastic cargo ship was in reality the *Buckau*, a schooner refitted by the inventor Anton Flettner, who conceived and patented the rotors that now bear his name. The wind-powered cylindrical rotors that made use of the so-called Magnus Effect to drive the *Buckau* were approximately 15 m (49 ft) tall and had a diameter of 3 m (9 ft), and although the ship sailed well and travelled from Germany to New York and the Caribbean, it proved to be less efficient than a conventionally powered ship of the day. This article was published at a time when traditional wind-powered sailing ships were still transporting a significant amount of the world's cargo and when dirty, inefficient coal-fired boilers were being replaced by cleaner and more economical oil burners in the larger passenger and cargo vessels of most shipping lines. Yet even at that time, there was clearly an urge to find the optimum source of free energy, then for economic reasons rather than for the ecological motives that drive the same quest today. And despite a recent surge of experimentation in response to global warming, that Holy Grail remains just beyond reach.

Today's futurologists envision a new generation of ships powered by a variety of innovative sails, kites and solar panels, thus making use of free and clean energy sources, the wind and the sun. In 1985 Flettner rotors, themselves, were revived and improved by Jacques-Yves Cousteau with the engineers Lucien Malavard and Bertrand Charrier, and renamed Turbosail, to provide supplementary power for the diesel-engine research vessel *Alcyone*. This is a hybrid wind-engine powered ship, its advantages being a reduction in the consumption of fossil fuels and a consequent lessening of pollutants. Ships remain the most efficient way to move goods around the planet, and because of their greedy dependency on fossil fuel and their dreadful record of polluting the seas their design should become a prime field of innovation in clean technologies. Yet *Alcyone* remains a rare experiment known to the world primarily through the medium of television and presented by Cousteau as a harbinger of things to come. Unfortunately, it has not had a great influence in the past quarter century thanks to the conservatism of the shipping industry, the relative cheapness of fossil fuels and a reluctance until recently to take global warming seriously.

The most far-reaching concepts remain essentially promotional in character and are known largely through widely circulated drawings and diagrams such as those published internationally to illustrate the *Kiteship*, a proposed vessel towed by a massive sea kite capable of augmenting the ship's conventional engine. The similar Skysail apparatus, invented by a German, Stephan Wrage, is also a very large kite attached to a ship by a towrope and controlled by a computerized autopilot, keeping the kite trimmed for optimal performance and guiding it to the best winds, those normally found at an altitude of around 30.48 m (1,000 ft). Such ships, equipped with what amount to auxiliary sails, as used on Brunel's early steamships, would also follow somewhat different routes from today's ordinary steamships in order to take advantage of prevailing winds. Thus far, however, only one large ship, the *Beluga Skysail*, has been fitted with this technology, and the modest predicted benefit of 10 per cent fuel saving is not yet proven.

Also at an early stage of development is a Norwegian project, the *Orcelle*, a cargo vessel that is intended to use rigid, rotating sails based on the Flettner rotor principle. These, however, also double as solar collectors when the wind is not sufficiently strong to power the vessel. Developed by the Norwegian firm Wallenius Wilhelmsen, *Orcelle* would have no conventional engines, powered entirely by wind, sun and waves, and it would emit no pollutants into sea or air. This 'ideas' vessel is proposed as a large vehicle carrier for the Britain–Australia route capable of carrying 10,000 vehicles, yet its

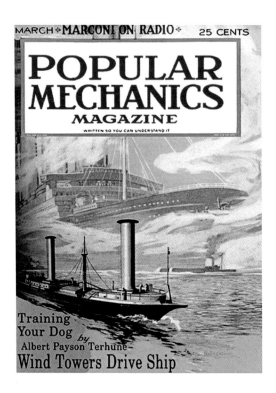

MARCH ✦ MARCONI ON RADIO ✦ 25 CENTS

POPULAR
MECHANICS
MAGAZINE
WRITTEN SO YOU CAN UNDERSTAND IT

Training
Your Dog *by*
Albert Payson Terhune

Wind Towers Drive Ship

technology could be applied to other types of cargo or passenger ships as well. Wave energy would be captured by a dozen fins attached to a slender monohull flanked by two sponsons for stability, while the wind and solar energy would be gathered by three large fin-shaped sails. This energy would then be stored in hydrogen fuel cells. Thanks to its innovative hull shape, the vessel would have the further advantage of carrying no ballast water, the discharge of which is now recognized as a major source of ecological destabilization. The development period for this technology is expected to extend another fifteen years, yet it is perhaps the most daring design for a clean vessel of the future. While the published

Science fiction meets technical reality in *Popular Mechanics Magazine*'s romanticized image of the converted cargo schooner *Buckau*, wind-powered by innovative Flettner Rotors, and seen at right operating in the 1920s.

images are exciting, they are simply renderings and diagrams that employ similar graphical descriptions and scale comparisons to those used in the magazines and newspapers of the early twentieth century to promote then new or unfinished liners such as the *Lusitania* and the *Normandie*, and experimental vessels such as *Buckau*.[19] As in other major transport industries, particularly trucking, motoring and aviation, fundamental technical innovation is still lagging behind the pressures of environmental pollution, and depictions such as those of *Orcelle* remain for the moment in the genre of science fiction.

Symbol

Both the mythology and imagery of the ship underwent a major transformation in the Jet Age. The middle-class clientele of the new cruise liners was not so newsworthy as had been the comings and goings of celebrities on global ocean shuttles up to the 1950s, when a gaggle of press photographers would turn out to photograph stars and politicians on deck for publication in the daily papers, fashionable monthlies and weekly fan magazines. Also, depictions of great ships disappeared almost completely from the fine arts during the 1940s and '50s, when all such figurative subjects became increasingly rare in the dominant climate of Abstract Expressionism and other subsequent non-representational movements in the arts. Even in figurative genres such as Pop Art, however, the ocean liner, like the train, rarely appeared, since it had become passé in relation to the airliner and automobile.

Yet the appearance of certain types of warship still conveyed a power represented by no other instrument of nationalism. Even the heavy, nuclear-armed B-52 bomber aircraft did not say Force as convincingly as a mighty aircraft carrier, which had not only the advantage of presenting its enormous bulk as evidence of defensive strength but also carried the highest-technology attack aircraft on its decks. The sheer spatial complexity of such a vessel as the US Navy's nuclear-powered Nimitz-class carriers attract attention not only from the general public, who visit such ships in large numbers whenever they are on display, but also from architects, who have continued to see in them models for high-density living in the postmodern period. These ships are as close to Verne's floating cities as have so far been built, although here the 'city' is a naval base at sea, housing an awesome arsenal of weaponry as well as a wide variety of distinct personnel communities.

In April 1968 the young Viennese architect Hans Hollein published in the journal *Bau* a manifesto accompanied by a series of montages collectively and individually titled *Everything is Architecture*. They included a giant sparkplug set on the side of a hill, rocks magnified to resemble a cityscape and, perhaps most famously, an image of an aircraft carrier, the USS *Enterprise*, placed in a landscape to suggest the military town it actually was. *Everything is Architecture* was very much a product of its time, representing an architectural response to the radical and inclusive ideas of Marshall McLuhan ('the global village'), Reyner Banham (*Megastructure*) and Buckminster Fuller (*Operating Manual for Spaceship Earth*), using a visual technique that Claude Lévi-Strauss called *bricolage*. Hollein's works published in *Bau* could easily be seen, then, as conceptual art: yet *Aircraft Carrier in the Landscape* defies such categorization. Peter Cook commented that:

> The image of the aircraft carrier sitting upon a hill is very compelling. It suggests that either the aircraft carrier is a city within a coherent structure; or it suggests that the ultimate in technology could poise itself on the land; or it suggests the irony of a ridiculous conglomeration of human functions sitting at a point on a hill, like a rock; or it suggests that there will always be a paradox between the involved man-made thing and the rest; or it can be seen as some mixture of all of these.[20]

Hollein said himself that his montages were both concept and proposal, and he asserted that they could be realized, fusing art and architecture. The surrealism surrounding the dislocated aircraft carrier does not negate the fact that such a vessel can house 7,000 people and serve all their needs just as a real town does, and perform that job more efficiently than many cities. It is then surrounded by natural landscape, much like the ideal post-war housing blocks, sitting in parkland, as proposed for the redevelopment of most major cities. Presented in such a context, the image of the ship aligned with the debates in and between architecture and the fine arts during the turbulent and inventive 1960s. Then, the emphasis shifted from homage for the machine to a more complex and ambivalent recognition of the largest and most complex of machines as environments with resonances for all other types of habitable structure.

The image of a land-locked carrier also resonates with one bizarre manifestation of naval history, the 'stone frigate', which according to a World War Two British naval intelligence officer, Alan Peacock, was:

> a rather contemptuous term for a shore-based establishment such as a barracks or training base masquerading under a title which gave the impression that it was a sea-going vessel. Thus the naval base at Rosyth was HMS *Cochrane*. Those serving in them did not have to suffer the discomforts and dangers of their sea-going counterparts. However, they tended to adopt naval parlance which suggested that they were simi-larly situated. For example, a sailor seeking to go off-duty would seek 'permission to go ashore' and, if granted, would 'go over the side' even though he might merely be going through the dockyard gate, down the street and into the nearest pub.[21]

Peacock's memoirs also recalled HMS *Royal Arthur*, a pre-war Butlin's holiday camp commandeered for the duration of the war, where 'a vestige of the camp atmosphere lingered. Surrounded by the (unheated) swimming pools and the now tatty decor of what had been the bars and restaurants, it was difficult to believe that one was going to be trained to face formidable enemies.'[22] In this way the definitions of ship, camp and town blur absurdly.

Although the tradition continues for the navies of the world to commission paintings of the ships in their fleets, just as the shipping lines of today commission both painted and photographic portraits of their new cruise liners, by the 1980s any representation of ships in contemporary art would, in the spirit of the time, be political and provocative. Such was the case of *Polaris* (1983), an installation work by the British sculptor David Mach. Sited on a riverside esplanade

outside the Royal Festival Hall in London, this was a full-scale replica of a Polaris submarine constructed using 6,000 used car tyres arranged in layers to simulate the form of a British nuclear-powered Resolution-class submarine, which was armed with sixteen Polaris A3 nuclear guided missiles. Two such boats of 129.5 m (425 ft) and 8,500 tons were built at Barrow-in-Furness by the Vickers Armstrong Company and named *Resolution* and *Repulse*, while two more, *Renown* and *Revenge*, were constructed by Cammell Laird of Birkenhead. HMS *Resolution*, the first vessel completed, was commissioned in 1967, and the fleet remained in service until replaced by the newer Vanguard-class submarines in the mid-1990s. Meanwhile, controversy raged throughout the later years of the Cold War over the British nuclear deterrent, and the very existence of nuclear weapons, a movement led most convincingly by the Campaign for Nuclear Disarmament (CND).

It was against this background that Mach presented his *Polaris*, a provocation to anyone with views on the nuclear debate, further

Like Noah's Ark, architect Shigeru Ban's and artist Gregory Colbert's Nomadic Museum conveys a message of salvation for nature's surviving animal species.

complicated by the use of commercial waste – the car tyre – as its material. The installation was aesthetically sophisticated and innovative as a work of art, but it also became notorious because of the dramatic response it evoked, when an irate viewer attempted to set fire to the piece as a gesture of protest, but was caught up in the conflagration and was, himself, fatally burnt. News images of the flaming sculpture altered the mythology of the ship significantly and irrevocably, drawing attention to the dark, elusive threat that stalks the depths of the world's oceans, unseen but widely feared, and demonstrating that even an artist's representation of such a sea monster can be fatal.

Perhaps the most provocative image of shipping in the early twenty-first century did not, in fact, take the form of a vessel, but used the basic element of modern global commerce, the steel container, as its fabric and symbol. The *Nomadic Museum*, a temporary, demountable structure, was built to accommodate an exhibition by the artist Gregory Colbert, *Ashes and Snow*, of large-scale photographs and film centring on the relationship between human beings and all other animal species. The *Nomadic Museum* was designed by the Japanese architect Shigeru Ban and sited on the legendary Pier 54 in New York, the former Cunard White Star Line pier where the greatest ships of the transatlantic shuttle came and went. There, the *Lusitania* embarked for the last time before being torpedoed off the Irish coast in 1915. There, too, the survivors of the *Titanic* returned from their ordeal at sea to meet the press. Like the ships of the past, Colbert's exhibition came and went, travelling to Venice, Los Angeles, Tokyo and Mexico City between 2005 and 2008.

The *Nomadic Museum* was constructed of 148 standard shipping containers stacked, chequerboard fashion, to create a linear space of 13,716 sq. m (45,000 sq. ft). Whereas, in the Smithsonian Museum in Washington, DC, a single shipping container is an exhibit in its own right, in the *Nomadic Museum* the collected containers are arranged as the enclosure for a vast public exhibition and depart from their normal function to carry a purely symbolic freight of ideas and images. The formal simplicity of the structure is equally reminiscent of a giant basilica or of the avenues created between stacked containers in a modern cargo port. But more symbolically, the *Nomadic Museum* forms an ark, providing an evocative backdrop for Colbert's giant photographs that depict the encroachment of human activity on the natural world; and like the Ark of Noah it conveys a message of salvation for nature's surviving animal species.

3 Conflict

Air Ships

On 2 May 2003, 30 miles off the coast of California, the US President George W. Bush, in the co-pilot's seat of a Navy S-3B Viking anti-submarine jet, landed on the deck of the aircraft carrier USS *Abraham Lincoln*. The four-seat aircraft was designated *Navy 1*, and 'George W. Bush Commander-in-Chief' was stencilled on its fuselage. The plane made a 241.4-kmph (150-mph) 'tailhook' landing, stopping in less than 121.9 m (400 ft). This was a spectacular and historic event, as the first time a serving president had landed a plane on the deck of an aircraft carrier. And such a carrier!

The *Abraham Lincoln*, known in naval circles as 'Abe', is the fifth of ten Nimitz-class nuclear-powered vessels to be designed and built for the US Navy by Newport News Shipbuilding (now Northrop Grumman Shipbuilding) in Virginia. Nimitz-class carriers are the largest capital ships ever built and are, today, the embodiment of US naval and aviation might. Launched in 1988, the 98,235-ton *Abraham Lincoln* is 332.8 m (1,092 ft) long, with 18210.5 sq. km (4.5 acres) of flight deck. It is powered by two Westinghouse nuclear reactors that propel the ship at more than 30 knots (56 km/ph) and can operate continuously for up to twenty years before needing to refuel. The vessel carries between 65 and 90

USS *Abraham Lincoln* dressed for an historic flying visit by President George W. Bush in 2003.

tactical and support aircraft, including transport planes, helicopters, early warning planes and the Navy's latest attack fighter, the F/A-18E Super Hornet. The ship houses a complement of around 6,000 personnel.

In addition to its statistical credentials, *Abraham Lincoln* enjoys a position in naval history as the first carrier to integrate a female aviator into the flight crew following the lifting of Combat Exclusion Laws in 1991 and the repeal in 1993 of the rule barring women from Navy combat ships, earning it the sobriquet 'Babe-raham Lincoln'.[1] Tragically, Lieutenant Kara Spears Hultgreen, the first female fighter pilot to join the crew, died on a routine attempt to land aboard the ship, when her F14 Tomcat suffered engine failure and crashed into the sea. Naval curmudgeons said 'Told you so!', but there was no serious evidence that Hultgreen could have avoided the accident. The ship also holds another unfortunate place in history for the hubris of the Bush visit, when the president made a globally televised appearance on deck declaring victory in America's war of liberation, 'Operation Iraqi Freedom', under a large banner stating 'Mission Accomplished', a premature claim in light of growing insurgency in Iraq at the time. The preposterousness of this public relations stunt, employing the imposing vessel as a presidential toy, created a media image of foolishness and arrogance outstanding in recent political history. As the entertainment industry newspaper *Variety* might have put it, 'Top Gun Lays an Egg'.

The *Abraham Lincoln*'s striking appearance is the result of form following function, in the strictest sense, and the culmination of more than 70 years of design evolution since the inception of the aircraft carrier. From any angle the ship has a terrible beauty consistent with the seriousness of its purpose, with the phenomenal resources that have gone into its design and construction, and with the technology embedded in each element of its enormous structure.

Beginning with the shape of its hull, the vessel is replete with dramatic forms. From the waterline, the bow flares up and forward in a graceful, dynamic curve to meet the underside of the flight deck. Below the waterline, it curves forward into a voluptuous, protruding bulb that modifies the flow of water around the bow to improve hull efficiency. Such bulbous bows, devised to raise speed, stability, economy and range, first appeared in 1910 when the US Navy's chief naval architect, David W. Taylor, designed an innovative hull with a bulbous bow for the USS *Delaware*, producing a much smaller bow wave, an indication of reduced drag. The later ocean liners *Bremen* and *Normandie* also employed bulbous bows in their radical hull shapes to reach Blue Riband-winning speeds, achieved on considerably lower horsepower and with greater fuel efficiency than their conventionally shaped rival, the *Queen Mary*.

Along the sides of its hull the *Abraham Lincoln* bristles with purposeful protuberances, including four massive lifting platforms that can each carry two aircraft at a time from the hangar deck up to the flight deck, vast loading doors for cargo containers and large vehicles, radar domes, housings for optical landing systems and rocket launchers. The flight deck, itself, is kept clean of any potential obstacles to take off or landing, although moveable elements such as the catapult control pod, which allows the catapult crew to view activities on deck, are retractable. Four catapults for launching planes are located in two pairs, one in the bow and the other near the forward edge of the stepped-out deck. A carrier's flight deck can be one of the busiest and most dangerous workplaces of any kind, with aircraft parked, some moving into position for launch and others landing, all at the same time. Personnel on deck perform their jobs in a strictly choreographed routine of movements, and they wear highly visible, brightly coloured uniforms that signify their rank and role.

The geometry of the modern carrier deck, itself, is devised to ease simultaneous take-off and landing and is therefore stepped out and angled toward the port side to provide space for multiple activities, including parking. The angled flight deck was the idea of Rear Admiral Dennis Campbell, a British Royal Navy test pilot who flew with carrier squadrons during the 1930s. It was his flight experience that led him to the angled-deck concept, which was applied for the first time by the US Navy in the conversion of the USS *Antietam* in 1952. Subsequently, that carrier engaged in test operations with both US and British navies, demonstrating the advantages of the angled-deck principle; it enabled pilots to approach the deck faster and provided them with the option to abort the landing in an emergency. Campbell described 'many self-inflicted near-misses and other close contacts with the Grim Reaper' that inspired his design breakthrough.[2] This is typical of the cross-disciplinary nature of carrier design, which involves the performance of the vessel itself,

Credited to the chief naval architect, David Taylor, and first used on a US warship in 1910, the bulbous bow improves speed and fuel efficiency of large ships with long, narrow hulls.

the design of its weapons and aircraft design, each advocated by a different community of interests.

The most outstanding feature of the carrier's shape is the super-structure, also known as the 'island house', which is a multi-storey building located on the starboard side of the ship's deck. It contains a compact forward-facing bridge, the main flight control room with windows at the side overlooking the flight deck, and a tower bristling with radar and other electronic communications equipment. The *Abraham Lincoln*'s island is positioned about two-thirds of the way aft from the bow, lending the ship's profile an almost jaunty aggressiveness, similar to the long-nose, short-rear proportional

George H. W. Bush watches the island house lifted into place during the construction of the Nimitz-class aircraft carrier named after him.

formula used in traditional sports car design. Its placement is not, however, an aesthetic choice, but rather a decision based on the ideal location of the ship's aircraft elevators. Like other major elements of the carrier, the 650-ton island house is entirely prefabricated at a facility near to the dry dock, where the ship is assembled; and then it is lifted into place on the deck. The 'island house lift' is a key moment in the construction of a carrier, when the vessel takes on its finished appearance.

Nimitz-class carriers are the most complex and expensive naval vessels ever constructed. They operate typically as the command centre of a battle group including destroyers, frigates, missile cruisers, submarines and supply ships. The carrier's air wing is used to conduct strikes supporting land-based artillery or to protect military and commercial ships. As floating air bases, carriers also host conferences, diplomatic functions and special events such as the visit of President Bush. In the early days of the NASA space programme they were the conspicuous rendezvous destinations for astronauts landing their tiny space capsules in the vastness of the world's oceans. Perhaps most importantly in times of international tension, the carrier is the greatest signifier of a nation's military strength.

Their interiors centre on the enormous hangars, located directly below the flight deck, where the aircraft on board are sheltered and serviced. Further down in the ship are the crew facilities, which comprise an entire town, with residential quarters, canteens, hospital, galleys, gymnasium and recreation areas for the 6,000 people in the combined crew and air wing. Additional workplaces include the internal operations room, where all activities of the flight deck are monitored on video screens, as are the flight paths of all aircraft within the ship's airspace. The two Westinghouse A4W nuclear reactors that power the ship are controlled remotely from another office-like facility, where work is centred on the computer terminal.

Pumping rooms ensure a constant supply of filtered aviation fuel to the flight deck as required by the air wing. Thus the aircraft carrier is a multi-purpose giant launched on to the sea, part ship, part office building, part airfield and a hybrid product of the modern age.

Such a ship can be best understood as a floating garrison rather than as a civilian town. Here, many residents rarely get outside. Views from the flight deck may be magnificent, but the pace and danger of its operation inhibit much reflection on the beauty of sky and sea, even for the lucky members of the air wing who get to go there. Sailors working in the bowels of the ship may not see the sun for days or weeks. Jim Prender, stationed aboard the USS *John F. Kennedy* in the 1970s, recalled the discomfort of his job as an apprentice fireman:

> I worked in the engine room where we made the steam to propel the ship and launch the F-15's. I was a Boiler Technician . . . We worked 16 hours a day every day in hot, oily, noisy and potentially dangerous conditions seven stories below sea level. Nobody went down into the engine room unless you had to. I can remember opening the hatch [door] onto deck to stumble back to my rack [bed] to sleep after a hard shift and sailors walking by the opened hatch would feel the blast of heat and ask how the hell we could work down there. Hell was an appropriate word. We would routinely go 10–12 days without ever seeing daylight or feeling fresh air in our nostrils.[3]

Despite the vast size of such ships, their interiors are cramped. Stairs are near vertical; corridors are narrow; and berths are stacked three high. Sailors may share a room with 50 other ratings, and their personal possessions and clothing are kept in a small locker. While officers have more space and the top ranks may enjoy more privacy, their personal accommodations are also minimal and efficient.

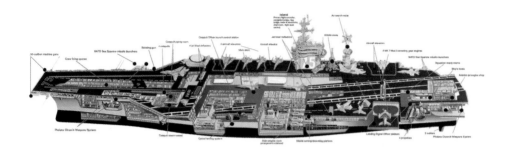

In earlier years and during wartime blackouts, conditions were poor even for officers. A World War Two British intelligence officer, stationed aboard the escort carrier HMS *Vindex* in the North Sea, recalled in a letter to his former senior officer that

> our office was the cleared-out flag locker just off the flight deck. Conditions were dreadful, cramped, cold, condensation on the bulkheads from the breath of those working there. You, in your considerate and practical way, used to let us go one at a time on the flight deck for five or ten minutes, if nothing was happening.[4]

It was in this dismal setting that significant enemy messages regarding fleet movements and attack plans were intercepted and interpreted by the first generation of sea-going personnel to use information supplied by the Enigma code-breakers of Bletchley Park, an estate near London often called the birthplace of computing.

When Hans Hollein displaced the aircraft carrier from its conventional aquatic habitat to a rural hilltop in his montage *Aircraft Carrier in the Landscape*, he could do so with plausibility, since the configuration of such vessels relates conceptually to that of a megastructure. The megastructure became a recognized building type in the 1960s, when the term was coined by the British architectural

Cut-away view of nimitz-class aircraft carrier, USS *Theodore Roosevelt*.

historian Reyner Banham, who defined its characteristics. According to Banham, the megastructure was built of modular units; it was extendable; it was a structural network to which smaller units could be 'plugged in' or 'clipped on' after having been prefabricated elsewhere; and it was expected to have a useful life exceeding that of the smaller units it would support.[5] *Abraham Lincoln* embodies all these characteristics as well as the mobility so admired by Banham and his friend, the architect Peter Cook. Cook's scheme for a *Plug-In City* (1964) was an expandable and flexible continuous structure into which all the changing necessities of the city – housing, offices, shops, transport – could be 'plugged' or unplugged as required. One can thus understand the role of the aircraft aboard a carrier as one such removable element.

In reality, the megastructure had become a familiar, popular image from science fiction long before architects took it up as a subject worthy of serious examination. It was in Verne's description of ships in *A Floating City* and *Propeller Island* that the concept of a vessel the size of a town and what would later be called a megastructure first converged. Like Verne's *Standard Island*, the *Abraham Lincoln* is an enormous ocean-going structure with a lifespan longer than its minor elements. It is assembled from prefabricated parts that can be replaced if they are damaged or can be upgraded with more advanced pieces to improve performance, add new capabilities or extend the vessel's useful life. It could be lengthened if required, in the same way that many cargo and passenger vessels have had new hull sections inserted to create additional capacity. Typically, *Abe*'s entire superstructure, the island house, can be 'unplugged' to make way for a newer and better component. And through its air wing, the ship's *raison d'être*, it extends or expands itself into the atmosphere over oceans and land to achieve its military objectives.

By the 1920s the high-density urban fabric and the airplane had already become closely linked in the public mind, when the epic German science fiction film *Metropolis* (1927) was being planned. Among the many apocryphal legends in the history of cinema, it has been said that the film's director, Fritz Lang, conceived his vision of the city of the future while gazing at the Manhattan skyline from the deck of an ocean liner moored briefly in New York harbour. Designed by Edgar E. Ulmer, the film's metropolis set was a dense ensemble of skyscrapers connected at various floor levels by bridges, crowded with vehicles and pedestrians. And between the skyscrapers, weaving their way through the spires and bridges, were flying machines that could, apparently, land on any roof or terrace. Thus, the building and aircraft became parts of the same megastructure, as are the jets, helicopters and pilots of a carrier's air group, intimately yet invisibly tied to the host machine by food, fuel, maintenance, sleep, radar and other electronic guidance and communication systems. The ship is the pilots' mobile base and, in the case of Nimitz-class ships, is also presented as a floating city assigned its own American postal zip code. Its community of mainly young crew members are there for a variety of reasons, which may not be primarily patriotic, but over a long tour of duty the ship can come to seem like their peripatetic home town.

Aeronauts

The concept of naval aviation extends back beyond the invention of the heavier-than-air flying machine to the days of balloon reconnaissance, first attempted seriously during the American Civil War, when observation balloons were tethered to barges and other vessels to monitor enemy activities.[6] Then, during the first decade of the twentieth century, rapid advances in the technology of the newly

invented airplane made its naval uses demonstrable. The first pilot
to take off and land in a fixed-wing aircraft from a ship was the
American Eugene Burton Ely, a sportsman pilot who went to work
for the brilliant pioneer aviator and aircraft maker, Glen Curtiss in
1910, when the first public demonstrations of the *Wright Flyer* were
only two years past. Through Curtiss Ely met Captain Washington
Chambers, who was investigating potential applications of aircraft
for the Navy.

Together, they arranged for Ely to test-fly his Curtiss Model D
pusher biplane from the specially adapted deck of a US warship,
Birmingham. In January 1911 Ely won a $500 prize for both taking
off and landing on the deck of the cruiser USS *Pennsylvania*, which
had a wooden platform (10 by 40 m wide [33 × 130 ft]) in length
fitted above its armoured deck for the event. This important experiment proved the viability of ship-based aircraft and introduced basic
carrier flight technologies, including use of the first ever tail-hook
to stop the un-braked plane rapidly when landing. The tail-hook
was the invention of Hugh Robinson, another daredevil stunt flyer
and pioneer aviation engineer, who also worked for Glen Curtiss.
Ely himself continued stunt flying in public exhibitions for several

A Curtiss pusher biplane, piloted by Eugene B. Ely in November 1910, was the first aircraft to
take off from a ship, USS *Birmingham*, anchored off the Virginia coast.

more months but met his inevitable fate in October 1911, when his plane failed to pull out of a dive at an air show. He had told the local press shortly before: 'I guess I will be like the rest of them, keep at it until I am killed.'[7] This was extreme sport!

The experimental phase of carrier development lasted for more than a decade, although the British navy had a plan for a purpose-built carrier as early as 1912. Two British ships, the battle cruiser *Furious* (1916) and a converted ocean liner, *Argus* (1917), were fitted with flight decks and were used with lesser and greater success, respectively, but neither made a major impact on the future development of the carrier. The world's first purpose-built carrier was the British *Hermes*, constructed by Armstrong Whitworth and launched in 1919, but not commissioned into the Royal Navy until 1923. It was built to the specifications of an armoured cruiser, making it a small carrier, and it remained in service until it was sunk in action by a Japanese naval air squadron off Ceylon in 1942.

The British carrier *Eagle*, converted from a battleship in 1924, was the first vessel to present the appearance of a mature aircraft carrier thanks to the innovation of its island superstructure, offset to the starboard side of the flight deck. Alternatively, the Japanese and American carriers of the early 1920s employed completely flush-deck designs, like the earlier training carrier *Argus*, to avoid any obstacles in landing what were still inherently unstable aircraft. Such was also the shape of the first US aircraft carrier, *Langley*, a converted collier, of 11,500 tons and 165 m (542 ft) and the first electrically propelled United States naval vessel. The Japanese continued the flush deck model, while later American carriers adopted the British island house, although the controversy over flush deck carriers continued in the US until after World War Two when the introduction of the angled deck concluded the argument in favour of the island.[8] Nevertheless, these experimental ships all led to the

development by the end of the decade of the carriers that would become major participants in the Battle of the Pacific during World War Two. The American ships *Lexington* and *Saratoga*, both built in the late 1920s, and the *Yorktown*-class vessels of the 1930s advanced the development of the carrier as the centre of a fleet of diverse ships and expanded the notion of a weapons system, an integrated set of equipment coordinated to achieve various objectives on air, sea and land.

Since the recognition, during World War Two, of aircraft as the most effective tools in modern warfare, the carrier has displaced the battleship as the capital ship of a naval fleet. Yet carriers lack the defensive capability of the battleship, and although some significant technological developments, such as radar, have helped to defend carriers from air attack, they still frequently travel in a

The first permanently adapted US aircraft carrier, *Langley*, built in 1911 as a collier and converted in 1920, was the first electrically propelled US naval vessel. In addition to aircraft, carrier pigeons were housed on its flight deck.

flotilla of more heavily armed vessels to protect them. As they have grown in importance, carriers have also got bigger; this is partly because the planes they carry have become larger and heavier, particularly since the advent of jet propulsion and also because of their vastly increased flight equipment and weightier weapons. The *Abraham Lincoln* is nearly four times the displacement of the World War Two carrier USS *Intrepid* (27,100 tons), yet accommodates roughly the same number of airplanes.

Aircraft designed specifically to operate from carriers have developed certain characteristics that differ from their land-based siblings. Typically, their airframes are reinforced, 'overbuilt', to compensate for the rapid acceleration of a catapult take-off and the sudden deceleration of a mechanically arrested landing. This makes them heavier than equivalent land-based planes. They are also designed with more fail-safe systems as a result of the particularly dangerous situation of a naval pilot operating over water, should a fault occur. Because of the possibility of salt-water corrosion, especially problematic aboard earlier carriers that could not store all their planes inside, they wear extra-heavy protective coatings. Carrier planes have developed very specific design features such as folding wings because of space limitations, both inside the hangars and on the flight decks.

The first folding-wing carrier planes were designed and patented by the British aircraft manufacturer Short Brothers as early as 1913.[9] The company subsequently produced a dozen types of innovative carrier aircraft known generically as Short Folders. During World War One the *Short Type 184* biplane was used for reconnaissance and torpedo bombing and was stationed, along with the *Sopwith Pup* fighter, aboard a number of ships including HMS *Campania*, which had been built in 1893 for Cunard as a Blue Riband-winning North Atlantic ocean liner. Requisitioned from passenger service in

1914, *Campania* was converted by the Royal Navy to a fast aircraft carrier, fitted with a 48.7-m (160-ft) wooden flight deck at the bow. *Campania* holds the historical distinction of being the first aircraft carrier to launch a plane while moving.

In the years just prior to the outbreak of World War Two folding-wing planes such as the American Vought *Corsair F4U* were designed specifically to enable the next generation of larger carriers to accommodate increased contingents of aircraft both inside their hangars and parked on the flight deck. The *Corsair* was a highly successful carrier plane because of its very high power to weight ratio, facilitating a short take-off. It could achieve a top speed of over 643.7 kmph (400 mph), and its very slow stall speed made short carrier-deck landings possible.

While the parameters of carrier-flying influenced the shape of new aircraft, conversely, developments in aviation technology had a fundamental effect on the design of new carriers, and it is not possible

Folding-wing FA-18 Hornet carrier jets are seen here parked on the flight deck of USS *Carl Vinson* in the harbour of Rio de Janeiro, 2008.

to discuss the evolution of the carrier without also considering the aircraft that have flown from their decks, so entwined are their specifications. As one founder member of the US Navy's Bureau of Aeronautics said in 1920, 'You won't be able to get a plane until you get a ship, and we cannot design a ship without the plane.'[10] This relationship was particularly apparent in the change from propeller-driven planes to jet-powered fighters in the post-World War Two period. According to the naval historian Norman Friedman:

> The transition from propeller to jet propulsion which naval aircraft are undergoing has likewise thrown the design of aircraft carriers into a transition stage . . . Up to and including *Midway* Class (1945–1992), it was possible to make the generalization that the number of aircraft to be carried and operated from an aircraft carrier was the most important aeronautical feature affecting the size of the ship. This was still true to a certain extent on *Forrestal* (1955–1998) but, for any new designs taken in hand now, we can foresee a definite change. Individual airplane performance, specifically maximum airborne speed, has begun to control flight deck lengths and, through this dimension, the size of the aircraft carrier.[11]

Thus, with its ascendancy to the prime position among naval ships in the years since 1945, the aircraft carrier has evolved along side developments in aeronautics. The advent of the helicopter, for example, opened a new chapter in the carrier's history. Whereas before the perfection of the helicopter as a fighting vehicle only unobstructed beaches provided suitable landing places for invasion forces (e.g. the Normandy beaches), the combination of the vertical take-off (VTO) vehicle and a purpose-designed helicopter carrier in the 1950s made virtually any coast assailable. The British and US navies led in the development of such vehicles and vessels, the latter known

as 'amphibious assault carriers' or 'commando carriers', deployed mainly to support ground invasion forces. Early examples were converted from smaller, light aircraft carriers, the first of which was the 13,190-ton HMS *Ocean* (1945), which also holds the distinctions of hosting the first take-off and landing of a jet aircraft from a carrier and of having participated in the first-ever large-scale helicopter assault launched from a ship, an event that took place at Port Said during the Suez crisis of 1956. Although amphibious assault carriers and similar-sized ships known unromantically as helicopter platforms often look like their larger siblings, they incorporate different, specific design criteria related to their deployment. These include the capability of carrying fleets of landing craft, either internally or on davits, for coastal assaults. Some also include a 'well deck' that

Sleeping giants. Built in the 1950s and then the world's largest warships, decommissioned sisters *Forrestal* and *Saratoga* lie side by side in the harbour at Newport, Rhode Island, awaiting their fate in 2009.

can be flooded to allow amphibious craft to float in and out of the host ship.[12] Because of the vertical take-off capabilities of their air wing, they are normally smaller and designed with shorter decks than other carriers.

In addition to carrying helicopters, which came to prominence particularly during the war in Vietnam in the 1960s, commando carriers were the natural home for other radically new aircraft such as the Sea Harrier 'Jump Jet', the only widely successful vertical/short take-off and landing (V/STOL) attack fighter in operation since the 1960s. Although an unladen Harrier can take off vertically, when it is carrying a full load of fuel and armaments it requires a short runway to launch, and as a result some carriers, including HMS *Invincible*, and its two sister ships *Ark Royal* and *Illustrious*, have been constructed with an upward-curving ski-jump deck at the bow to add capability for Harriers. Such carrier designs have been used by many navies including those of Britain, France, Russia, Spain, Thailand and the US, although a raging controversy continues about

Innovative vertical take-off Harrier jets require a ski-jump deck ramp, such as this one on HMS *Invincible*, for extra lift when taking off fully loaded with fuel and weapons.

the relative merits of 'big deck' versus smaller V/STOL carriers. The carrier's future resides in the midst of such debates.

Stealth

Although at the beginning of the twenty-first century the aircraft carrier is the supreme naval vessel, its conspicuousness, relatively light defensive armament and vulnerability to guided missile attack may ultimately compromise its effectiveness. By contrast, the submarine has the obvious advantage of stealth, which suggests its increasing importance in future naval operations. The earliest submersible boats were invented as stealth weapons, to be operated in harbours where they would drill or ram a ship's hull and plant an explosive charge, which would then be detonated by a time-delayed fuse. During the American Revolutionary War, the Connecticut patriot David Bushnell designed and constructed a 2.4-m (8-ft) long vessel, *Turtle*, controlled by hand-cranked screw propellers for both vertical and horizontal movement, the first known use of screw propulsion applied to a ship. This barrel-like submersible was deployed only once, to attack a British warship anchored in New York Harbor, where the fast local currents prevented the unstable boat from planting its charge. When the twenty-minute air supply within the *Turtle* was becoming exhausted, the attempt was abandoned.

The next significant design was developed by another American, Robert Fulton, who was living in France in the 1790s. There, he built the *Nautilus*, a 6.5-m (21-ft) boat constructed of copper plates over an iron frame and powered underwater by a screw propeller hand-cranked by two crewmen. For travelling on the surface, *Nautilus* was rigged with a sail. Initially, Napoleon supported the development of Fulton's submersible vessel, and although he soon lost interest in the project, this hydrodynamic design was prophetic.

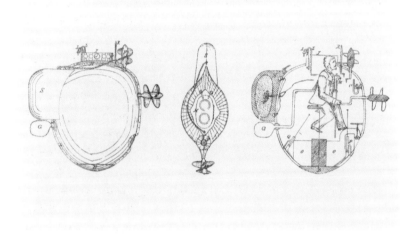

In the 1850s the Catalan socialist writer and inventor Narcis Monturiol turned his attention to the development of a submarine to be used for gathering coral and for scientific exploration, not for military purposes. In 1859 he launched the *Ictineo* of 7 m (23 ft) and 8 tons, driven by horizontal and vertical screws powered by four men turning cranks in the cramped space of a cylindrical, internal pressure hull concealed within a smoothly streamlined external shell. Between the two hulls were four ballast tanks that controlled dive and ascent. The hull was also fitted with three fish-eye portholes allowing the occupants to view the sights of the deep. Built in the Nuevo Vulcano shipyard in Barcelona, and involving the naval architects Joan Monjo i Pons and Josep Missé, the ship was demonstrated successfully in Barcelona harbour to the delight of hundreds of small investors, whose subscriptions had funded the boat's construction. One of them, Josep de Letamandi, invited aboard by Monturiol for a dive, described the experience with mixed feelings:

American Revolutionary David Bushnell designed and constructed this 2.4-m (8-ft) long submersible, *Turtle*, which made a single unsuccessful attempt to sink a British warship in New York harbour in 1776.

The silence that accompanies the dives; the gradual vanishing of sunlight; the great mass of water, which sight pierces with difficulty; the pallor that light gives to faces, the lessening of movement in the *Ictineo*, the fishes passing outside the portholes – all this helps stir the imaginative faculties, and shows itself in the shortened breath and the utterances of the crew . . . there are times when nothing can be seen outside by natural light. All noise and movement stops. It seems as though nature is dead, and the *Ictineo* is a tomb.[13]

A second and much larger boat, *Ictineo II*, launched in 1864, contributed to the subsequent development of the submarine by solving two basic problems, air and power. The boat was driven by a six-cylinder steam engine powered by a coal-fired boiler for surface running and by a chemical mixture that generated both steam for the motor and oxygen for the crew when running submerged. This was an innovative example of hybrid power for ships in keeping with the age of sail-assisted steamships. Although a technical success,

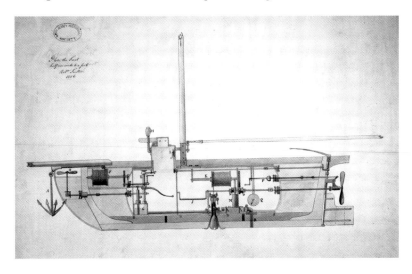

Famous for constructing the first practical steamship, *Cleremont*, in 1807, Robert Fulton also designed the innovative submersible boat *Nautilus* in 1806, which he hoped to sell to Napoleon, but the emperor declined.

the vessel never attracted government funding, possibly because it was presented as a research instrument rather than as a war machine. The historian Robert Hughes compared Monturiol, himself, to Jules Verne's Captain Nemo in respect of his scientific curiosity about the deep and in his commitment to social justice for working people.[14]

Despite Monturiol's utopian effort, naval warfare was the future of submarine development, and the nineteenth century was peppered with experimental submersible fighting boats. During the American Civil War the Confederate submersible *Hunley* was built along similar lines to the first *Ictineo*; 13.2 m (40 ft) long and operated by an eight-man crew turning its hand-cranked propeller, it was put into action in 1864 and, using an explosive charge rammed into the hull of its prey, sank the steam warship USS *Housatonic* off Charleston, Virginia. This was the first ever wartime sinking of a vessel by a submarine.

Later in the nineteenth century other navigation pioneers followed Monturiol's experiments with steam-powered submarines. The British clergyman George W. Garrett successfully demonstrated a functional

Catalan socialist Narcis Monturiol developed submarines for gathering coral and for scientific exploration, not for military purposes. His most successful vessel, *Ictineo II*, was launched in 1864. This is a modern replica.

submersible steamboat, *Resurgam*, in 1880. This ship used its steam engine conventionally for surface running and relied on 'accumulated steam' for power when submerged. Garrett took his ideas to the Swedish inventor and manufacturer, Thorsten Nordenfeldt, whose company constructed a 19 m (62-ft) vessel of 56 tons, based on the Garrett pattern, with a 100 horsepower steam engine that gave it a maximum speed of 9 knots. It was armed with a 25mm machine gun and a single self-propelled torpedo driven by compressed air, a weapon invented in 1866 by the British engineer Robert Whitehead. Nordenfeldt subsequently built and sold to European navies three successively larger prototypes (up to 30 m/100 ft) that advanced submarine technology but never saw active military service.

It was not until the development of a vessel using an internal combustion engine for surface running in combination with an electric motor for underwater propulsion that a truly effective submarine was achieved. This boat, the *Holland VI*, was the work of John Philip Holland, an Irish-American inventor who had built several previous

Stealth weapons were considered inherently ungentlemanly in the 19th century.

prototype vessels before succeeding at his sixth attempt. Holland worked in conjunction with the naval architect Arthur Leopold Busch of the Crescent Shipyard in New Jersey, where the boat was built. *Holland VI* was a 16.2-m (53-ft) craft that embodied the main elements of the modern submarine; its dual propulsion system (conceptually similar to the petrol-electric hybrid technology pioneered by Toyota for its Prius automobile), on-board compressed air supply, separate large tanks for submerging and smaller ones for trimming the boat, a fixed longitudinal centre of gravity and torpedo weaponry. These were the necessary constituents of a useful,

In 1900 John Philip Holland demonstrated a submersible vessel using an internal combustion engine for surface running with an electric motor for underwater propulsion. His *Holland VI* was the first effective submarine.

seaworthy submarine. The boat (regardless of their size, submarines are traditionally referred to as 'boats') could dive to 30.5 m (100 ft) and remain submerged for more than 24 hours, necessitating the provision of a toilet. It had a theoretical surface cruising range of 1,609 km (1,000 miles) at a maximum 6 knots and could travel at 5 knots for 32.1 km (20 miles) while submerged. The *Holland VI* was armed with a compressed air dynamite gun and three Whitehead torpedoes that could be launched consecutively through a single covered torpedo port in the bow.

In 1900, following a series of charismatic public demonstrations, the re-designated USS *Holland* became the first submarine to join the US naval fleet. The Navy quickly ordered the construction of six additional boats, prompting the formation of the Electric Boat Company in Groton, Connecticut, one of America's first industrial conglomerates.[15] The 75-ton *Holland* was a graceful craft with a streamlined, organically shaped hull, a clear deck and a cylindrical conning tower joined to the deck by a streamlined faring. Windows in the tower provided the only forward visibility from inside, leaving the crew blind when the boat was submerged and thus severely inhibiting its stealth capability. Inside, cabin space was cramped for the five crewmen. Despite their limitations, Holland boats served the US and the navies of Britain, Japan, the Netherlands and Russia until the start of World War One, by which time they were obsolete.

In the early years of the twentieth century the image of the submarine was that of a cheat. Perhaps it was partly the myth of Captain Nemo that created a feeling among some naval observers and tacticians that the submarine was inherently ungentlemanly, the weapon of an unprincipled renegade. In an age before fully mechanized warfare, combatants were expected to see and recognize each other before firing a weapon. Yet the submarine operated by stealth. The Royal Navy had quickly ordered five *Holland* submarines while their top officers discussed the legality of submarine warfare, considering whether it should be deemed piracy. Senior naval staffs of most countries were traditional in their views not only about ethics but also concerning the types of ship they believed in, and the battleship was the capital ship of the day. As yet, they had no experience of the submarine's capabilities, and there were no submariners in the top ranks to advocate for them. The general attitude was that only navy 'scum' went into 'pig boats', as the submarine was derisively known. Yet their realistic concern that enemy nations would not be inhibited by politeness or scruples in the use of a new weapon eventually overruled the moral argument. And within fifteen years the submariner would attain a uniquely heroic status.

Such resistance to progress in regard to the submarine echoed the dislike of steam voiced in the second quarter of the nineteenth century, when the Royal Navy's First Lord declared that:

> Their Lordships feel it their bounden duty to discourage to the utmost of their ability the employment of steam vessels, as they consider the introduction of steam is calculated to strike a fatal blow at the supremacy of the Empire.[16]

At that precise moment in history, the sprawling British Empire was in desperate need of the speed and regularity of service offered by steam propulsion to link together a disparate agglomeration of colonies spanning the entire globe. Yet such simple logic took decades to penetrate the hidebound attitudes towards change embodied in the orthodox military thinking of the time. It was mainly for the thrusting commercial shipping lines, led by innovators such as Brunel and Cunard, and the shipbuilders of England, Scotland and Ireland to experiment over the next thirty years in a quest to perfect steam power, iron construction and screw propulsion for passenger and cargo ships, before the greatest navies of the world would follow their lead and actively modernize their fleets.[17] However, there was no such commercial application for the submarine, and so it was thanks to the efforts of inspired individual inventors, manufacturers such as Electric Boat and motivated middle-ranking naval personnel that the technology of the submarine developed so rapidly in the years leading up to World War One.

Among the limitations of the early submarine, the problem of visibility while submerged was partially solved in 1902 by the designer and manufacturer Simon Lake, who invented the omniscope, a device using lenses and prisms to enable the crew to see forward when they were running just below the surface. This was an early type of periscope, which was perfected during World War One by the British optical instrument manufacturer Sir Howard Grubb, whose early periscopes were first tried in the Royal Navy's Holland submarines. Grubb's periscope remained the standard means of seeing while

British optical-instrument maker Sir Howard Grubb solved the problem of limited visibility while submerged by perfecting the periscope, seen here guiding a D-class diesel-electric submarine of 1911.

submerged until the mid-1950s, when for the first time television cameras were installed aboard the nuclear submarine *Nautilus.*

In 1904 a French submarine, *Aigette,* was the first to be fitted with a diesel engine for surface propulsion, producing fewer fumes inside the hull and consequently improving both habitability and safety. By 1911 the US Navy was finally beginning its move towards diesel power in part as a result of the enthusiasm of the submarine commander Chester Nimitz, who skippered the first American sub-marine powered by a diesel engine, the highly advanced *Skipjack.* Built in 1909 by Electric Boat, *Skipjack* was not only the Navy's first diesel-electric powered submarine, but it also carried a radio for experiments in submerged communications, used an early Sperry gyrocompass for navigation, and employed the newly invented bow planes for improved underwater manoeuvrability. It was 41.15 m (135 ft) and 342 tons with two 350-horsepower diesel engines achieving 13 knots on the surface. Nimitz took command of *Skip-jack* and its nineteen-man crew in February 1912 as his first step to becoming the Navy's chief expert on diesel power. He then spent the summer of 1913 visiting German diesel engine manufacturers, adding to his unique knowledge of the subject. According to the naval historian Commander Walter Karig:

> He took off his coat and rolled up his sleeves in every important Diesel factory in the country. He talked, ate, slept Diesels until even his wife, so she says, '. . . learned the lingo of wrist pins and bushings.' When he returned, he was the Navy's last word on the subject.[18]

Nimitz exploited his relative freedom from regulation and interfer-ence in the undeveloped field of submarines to explore the tactical as well as the technical potentials of the vessels. In December 1912 he published 'Defensive and Offensive Tactics of Submarines' in the

US Naval Institute Proceedings, the text of a lecture he had recently delivered to the US Naval War College.[19] Thus, on the brink of the first truly global conflict, Nimitz was becoming the Navy's pre-eminent expert about a novel but promising type of ship. It is not surprising, then, in honour of his long and varied career, that Nimitz was the namesake for the present class of innovative, nuclear-powered aircraft carriers, the capital ships of our age.

By 1910 hull shapes also had evolved. The British *D-1* of 1908 featured a much more ship-like form than the earlier Holland boats, with their dolphinesque hulls. This change was the result of a general recognition that submarines spent most of their time travelling on the surface, rather than underwater, and would need to be designed for maximum seaworthiness in all weather and sea conditions, qualities lacking in the organic forms best suited to underwater running. There followed a growing realization that the uses of the submarine went far beyond the coastal and harbour-based stealth deployment that was possible for the ships of very limited range in the early years of the submarine's development. With increased size and power, they would go into the open ocean as attack, reconnaissance or escort vessels, and their design evolution from then on would reflect these much wider ambitions.

U-1, the first German U-boat (*Unterzeeboot*), was built in 1905 to a design by the Spanish engineer Raymondo Lorenzo d'Equevilley Montjustin. The first of the Karp-class vessels, *U-1* was 42.3 m (139 ft) and 239 tons. It was powered by a kerosene engine that could push the boat to 11 knots on the surface and 9 knots submerged and gave it a potential range of 2,000 miles. Like the Holland boats used by the American and British navies, it had a single torpedo tube, a limitation corrected in 1908 by a much-enlarged *U-2*, which had space for twin torpedo tubes. The German Navy had been comparatively slow to develop their own submarine technology in the first decade of the twentieth century and, typically, did not switch to diesel-electric power until the construction of their U-19 class boats in 1912. From then on, however, they began to construct a fleet of boats using the highest available technology in the two years remaining before the start of the war. This gave them an advantage over other combatant nations, whose larger but older fleets were quickly becoming obsolete. Among these later German boats, the fast '30'-series diesel-electric powered boats of 64.7 m (212 ft) and 685 tons could cruise at approximately 16 knots on the surface and nearly 10 knots submerged, with a maximum range of 12,552.8 km (7,800 miles) at 8 knots. They were armed with a powerful 88mm deck gun and six torpedoes, making them formidable fighting machines.

In September 1914 the German Navy had 28 state-of-the-art submarines with seventeen more under construction; and during the war they built an additional 360. At the same time Britain had the largest submarine fleet in the world with 74 in service and 45 planned or under construction. France was operating 62 boats with another nine being built. The US had 30 active submarines and ten more pending completion. Russia had 48, Italy 21, Japan thirteen and Austria six. But what could be done with them? Most of these primitive boats, and particularly those of the Allies, were capable only of harbour or coastal assignments because of their small size, limited range and general unseaworthiness. Although there were no effective ways yet to detect or destroy a submarine, the battle tactics that had been developed by Nimitz and others remained entirely theoretical. It was a weapon without a clearly defined mission in a service heavily dependent on prescribed methods of operation, particularly in Britain, whose navy relied on sailing and fighting instructions dating back to 1653.

All of this would change in the crucible of the 1914–18 war, when the submarine came into its own as an instrument of blockade, as an attack ship, a mine-layer, a reconnaissance vessel and even as an aircraft carrier. This became a time of practical experimentation in the harsh environment of an empire-wrecking struggle played out on a global stage. During the war the submarine progressed rapidly from a highly suspect novelty to a deadly and essential element in naval warfare and, along with the airplane, it pushed the boundaries of military behaviour away from the traditions of chivalry and towards the abstract, impersonal activity it has become in the age of the atomic bomb and the electronically controlled 'surgical' air strike. Nevertheless, successful U-boat captains of both World Wars became 'aces' comparable with the most deadly aviators, such as Manfred von Richthofen; they were scored according to those sinking the highest number of ships and destroying the most overall tonnage. And their successes were celebrated in their country's popular press and in folklore.

However, the U-boat relied on well-disciplined teamwork and its daring took place invisibly, beneath the waves, the crew working in a hot, stuffy and distinctly unglamorous environment in contrast with the lone open-cockpit air ace, whose singular exploits were frequently witnessed by other flyers and were often visible to observers on the ground. Unrestricted submarine warfare, authorized by the German High Command during the first and last years of the Great War, struck terror into merchant shipping. Yet, in both World Wars there were also episodes of gallantry conducted by those U-boat captains retaining an old-school naval ethic. In such instances, captains allowed crews and passengers of targeted vessels to abandon ship and gave them advice on reaching land, before sinking the vessel. More often, however, both naval and merchant ships were targeted and sunk without warning from the submarine. Such was the case of the Cunard liner *Lusitania*, which was torpedoed with the loss of 1,198 mainly civilian passengers on 7 May 1915, an incident that helped to turn neutral America's public opinion against Germany and contributed to America's eventual entry into the war.

In addition to attacks on merchant shipping in the Atlantic and Mediterranean, Germany also employed specially designed U-boats as blockade-running freighters. The first of these was the *Deutschland*, privately funded and unarmed, built with a wide beam providing a large cargo hold. It evaded the British blockade of German shipping and famously carried a cargo of chemical dyes to Baltimore in the still-neutral US, where it arrived in July 1916. According to Frederick Simpich, the withdrawal of German coal-tar dyes from the textile and printing industries during the war had demonstrated the problems of America's material dependency on unstable foreign countries:

> everybody remembers how the submarine *Deutschland* sneaked into Baltimore with dyes that sold for dizzy prices. We had so few dyes, and such poor ones, that our coat collars turned our necks blue and green, and Uncle Sam couldn't even properly color his postage stamps.[20]

Although this was mainly a propaganda stunt, it also proved profitable for Germany since the boat returned safely home carrying a valuable cargo of American rubber, tin and nickel. It also demonstrated an unexpected commercial benefit of stealth.

Techniques and tactics for detecting and destroying submarines began evolving rapidly after 1914. Whereas the German boats were technically superior to the Allied fleets, the British and Americans were relatively more successful at developing deterrents. The British devised 'Q Ships', which were decoys, apparent easy targets, secretly armed with heavy deck guns and other weapons, sometimes including torpedoes, and sent out to lure submarines into surface battle. Both sides laid vast minefields to prevent submarines from leaving their ports and reaching open sea. After Germany developed an early lead in mine construction, by 1917 the British were using the 'Mark H2', based on a German mine, and eventually evening the odds.

Following a concept proposed by Admiral Sir Charles Madden, the British also perfected the depth charge, the first weapon capable of targeting a submerged submarine. The Admiralty developed the *D Pattern Mark III* depth charge, which was a canister packed with 135 kg (300 lb) of high explosive TNT. The canister was fitted with a pressure-sensitive detonator that could be calibrated to set off the charge at various depths down to 180 m (600 ft). The depth charge was combined, by 1918, with a 'projector' that could hurl the charge up to 70 m (225 ft). A destroyer fitted with four projectors located at the stern could create a mass of underwater explosions calculated to engulf the hunted submarine.

Another important detection device developed by the British was the 'hydrophone', an invention based on early telephone technology, which was a primitive underwater directional microphone that could be tuned by a shipboard operator to detect sounds beneath the surface of the sea. It was unreliable, and often picked up sounds emanating from its own ship rather than those of the boat it was pursuing. Nevertheless, it was a first tentative step towards sonar. By the early 1940s more effective anti-submarine technologies made the submarine's survival even more precarious, cancelling out the technical developments that increased their stealth capability. A World War Two U-boat seaman recalled hearing 'the un-mistakable "pings" of a warship's *Asdic* underwater detection device. *Asdic* pings are like a woman's labor pains; the shorter the interval between them, the closer the moment of truth. These pings were getting closer – and at a very alarming rate!'[21]

Aerial reconnaissance also became a useful tool in anti-submarine warfare. The Allies employed early flying boats to attack U-boats discovered sailing on the surface, sinking or damaging 47 between 1914 and 1918. Despite these advances in anti-submarine counter-measures, the early German U-boats were very successful vessels. By the time of the Armistice in November of 1918, they had sunk nearly 5,000 Allied ships, while losing 178 U-boats; and they had killed nearly half of the Allied navies' 13,000 crewmen lost at sea and an estimated 15,000 civilians.

Inventions of World War One that continued to be used during World War Two included a type of dirigible known as a 'blimp', a powered, non-rigid lighter-than-air craft, which accompanied merchant vessels and warships at sea. These fantastic machines could cruise along with a ship, exploiting their own high altitude and greater field of visibility to give advanced warning of approaching vessels. The Royal Navy first used blimps in 1915 as anti-submarine patrol vehicles. Also between 1914 and 1918 various navies built experimental aircraft-carrying submarines; these boats were capable of launching a small seaplane from the deck to undertake rapid aerial reconnaissance. Although this technology did not contribute meaningfully to the World War One effort, its implications for the future were significant.

Perhaps the most effective deterrent against submarine attack was not an instrument but a tactic – the convoy. During the early years of World War One the British Admiralty tended to underrate the impact on merchant ships of the 'cowardly' submarine. They believed that convoys were nannyish and not sufficiently thrusting a use for their prized destroyers, which were designed for speeds far in excess of those achieved by any convoy, which could only move at the rate of its slowest vessel. Consequently, as policy they rejected the historic tactic of armed convoys until as late as 1917. By then, however, it had become clear that despite any objections or misgivings about either the utility or the dignity of the convoy, the tactic was able to defend effectively the great majority of merchant ships, which were essential to British survival. By the outbreak of World War Two it was taken for granted. David Stevenson described a well-organized Atlantic convoy bound for America in 1944 and the aerial support provided for his ship, a tanker carrying precious oil:

> Another routine convoy, boring in its monotony and safety. I almost wished that something would attack us just for a change. The U-boats were having a lean time. Though we had heard of the Schnorkel Tube, which meant a U-boat need not surface to charge batteries, the Hunter/killer groups of allied warships ensured the safe passage of convoy after convoy . . . Six days from New York we were detached from the convoy and ordered to Guantanamo Bay, Cuba. For the first few days our escort was a Martin Mariner flying boat, which visited us daily to see if we were OK. As we neared Cuba we got a blimp escort. I had not seen one since early '42, on the Eastern Seaboard. It was like meeting an old friend. The situation at sea must have been well under control if so much attention could be lavished on one ship.[22]

Yet it was not always such plain sailing. The convoy was countered by ever more sophisticated U-boat tactics such as the 'Wolf Pack'. The German admiral Karl Doenitz had created the concept of the Wolf Pack in the 1930s, declaring: 'U-boats are the wolves of the sea. Attack, tear, sink [by] herd or pack tactics'. In the first six months of 1942 alone, 360 ships were sunk by the Wolf Packs, totalling some 2.25 million tons of Allied shipping with the loss of only eight U-boats.[23] Nevertheless, U-boat duty remained the most dangerous assignment of World War Two. Stevenson noted with compassion:

> It is perhaps the ordeal of the U-boat crews which stands out most starkly . . . Of the 39,000 who served, 32,000 were lost. The highest

proportion of fatalities suffered by any branch of the Armed Forces of any of the combatants. How many of the souls must have died slowly, in suffocating terror, trapped beneath the surface of a cold ocean in the flooding hull of a crippled sub-marine. In a most cruel war theirs was the most cruel fate of all.[24]

Between the wars the technical development of the submarine continued more slowly. After 1919 Germany was prohibited from developing weaponry, and so the major advances up to the mid-1930s were made by Britain, France, Japan and the US. Britain, France and Japan all built more successful aircraft-carrying submarines with pressure-sealed deck hangars and catapult launchers. These included the British HMS *M2*, several enormous Japanese submarines commissioned shortly before their attack on Pearl Harbor, and the French underwater cruiser *Surcouf*. The last was the largest submarine in the world at the time it was launched, in 1929, and one of the most

Sketch of a World War Two convoy by Victor Lundy. The convoy proved an effective deterrent to submarine attacks on merchant shipping during both World Wars and remains a significant defence against 21st-century piracy.

mysterious and fabled boats of World War Two, deeply immersed in Vichy intrigue, and the subject of a highly contested disappearance in 1943. In addition to increasing size, power, speed and range, by the 1930s some attention was being given to habitability. The first US Navy submarine to be fitted with full air-conditioning was the *SS-179 Plunger*, a state-of-the-art Porpoise-class boat launched in 1935, which also carried another significant new device, an early radar set. Porpoise-class boats were also the first submarines of welded rather than riveted construction, permitting deeper dives.

After Adolf Hitler came to power in 1933, the German military began to rebuild rapidly and used the most advanced science in the development of more sophisticated weaponry. Their Class-IX submarines of 1935–6 were able to support a new type of torpedo superseding the Whitehead type, which because it was powered by compressed air had the disadvantage of leaving a visible trail of bubbles in its wake. The Class-IX boats were large enough (77 m, 252 ft) to accommodate up to 22 electrically powered torpedoes, each containing a massive battery. The great advantage of these large new torpedoes was that they left no trail on the surface of the water, increasing their surprise factor while also concealing the position of the submarine that launched them, although they required a much bigger boat to carry them.

Yet even the Class-IX boats suffered from severe limitations. Their Siemens battery-powered electric motors for underwater running gave them a top submerged cruising speed of 7 knots with a range of only 65 miles. Otherwise, they had to travel by diesel power on the surface; and it took seven hours of surface running to recharge their batteries, during which time they were vulnerable to detection by enemy radar. Their Allied counterparts, however, shared these limitations. Able seaman Charlie Andrews recorded in the log of a similar British boat, HMS *Safari*, 'June 9th. Night alarm

0100 . . . either sighted or R.D.F. [radar detected] by destroyer, depth charged, and were kept down for 21 hours after unsuccessful attempt to get away on the surface, and fully charge our battery.'[25] The Germans solved this problem late in the war by adopting a Dutch invention, the snorkel. This was a ventilation tube that enabled submarines to take in air and recharge their batteries while submerged just below the surface. Thus equipped, submersible ships became significantly stealthier and harder for an enemy to detect. It also transformed them into true submarines that could operate invisibly nearly all the time.

Although technically progressive, the World War Two-generation submarine was a crude affair inside. The atmosphere inside these vessels was typically damp, noxious and claustrophobic. With large motors, batteries, fuel and ballast tanks, in addition to the bulky cargo of armaments taking up much of the available space in the hull of the ship, crew accommodation was nightmarishly cramped, and no effort had yet been made to conceal the vessel's mechanistic character. All surfaces and details of the interior clearly belonged

HMS *Safari* surfaces to launch a surprise attack on an Italian steamer in 1942. Such boats were as dangerous fighting on the surface as they were firing torpedoes when submerged. Illustration by William McDowell.

to the machinery of the boat. The bunks in which the crew slept were spartan metal-framed structures within which the crewman's body was contained for a fixed period of time before another sailor took his place in a round-the-clock rotation.[26] Control room mate Hans Goebeler described the conditions aboard *U-505* sailing off the coast of North Africa in 1942:

> As we crossed the Tropic of Cancer, the boat began to heat up like a furnace during the daytime. German submarines were not equipped with air conditioners, so we used every imaginable excuse to get out onto the deck and escape the roasting temperatures inside the hull. When we dived, the ocean water cooled the pressure hull, causing drops of condensation to rain down upon us.[27]

Later in the war, when it was necessary to run submerged most of the time to avoid air attack, he wrote:

> Instead of the wild surf and pounding diesel noise, we experienced day after day of the monotonous, mechanical hum of the electric motors. The weather was quite cold too. We shivered in our bunks as ice cold drops of condensed moisture soaked our clothing. The long periods under water also influenced the smell of the boat. We were steeped in the stench of rotting potatoes, the reek of the 'shit' bucket in the engine

The ace submarine skipper was a charismatic figure equal to the ace fighter pilots of the air, much celebrated in the press of their home countries. *Safari*'s Commander, Ben Bryant, is pictured here with his crewmen.

room, and the stench of our own bodies . . . the fetid stink of rot and decay made our boat seem like a cold, clammy coffin in which we were already decomposing.[28]

The Raymond Loewy industrial design consultancy began designing for the American Navy during World War Two 'to improve the life of the crew in extreme conditions of warfare . . . Our goal was to limit noise and heat . . . and save money at the same time. We had established new standards of comfort and work efficiency for US Navy warships.'[29] Although the concept of comfort had now been considered, Loewy's standards were realized only for a small number of the vessels in which American soldiers fought during World War Two. The rest more closely resembled the harsh environment of *U-505*.[30]

However, submarine habitability did improve considerably in the post-war period primarily as a result of two major technical advances in life support and propulsion. The ability to extract oxygen from sea-water through electrolysis prolonged submersion time indefinitely, enabling boats to avoid the uncomfortable effects of surface turbulence. And the development of a nuclear reactor small enough to power a submarine eliminated the need for refuelling and for the storage of diesel fuel and batteries, making more space for crew and for weapons. The first operational nuclear-powered submarine, USS *Nautilus*, was designed by John Burnham, built by the Electric Boat Company for the US Navy, and named by the First Lady, Mamie Eisenhower, in 1954.

During the most aggressive years of the Cold War, *Nautilus* was the first of 27 similar vessels to be commissioned by 1960. Because the nuclear submarine could cruise underwater as long as food supplies lasted, or almost indefinitely, the quality and appearance of its interior spaces and the level of comfort it provided the crew became

more important. One of the original *Nautilus* crewmen described its interiors as being 'like the *Queen Mary*'.[31] In fact, the boat was spacious enough to provide an internal 'grand staircase', the first genuine staircase aboard a submarine, a large mess room that doubled as a cinema, and individual sleeping accommodation for the entire complement of 105 crew and officers. Its relatively spacious interiors were humanized by the decorative use of wood veneers trimmed in stainless steel and brightly coloured leatherette upholstery, creating a well-finished appearance in the crew quarters.

Nautilus was developed by the Naval Reactors Branch of the Atomic Energy Commission under the leadership of Admiral Hyman G. Rickover, known as 'the father of the nuclear navy'. The 2,980-ton, 97.5-m (320-ft) boat broke all submerged speed and distance records in its first year of service. Its shakedown cruise of 2,222.5 km (1,381 miles) was by far the longest submerged distance yet

Launched in 1954, the first nuclear submarine, *Nautilus*, by 1957 had logged 60,000 nautical miles, the same distance travelled by the fictional *Nautilus* in Verne's *Twenty Thousand Leagues Under the Sea*.

travelled. It also maintained the highest average speed of 16 knots recorded for a submerged boat running for more than one hour. By 1957 *Nautilus* had logged 60,000 nautical miles, the equivalent distance travelled by Verne's *Nautilus* in his novel *Twenty Thousand Leagues Under the Sea*, which remains a touchstone for submariners today. In the following year *Nautilus* was the first vessel to sail under the North Pole after an epic underwater journey ironically named 'Operation Sunshine', approximating Monturiol's dream of an underwater research vessel.

This record was notable among many tests of underwater speed and endurance undertaken by the boat in accordance with one of its primary purposes – development testing. Through its trials, performance faults such as noise and vibration were identified and led to improvements in the design and construction of later nuclear vessels. Tests also demonstrated that the speed and flexibility of *Nautilus* had rendered conventional detection methods such as sonar useless. *Nautilus* went on to travel the world demonstrating both the capabilities of a nuclear submarine and the ingenuity and technological accomplishments of the United States during some of the most difficult years of the Cold War and particularly following the humiliating launch of the Soviet orbital satellite *Sputnik* in 1957. *Nautilus* had a long and significant career up to its retirement in 1980, and in 1986 the boat became the centrepiece of the Submarine Force Museum in the town of Groton, Connecticut, where it was built.

In the twenty-first century the submarine continues to evolve and to develop new capabilities. Yet the largest-ever nuclear submarines remain the Russian Typhoon-class boats commissioned in 1981, of which only the first, *Dmitry Donskoi*, remained in active service after major military cutbacks following the dismantling of the Soviet Union. Typhoon-class boats were not only the largest (48,000 tons) but also the quietest submarines of their day, employing 'low-cavitation' noise-reducing propellers, making them ideal platforms for launching intercontinental ballistic missiles (ICBMs). They were the vessels on which Tom Clancy based the portrait of a super-submarine central to his novel *The Hunt for Red October* and the subsequent film of the same title, directed in 1990 by John McTiernan. Following the dismantling of the USSR, Russia cut back its nuclear arms programme, and so the Typhoon-class remains one of the last great examples of the giant Soviet war machine, alongside the *Antonov AN-225* space-shuttle-carrying aircraft.

The Cold War generated a constant stream of technical 'firsts' in a game of one-upmanship conducted on both sides of the 'Iron Curtain'. For example, the Soviets built the first nuclear-armed submarine, but the US developed the first boat to be capable of launching nuclear missiles while submerged. Meanwhile, certain technical developments improved the performance of all new submarines. Its manoeuvrability was enhanced by the development of ever more sophisticated tailplanes and foreplanes that enabled the skipper to 'fly' the vessel very much like an airplane under the water. Similarly, the latest generation of robotic torpedoes aboard a boat such as the 17,000-ton USS *Pennsylvania* can be steered towards their target, changing direction and depth by means of fibre optic controls linked to the submarine; thus, they perform as underwater guided missiles.

A persistent challenge for submarine designers was the improvement of vision while submerged, and the nineteenth-century dream of using the vessel as a sub-aquatic roving eye has not been realized. Today's denizens of the deep still cannot view the undersea world as would Nemo through the great picture windows of his fictional *Nautilus*. Yet the practical issue of sighting surface ships from a submerged vessel has been solved in the electronic age by the development of new types of optical instruments. Such devices include the hull-penetrating periscopes used today on the US Navy's Los

Angeles-class and Seawolf-class submarines. These stabilized digital periscopes offer low-light image intensification, day-and-night viewing capabilities, multiple magnification levels, plus digital photography; and they beam their images to TV screens located around the ship. Not only do such instruments offer clear 360-degree views of the ocean's surface from boats sailing as much as 18.3 m (60 ft) below the surface, they are almost invisible themselves.

The next generation of 'eyes' for American Virginia-class submarines will no longer penetrate the hull with a mechanical device; instead, these telescopic 'photonics masts' will send images via a fibre optic system directly to a control room that no longer needs to be located in a cramped space directly below the 'sail' or 'fin' with which it was previously linked by the periscope. Fibre optics made it possible to relocate this facility to a lower, more spacious deck where the commander can sit comfortably to view surface activity on a flat-panel display screen. Thus, commanders will no longer 'dance with the Grey Lady', that is, stand to manipulate and mechanically rotate the traditional control and viewing device of all earlier periscopes. This last technological advance represents a complete break from the historic ritual and symbolism of submarine life.

The Fleet

The twentieth century saw naval opinion turning decisively away from battleships as capital ships and gradually transforming destroyers, frigates and other conventional surface ships to new purposes in response to emerging threats and opportunities. Yet earlier, in the age of steam, radical innovations had transformed the design of conventional surface warships, some of which also foreshadowed the features of entirely new types of ship, such as the destroyer and the submarine. Among the most significant inventions of that era were the works of a Swedish engineer, John Ericsson, one of the most important inventors of the nineteenth century.

Ericsson's first notable device was the steam condenser, which enabled a steamship to produce fresh water for its boilers when at sea. While in his twenties, Ericsson invented a hot air 'caloric' engine in which repeatedly heating and cooling air in a chamber produced sufficient expansion and contraction of the air to move a cylinder. His later patent for twin screw propellers dramatically improved the operation of steamships thus equipped. Ericsson also assisted John Holland in the development of his early experimental submersible boats. His greatest achievement, however, was his conception and realization of the radically innovative US Navy ironclad, *Monitor* launched in 1862.

Although the French warship *La Gloire* of 1859 was the first true ironclad, *Monitor* represented a quantum leap in both design and construction of military vessels. The 1,000-ton, 52.4-m (172-ft) ship's armoured deck was just above the water and revealed only a small bridge-house, a collapsible smokestack and a revolving gun turret constructed of 20-mm (8-in.) thick iron plates for protection. The turret, designed by Theodore Timby and fitted with twin Dahlgren guns, was rotated by a dedicated steam engine enabling crew to direct fire for fully 360 degrees. Despite its innovations, and because of Ericsson's pioneering use of prefabrication, the *Monitor* was built in only 120 days. Nine New York foundries made parts that were assembled at the Continental Iron Works in Brooklyn, where the vessel was launched. The DeLamater Iron Works in Manhattan built the machinery and engines that drove Ericsson's inventive marine screw propeller, making the ship efficient and reliable enough to forego the usual rigging for sails. Monitor's low, stealthy profile protected its vulnerable hull from damage and established a precedent as the first semi-submersible warship.

The US Navy ordered three such vessels, which became models for subsequent Monitor-class ships adapted for either river or sea deployment and used widely in the later stages of the American Civil War, a war that was fought on inland waterways as well as in coastal waters and open ocean. Ericsson's design was also sold to the Swedish navy, which commissioned fifteen such ships. Later American Monitors were increasingly large and were typically equipped with two or more turrets, anticipating and influencing the design of later nineteenth-century battleships and armoured cruisers. Following the Civil War, however, American government funding for navy ships dried up, and the subsequent development of the ironclad warship was taken up by European countries that were intent on building strong navies. Yet the American Monitors proved useful during World War One, when their low decks made them ideal ships to supply and tend the new generation of submarines,

Swedish engineer John Ericsson is memorialized holding a model of his greatest invention, the radically designed battleship *Monitor*, in a Manhattan park near the nine factories that prefabricated the ship's parts in 1860.

boats that incorporated both the attack capabilities and the stealth qualities first demonstrated by Ericsson's original *Monitor*.

Despite great advances in battleship design and the development of new tactics to exploit their speed and powerful armaments, following the Great War major navies increasingly favoured the hybrid aircraft carrier and the stealthy submarine. The intermediate-size frigate and the smaller, more manoeuvrable corvette, used mainly for coastal defence, continued developing as anti-aircraft and anti-submarine vessels. Large modern destroyers are essentially nuclear-armed guided missile platforms equivalent in tonnage to the biggest battle cruisers of World War Two. While the weaponry and the deployment of these surface ships have evolved, their most significant visible change has been the incorporation of stealth geometry into their design. Thus, these conventional surface ships have absorbed both the hybrid nature of the aircraft carrier, by accommodating airborne attack weapons, and the stealthy character of the submarine, through their advanced forms.

Theodore Timby designed the *Monitor*'s steam-powered revolving gun-turret, which revolutionized naval firepower.

A recent example is HMS *Daring*, a Type 45 air defence destroyer of the Royal Navy, commissioned in 2008 as that force's most powerful ship. This 8,000-ton, 152-m (500-ft) vessel is deployed to protect escorted ships against any form of aerial attack. Employing its *Aster* surface to air, anti-aircraft and anti-missile missiles in conjunction with a Sampson multi-functional long-range radar system effective up to 400 km (250 miles), and equipped with Lynx and Westland helicopters, the ship can operate at sea or close to shore in defence of troops engaged in amphibious landings and is capable of intercepting low-altitude attacks by sea-skimming missiles. The hard-edged design of this ship's superstructure and the cleanliness of all exterior surfaces are intended to reduce its radar profile or 'cross-section' to that of a small boat. In addition to its advanced geometry, the coating material used on the surface of hull and superstructure, its low bow wave and wake, and its overall appearance are also factors in limiting the ship's 'noise' and making it hard to recognize by visual reference, radar, sonar or infrared techniques.

Following the early contributions to stealth, embodied in Ericsson's design for the *Monitor*, the concealment and disguise of ships has also been accomplished in other ways. Artists working for the Royal Navy developed a technique of camouflage known as Dazzle painting, which was used extensively during World War One to obscure the type and size of a ship observed by an enemy at sea, particularly as seen through the periscope of a submarine. Dazzle painting used geometries inspired by Cubism and Vorticism (British Cubo-Futurism) to break down visually the form and silhouette of a vessel. It represents one of the more significant and practical contributions of modern painting to modern warfare. In more recent times, particularly during the Cold War, various design features of Soviet and Western Allied ships were calculated to reduce their radar cross-section. One such feature was the 'tumble-home' of the hull and

superstructure, a sloping inward of all surfaces from the waterline upwards. This particular form can be traced back to warships of the eighteenth century and is a familiar design term in automotive styling studios, as well as featuring in the shape of HMS *Daring*. With its state-of-the-art electronics and low-detectability profiles, *Daring* is one of the most 'invisible' air-defence surface warships.

In addition to its high-tech design, this vessel has been noted for its crew comforts, including common twenty-first-century civilian amenities such as email access and iPod docking facilities. Yet the ship was also designed to recognize the more heterogeneous composition of the modern crew, with gender-neutral social spaces where male and female seafarers can socialize informally. Sleeping quarters, however,

With the development of radar, the complex and distinctive shapes of warships became a greater liability than they had been in the era of visual reference, when camouflage painting was considered sufficient disguise.

remain separate, and *Daring* provides individual shower stalls, replacing the communal facilities still found on most Navy ships.

In the modern age of armed conflict or stand-off at sea, a successful ship must have flexibility and reach. The aircraft carrier has both, since it is a mobile airfield that can go nearly anywhere on the planet; and its air wing can respond to almost any type of emergency – suspicion or outright attack. But the carrier needs the additional defence of its fleet to protect it from aerial or underwater attack. Its size makes it vulnerable, and so the development of new air-defence escort vessels, such as HMS *Daring*, remains a high tactical ambition. The modern submarine can sail on or below the surface of the sea almost indefinitely and can carry an increasingly large cargo of devastating airborne nuclear weapons with a reach of thousands

World War One freighter camouflaged with 'dazzle painting', patterns derived from modern abstract art, used to disguise the ship's size and type.

of miles. It operates in the stealthiest manner possible at sea, and it can work alone, like the seafaring pirates of days gone by. Surface ships in a wide variety of types still have a role in coastal defence, in the protection of a convoy and in the long-range delivery of troops and equipment; with their own torpedo, cruise missile and nuclear weapons capabilities, they too have an extensive reach beyond their geographical position. And so, a modern navy is significantly more varied than ever before, its vessels blending aerial and seagoing capabilities, in a dizzying range of permutations intended to address any known type of military threat.

Yet some aspects of the warship have remained the same throughout the past two centuries of political, military and technological change. It is still the biggest and most expensive piece of kit in which maritime nations invest heavily to pursue and protect their national and global interests. The warship is still one of the world's most dangerous places to work. Fires, explosions, crashes and sinkings still claim the lives of many a mariner, submariner or naval aviator, even in peacetime. And even the largest warship is still cramped internally, requiring great sacrifices of comfort and freedom from its crew. Bunks are narrow, storage minimal, the regime unremitting, the worst jobs on the lowest decks punishing. It must still strike its enemy targets, be they on land, sea or in the air.

The fighting vessel is a significant contributor to the CO_2 emissions causing global warming and to the pollution and destabilization of ocean habitats. And despite the efforts of the US Naval Sea Command's Energy Conservation Program and comparable programmes operated by other navies to reduce the fuel consumption of their fleets, the warship remains very dirty in an environmental sense and potentially devastatingly so, should an outbreak of nuclear violence occur. The very existence of the armed vessel depends on an accepted global political system of checks and balances ensured

by military strength, although many in the world would contend that this system has failed, that the inevitability of war is unacceptable, and that armies and navies, themselves, are the problem. Yet warships exist to engage in various types of conflict: all-out nuclear war between nations, local clashes that require outside peacekeeping (these could involve terror attacks and piracy), and genocidal civil wars that call for humanitarian intervention. Utopian anti-militarists may contend that all these rationales are unacceptable in the world today, while more mainstream views may allow for the peacekeeping and humanitarian functions of navies to justify the continued development of some types of warship. Hard-line militarists demand ever more potent warships in their belief that might is right. Yet at the moment of writing no significant argument is in progress that

The clean surfaces of the guided missile destroyer USS *Zumwalt*, scheduled for completion in 2013, are designed to reduce its radar 'cross-section', bringing the stealth capabilities of the submarine to the surface warship.

would fundamentally change or undermine the development or deployment of the modern naval vessel.

Finally, at the most basic level, the warship must still resist the vagaries and violence of the world's oceans, potentially its most lethal foe.

4 Cargo

Before the Box

'Shipping is the lifeblood of the world economy'[1]

> LOS ANGELES, 29 January, 2009 (Reuters) – A dramatic slowdown in activity at US ports may extend well into 2009 as the recession deepens, spelling weak demand for diesel from the shipping and trucking industries.
>
> Cargo volumes at major US container ports have fallen for 17 straight months, and 2008 ended as the weakest year since 2004, according to the monthly Port Tracker survey by IHS Global Insight for the National Retail Federation.[2]

The world economic crisis, gathering pace in 2009, was as closely tied with shipping as it was with soaring energy prices, the US and British housing bubbles, over-ambitious banking practices and orgiastic domestic consumption in developed nations since the 1980s. The link between the trucking and shipping industries is also an intimate one stretching back to the inter-war years, with post-World War Two containerization having emerged conceptually from road and rail networks (both linked to inland, coastal and ocean shipping) and technically from trailer bodies and railroad boxcars.

Riding high in Singapore. The 2008 economic crisis quickly stalled the global shipping industry, leaving all types of cargo vessels anchored and empty. Ships are earning only when they are moving freight.

Yet following the credit crisis the landscape of the world's cargo ports, which have been increasingly busy since the development of container shipping, quickly retreated to an appearance of suspended animation. Vast new ships sit at anchor waiting for cargoes that cannot be sold and will not be dispatched, while crew members hold their breath in anticipation of seemingly inevitable lay-offs and the prospect of returning home to less-developed countries where a living will not easily be found. Observers report on the ominous appearance of formerly busy ports:

> Idle ships are now stretched in rows outside Singapore's harbour, creating an eerie silhouette like a vast naval fleet at anchor. Shipping experts note the number of vessels moving around seem unusually high in the water, indicating low cargoes.[3]

How did the 'lifeblood of the global economy' come to this?

During the last major depression, in the early 1930s, Malcom McLean was struggling to build a small trucking business in his native North Carolina. Progressing from hauling freight in a trailer attached to the back of an old car, McLean obtained sufficient work from the WPA (Works Progress Administration), hauling gravel for road building, to purchase two second-hand lorries and expand his business, which eventually saw him running a small fleet of tractor-trailer trucks up and down the eastern seaboard. But his trajectory was not firmly upward, and by 1937, with yet another downturn in the American economy, McLean's business was in trouble. However, at that low point, he had an experience that led to the most radical change in twentieth-century cargo shipping and eventually made him his fortune.

Losing a day's work while his rig was parked in a queue at New York's Jersey City dock waiting for longshoremen to transfer its cargo of textiles onto the 5,590-ton American Export Line freighter *Examelia*, bound for Istanbul, McLean observed the nature of this slow, laborious task:[4]

I watched all those people muscling each crate and bundle off the trucks and into the slings that would lift them into the hold of the ship. On board the ship, every sling would have to be unloaded by the stevedores and its contents put in the proper place in the hold. What a waste in time and money! Suddenly the thought occurred to me: Wouldn't it be great if my trailer could simply be lifted up and placed on the ship without its contents being touched? If you want to know, that's when the seed was planted.[5]

Loading and unloading cargo by hand was always a labour-intensive and time-consuming process for stevedores.

Although the colourful story of McLean's eureka moment has an apocryphal ring, there is little doubt that he identified a problem, an opportunity and, through his likely knowledge of other innovative and well-publicized cargo handling techniques, became the first commercial shipper to implement all the constituents of the modern containerization system.

Among the innovative shipping methods that provided useful models for containerization, Seatrain stands out. In the 1920s railways had been using various sorts of coastal vessels, ferries and barges for decades to move fully-loaded freight cars across rivers, lakes and bays. However, Seatrain was the first company to outfit ships and docks specifically to streamline a water–rail cargo service. Graham M. Brush developed the Seatrain system to provide an economical freight service connecting the American south's busiest port, New Orleans, with Havana, from which a US-standard rail network fanned out across Cuba. Brush's first ship, *Seatrain New Orleans* (1929), was a converted British-built tanker, its three newly installed cargo decks and the main deck fitted with parallel sets of standard gauge rails, running the length of the ship, onto which fully loaded freight cars could be lifted by a 125-ton car-lifting crane and then rolled into position within the deck, and their wheels fastened down for the voyage. Thus, the combination of a specialized ship, a gantry crane permanently located on the pier and a standard pre-packed container (the rail freight car) established the essential elements of all subsequent container systems.

The successful *Seatrain New Orleans* was joined in service in 1932 by two newly constructed ships, *Seatrain New York* and *Seatrain Havana*, both larger at 145.7 m (478 ft) and 16,480 tons and capable of 16.5 knots, to carry 100 loaded freight cars from the port of New York to New Orleans via Havana. These 'floating freight yards', as the press called the ships, were loaded and unloaded through a central hatch, the gantry's cradle functioning as a lift serving all four decks. Speed, both at sea and at the dock, was the benefit, and an advantage that would not be lost on Malcom McLean. In ten hours Seatrain ships could unload and load a cargo that would take an ordinary ship, using the conventional break-bulk method of handling cargo, six days to complete. Break-bulk, as McLean noted, required every piece of cargo to be loaded by hand and fitted like pieces of a gigantic puzzle into the irregularly shaped hold of the ship, a hugely labour-intensive task. And so, while the Seatrain system was highly economical, avoided pilfering and reduced damage to the cargo, it also directly threatened the livelihood of longshoremen, who loaded the ships. And it was not only the longshoremen who were worried by this new phenomenon of mechanization. *Time* magazine sounded the alarm at the launch of *Seatrain New York*:

> Wind & wave were not the only hazards faced by a strange looking craft which set out from Hoboken, NJ via Havana for New Orleans last week. At the last moment, the *Seatrain New York* was almost scuttled by a Shipping Board ruling.
>
> Atlantic shipping lines, Seaboard Railways and unfriendly shippers protested bitterly to the Shipping Board and the Interstate Commerce Commission that the Seatrain . . . was damagingly unfair (to) competition. . . The Shipping Board handed down a last-minute decision while *Seatrain New York* was fidgeting in New York Harbor: Seatrain Lines Inc. will be suffered a six-month trial period. The vessel cleared South with a cargo of cotton manufacturing machinery, paper, beans, steel, olive oil, whale oil, soap grease, soap stock, cement. [Seatrain] cut 40% off the usual stevedore charges, saved two loadings for shippers using rail–water transportation between the US and Cuba. In the past three years Seatrain Lines Inc. has carried twice as much tonnage

between New Orleans and Havana as the three competing shipping lines which operate four times as many vessels.[6]

Regulatory problems and difficult labour relations dogged Seatrain, as a pioneer of what later became known as containerization. The company's innovative methods and their effect on labour also drew the attention of organized crime, whose interests became widely established in trucking and shipping. In response, an investigative journalist, Malcolm Johnson, published a Pulitzer-Prize-winning series of exposés in the *New York Sun* in 1949 entitled 'Crime on the Waterfront', which described massive corruption in the docks of Brooklyn, Manhattan and Hoboken. These articles provided the material for Elia Kazan's 1954 feature film, *On the Waterfront*, which dramatized the racketeering then being perpetrated in the ports of New York, New Jersey and, by implication, elsewhere in America. The

The International Longshoremen's Association became one of the world's most powerful labour unions, and the highly publicized site of racial animosity, political ferment and criminal activity in its long and turbulent history.

film's Oscar-winning portrayals of key figures in the Waterfront Commission's investigation of dockland crime were based on the real-life participants: whistle-blowing longshoreman Anthony DiVincenzo; Murder Incorporated hit-man, Albert Anastasia; and Longshoreman boss Michael Clemente.

Despite such unsavoury associations, during the later 1930s and in the years of World War Two *Seatrain* ships performed well, even heroically, when they were requisitioned by the US Navy to transport fighter planes and other large military hardware to the various theatres of battle. They became part of the largest arms-carrying cargo fleet in history. General cargo vessels, tankers, barges and ferries, along with the celebrated personnel-carrying ocean liners, plied the seas serving every war zone. Among them was the *Examelia*, the freighter whose slow loading had frustrated and inspired Malcom McLean back in 1937.

The artist Alfred Lundy recorded the hurry-up-and wait routines of sailors aboard merchant vessels carrying supplies to all theatres of war in the 1940s.

While *Examelia* has a special place in the history of twentieth-century shipping, the final episode in this jobbing freighter's 22-year-long story was a sad one typical of many cargo ships pressed into war work. In the early hours of 9 October 1942 the unescorted *Examelia* was following a non-evasive course off the Cape of Good Hope when it was struck by a torpedo from a German submarine, *U-68*, causing the ship to sink in seven minutes. Four officers, thirty men and thirteen armed guards abandoned the ship, but fourteen of them drowned in their attempt. One lifeboat was launched successfully with a small group of men aboard. The commander of *U-68*, Karl-Friedrich Merten, surfaced his boat and questioned the survivors before leaving them to be rescued.[7] Later that day they were found by an American merchant ship, *John Lykes*, and put ashore at Port Elizabeth from where they travelled by train to Cape Town. There, they joined the 10,000-ton 153-m (502-ft) cargo liner *Zaandam*, capable of 16 knots and recently converted to a military transport. On 2 November, sailing off the north coast of Brazil en route to the United States, that ship was torpedoed twice by *U-174* and sank within two minutes, taking 130 people with it. They included survivors of five US ships sunk previously, and 21 of those were from the *Examelia*.[8]

World War Two was a crucible for the improvement of all shipping technologies. In addition to bulk freight, other cargoes such as oil were required to be delivered in unprecedented quantities and at greater speed than ever before at ports and in seagoing refuelling exercises. The urgency of such work encouraged cargo handlers to push the boundaries of existing techniques well beyond their previous limits, as described by David Stevenson, who observed loading the Eagle Line tanker *San Amado* at Puerto La Cruz, Venezuela, in December 1941:

In the 1940s the normal cargo loading of petroleum was 600/500 tons per hour. The young Cargo Supervisor said, matter-of-factly to the Mate, 'Kay. We'll just hook up four lines and let you have it 3000 an hour!' '3000?'. Thinking in 'Barrels', the Mate started to say 'But that's only 75 tons'. His voice trailed off. A look of incredulity spread over his face. 'You mean – 3000 TONS per hour?' 'Yup! Tha's what Ah mean, Mr Mate'. So, with double banked watches, we loaded San Amado with twelve thousand tons of Venezuelan Crude in four hours . . . So fast was this, that, by watching carefully, it was possible to see the ship going down in the water.[9]

Following the war, as the American economy grew, the regulation of highway and rail freight traffic ossified beyond even the conservative standards of the 1930s, while a cold war between the railroads and trucking industries intensified, stifling the potentials for 'intermodal' transport initiatives – any system involving more than one means of transport. Meanwhile, McLean's trucking company had flourished and become the second largest road hauler in the US, and he was anxious to expand further. His eye was firmly planted on coastal shipping as an extension to his trucking enterprise and as a way of taking his cargoes off the increasingly crowded and ageing American highway system. First, however, due to legislation preventing ownership of both shipping and trucking lines, McLean divested himself of the trucking business to buy the Pan-Atlantic Steamship co., which he later renamed Sea-Land Shipping.

Although McLean was a lifelong trucker, he had a wider vision of transportation and instinctively sought links between various modes of transporting cargo to improve both efficiency and profit. Yet at the same time, he saw the ship as a giant lorry, which cruised the invisible and relatively unimpeded lanes of the sea. And like his lorry, losing money while stuck in a queue at port waiting to be unloaded, a ship was generating profit only while it was moving, out at sea. Initially, McLean had intended to build a service using newly constructed 198.1 m (650 ft) roll-on, roll-off vessels capable of 20 knots to revive the moribund coastal shipping industry while avoiding the high costs of cargo handling in ports. The concept was similar to the Seatrain system, but the technology was different, using lorries rather than railroad cars.[10]

In addition to Seatrain, other new freight handling models had appeared by the early 1950s. During the Korean War the US military made extensive use of the 90-cu. m (295-cu. ft) steel 'Conex' boxes to ship small articles such as medicines and spare parts. The Alaska Steamship Company had begun in 1953 carrying a combination of truck trailers and custom-made collapsible container boxes on converted World War Two Liberty ships. Both the Canadian White Pass & Yukon Railway and the north-west-based Ocean Van Lines were also using pre-packed custom-made containers to transport cargo on barges and coastal steamers. The latter used 9.14-m (30-ft) containers made by Brown Trailer Co., the same company that would soon supply McLean with his first shipping boxes.[11]

Boom Box

Inspired by such innovative enterprises, in the spring of 1956 McLean inaugurated his first container ship, although at that time it was described as a 'trailership', reflecting the connection with road haulage. The *Ideal X* had been built in 1945 as a Type T2 tanker of 180 m (523 ft) and 10,448 tons, capable of 15 knots and with a cruising range of up to 20,277.7 km (12,600 miles). McLean fitted the *Ideal X* with a wooden 'mechano' deck, a type of structure that had been used extensively during the war to carry heavy and oversized cargo such as tanks and aircraft. To withstand the rigours of sea travel, McLean ordered from Brown Trailer Co. 200 reinforced semi-monocoque aluminium trailers of 10 × 2.4 × 2.5 m (33 × 8 × 8½ ft), which would be removed from their wheels and chassis before they were lifted onto the ship. That operation would be carried out by a specially adapted revolving dockside crane fitted with a newly devised spreader apparatus designed by McLean's chief design engineer, Keith W. Tantlinger, which automatically gripped the container at its four upper corners for lifting. *Ideal X* was quickly joined in service by the *Almena*, *Coalinga Hills* and *Maxton*, also converted T2 tankers each capable of carrying 58 containers on deck. After nine months the company had moved more than 67,000 tons of cargo in containers from its home port of Newark, New Jersey.

From this point on, Malcom McLean began expanding and perfecting the system that would make him the Henry Ford of the shipping world. At the very moment when the passenger steamship was being rendered obsolete by the jet airliner, the containerized cargo vessel was becoming the key element in a system of freight transport that would revolutionize world trade and significantly alter the global community in the last decades of the twentieth century. Just as Ford did not single-handedly invent mass-production, Mclean was not the lone inventor of containerization. But both men earned their places in history by bringing together a set of existing ideas, the recent technological innovations of others, a team of people with complementary skills, a few original key inventions, and a genius for orchestration to create a viable system of enterprise that would revolutionize their respective fields of transport. It was their vision and their burning ambition to earn profits by reducing unit costs, first in the production of passenger cars and later in the global shipping of manufactured goods, food and materials, that led to their successes.

Following the breakthrough of the experimental *Ideal X*, Sea-Land Shipping began to buy inexpensive war-surplus Liberty ships from the US Government. Built as freighters rather than tankers, these vessels were converted to accommodate 226 containers of 10.67 m (35 ft), manufactured by Fruehauf Trailer Co., which were for the first time stacked within cellular steel guiding frames, five-high below deck and two-high above. The success of the new supporting framework was made possible only by another Keith Tantlinger invention, the twistlock device – a rotating bolt that enabled the crane to engage with the four top corners of each container and lower it into place within the dimensions of the newly devised cell guides, an apparently simple technology that became the industry standard.

Shanghai port machinery plant portal crane at the port of Bangkok. Purpose-designed dockside container cranes were required to maximize efficiency and safety.

These early ships carried their own collapsible cranes to facilitate loading and unloading at ports where dockside cranes were not compatible with the containers. Thus, they demonstrate a transitional, emerging technology.

By 1958 other shipping lines were beginning to introduce their own freight container services, among them the venerable Matson Line, which serviced the California to Hawaii routes. Matson's system reflected local conditions in certain choices, such as the use of 7.32-m (24-ft) containers, a dimension determined by two factors; first, California highway legislation allowed lorries to haul in tandem two 7.32-m (24-ft) trailers; second, this size provided an optimum volume for the shipment of pineapples, Hawaii's largest export crop. Matson adopted many of the innovations pioneered by McLean, but also introduced other new ideas, which improved efficiency and had a major impact across the industry. Their particular contribution to

Shipping containers stacked by straddle carriers in the port of Singapore.

the development of dockside gantry cranes is an example. Matson directors were convinced from the start that purpose-designed dockside container cranes were required to maximize efficiency and safety. They commissioned the Paceco company of California to design a high-speed A-frame gantry crane, fitted with anti-sway restraints, a product that was subsequently installed at docks around the world. They also improved storage at ports by stacking their containers and by employing both cranes and straddle carriers, vehicles that can move several stacked containers simultaneously, to convey boxes around the port and to the ship.

Matson's research into mechanization also led to significant developments in the troubled area of labour relations. The International Longshore and Warehouse Union (ILWU) and the Pacific Maritime Association (PMA), in response to the development of containerization by Matson, entered into a Mechanization and Modernization Agreement in 1960 to acquire subsidies for early retirement and redundancies in exchange for relaxation of union rules that would impede mechanization at the docks. This was a milestone in the normally toxic world of waterfront labour and a development that significantly eased the growth of containerization in the Pacific. Although many jobs evaporated, those ILWU workers who remained in the wake of mechanization were among the highest-paid manual workers in the world. Matson's modernization also brought improvements to the Hawaiian standard of living by increasing the importation of fresh food from the American mainland and South America, and by facilitating the export of Hawaiian pineapples.

Aside from a failed attempt in 1960 by the Grace Line to initiate an international container service from New York to Venezuela, all dedicated container shipping had thus far been conducted as domestic American trade. Although operating entirely within US territory, Matson ran the first container line on a long ocean route. Several other companies had carried containers on the decks of ships other-wise filled with break-bulk cargo, but the turn-around time for such ships at ports was only as fast as the break-bulk freight could be unloaded, and so they offered little real economic gain to the shipping lines. Yet 1966 became an historic year for ocean transport-ation when two companies, Sea-Land and US Lines, both launched successful international containerized transport services across the Atlantic employing all-container ships. The first was US Lines' *American Racer* in March. A month later, Sea-Land inaugurated its route from Port Elizabeth, New Jersey, to Bremen, Grangemouth (in Scotland) and Rotterdam, on which *Fairland* carried 226 containers.

Within three years both *American Racer* and *Fairland* were part of the American merchant fleet carrying supplies to battle troops in Vietnam. There, the difficulty of transporting massive amounts of armaments, medical supplies and other goods to the military via the rudimentary port facilities at Saigon was compensated by the use of efficient containers. And the government contracts were, in turn, good for the container lines, which then flourished in the Pacific. Both *American Racer* and *Fairland* survived rocket attacks while de-livering cargoes to Vietnam in 1968 and 1969. In these testing cir-cumstances, container shipping demonstrated its value on a global stage, and from that time on the industry started its exponential growth as the chief conduit of global trade. Ironically, *American Racer*, the world's first all-container ship to serve on an international route, has been rusting in the US Maritime Administration's Reserve Fleet at Suisun Bay, California, since 1983, its historical significance sadly unacknowledged. By contrast, a 7.32-m (24-ft) Matson con-tainer constructed in 1970 is exhibited proudly in the transport collection of the Smithsonian Museum in Washington, DC, a modern-day successor to the eighteenth-century hogshead barrel or the Greek amphora, the standard transport containers of their ages.[12]

The international reaction to the first North American transatlantic container services was swift. The Dutch-owned Holland-America Line initiated the formation of the Atlantic Container Line (ACL) in 1965 with the Swedish companies Wallenius, Transatlantic and Swedish American Line. The French Compagnie Générale Transatlantique and Cunard soon joined these, which together cooperated to employ coordinated containerization services from European ports. In the same year four British cargo lines joined forces to launch Overseas

The steel shipping box was a modern-day successor to the 18th-century hogshead barrel or the Greek amphora, the standard cargo containers of their time.

Containers Limited, a container route to Australia. ACL made an important contribution to the technology of the container ship by exploiting their prior experience with roll-on, roll-off ferries and applying it to the design of a new type of hybrid RO/RO/container ship. These were the first such ships designed for long-distance ocean routes. Such vessels demonstrated the potential for mixing cargo-handling systems of types that could be loaded and unloaded equally quickly and efficiently at ports, guaranteeing a speedy turn-around. Such ships grew in size and sophistication and continue to operate today on the Atlantic and other trans-oceanic routes.

Despite initial heavy resistance from labour unions and trad-itionalists in shipping management, the container revolution was apparently unstoppable; Europe joined in swiftly, and Japan followed very soon after. However, as Arthur Donovan and Joseph Bonney point out, the long maritime history of Europe, its traditions and the conservatism of its shipping management presented challenges that were just as difficult as the resistance of international labour unions:

> In the 21st century, 40 years after containerization was introduced on international routes, it is easy to overlook the anxiety and dread that this new technology aroused among many members of shipping's tight-knit fraternity of executives . . . they had good reason to resist and regret the kind of revolutionary change in well-established routines that containerization was about to loose on an industry they considered their own.[13]

Some carriers, however, saw in the new system an opportunity to expand and revive international shipping, just as manufacturers realized the potential of shipping their goods more quickly, at greatly reduced unit costs and with important benefits such as in-creased safety for their consignments. Wine and spirits shippers, for

example, had historically lost significant amounts of their cargoes to breakage and theft during loading and unloading at ports; among longshoremen, pilfered whisky was considered almost an unofficial bonus. The container system greatly reduced such losses and slashed insurance costs as well. During the later years of the Cold War, when substantial numbers of American military personnel were stationed both in Europe and the Far East, large quantities of household goods and other PX supplies were also prone to theft en route to bases, and so the military enthusiastically supported containerization for security as well as its per-unit economy.

While American container ships carried supplies across the Pacific to the war in Vietnam, *Toyota Maru*, an early hybrid roll-on/roll-off freighter designed for long ocean routes, was conveying the first wave of Japanese cars to the US.

Toxic Cargo

While they helped to avoid pilfering, containers did not always protect against damage to cargo at sea, since packing them was an art
not quickly perfected or easily learned. Cargoes in improperly packed
containers could suffer terribly in rough seas and could also endanger other containers or the ship, itself, if they shifted within the box
or caused it to break loose from its fixings. The other main concern
with the packing of containers is what they may contain, undeclared.
Since no inspector sees the contents of a box before it is loaded aboard
a vessel, only the shipper's declaration gives the master any idea of
what his ship is carrying. The hazards of undeclared dangerous
cargo were illustrated by events aboard the four-month-old *Hanjin*

Pennsylvania on the 11 November 2002 in the Indian Ocean, 150 km (93.2 miles) south of Sri Lanka. The 50,242-ton, 281.5-m (923-ft) ship was carrying 4,000 containers on only its fifth voyage to Europe. An explosion, thought to have been caused by an undeclared dangerous cargo, possibly of calcium hypochlorite, started a fire that four days later ignited a second, larger explosion of declared dangerous cargo – fireworks – and also engulfed containers filled with volatile magnesium ingots. In the ensuing conflagration two mariners were killed, and the ship was gutted. The actual cause of the initial blast remains unproven, but the result is clear enough: even a state-of-the-art ship with the latest fire-fighting equipment aboard is highly vulnerable to dangerous cargo, declared or undeclared.

Since the 11 September attacks in the US, the entire world has become more alert to the threats of terrorism, and concern has been raised in many quarters about the potential threat of container cargoes.

Hapag-Lloyd's 88,000-ton *Hamburg Express* has a capacity of more than 7,500 standard 40-foot containers (TEUs), carrying up to 100,000 tons of invisible and mostly inaccessible freight.

While port security has been tightened and new security technologies developed, it is still possible for anything from toxic chemicals to enriched uranium to be hidden in a container, the latter scenario portrayed in a 2002 Hollywood spy thriller, *The Sum of All Fears*, in which a nuclear bomb is set off in the port of Baltimore. This new awareness has revived an historic paranoia, stretching back throughout the history of navigation, inspired by the mysteries of a ship's cargo.

One need only go back as far as the late nineteenth century, however, to taste the delicious horror of the toxic cargo as represented in Bram Stoker's novel of exotic, central European vampyrism, *Dracula* (1897). In that story a cargo vessel arrives on the English coast during a ferocious storm and runs aground near its destination, the port of Whitby. Of its crew only the dead captain remains aboard, his corpse tied to the ship's wheel. The captain's log raises suspicion of a cursed cargo, a shipment of 50 large boxes suspected of containing something sinister. Yet Stoker's account begins matter-of-factly with a routine entry in the log:

> On 6 July we finished taking in cargo, silver sand and boxes of earth. At noon set sail. East wind, fresh. Crew, five hands . . . two mates, cook, and myself [captain].
>
> On 14 July was somewhat anxious about crew. Men all steady fellows, who sailed with me before. Mate could not make out what was wrong. They only told him there was SOMETHING, and crossed themselves.
>
> On 16 July mate reported in the morning that one of the crew, Petrofsky, was missing. Could not account for it.
>
> July 24. There seems some doom over this ship.

Stoker gives his narrative contemporary veracity by including an article from the fictitious Whitby daily newspaper, *The Dailygraph*:

9 August.

The sequel to the strange arrival of the derelict in the storm last night is almost more startling than the thing itself. It turns out that the schooner is Russian from Varna, and is called the *Demeter*. She is almost entirely in ballast of silver sand, with only a small amount of cargo, a number of great wooden boxes filled with mould. This cargo was consigned to a Whitby solicitor, Mr S. F. Billington, of 7, The Crescent, who this morning went aboard and took formal possession of the goods consigned to him.[14]

The banality of the article detailing the business of freight shipping and the blandly unreliable ship's manifest stand out sharply against the dark and bizarre emotions inspired by the cargo itself and foreshadows the disjointed relation today's world has with the cargoes carried in our modern merchant vessels. A very large container ship such as the *Emma Maersk*, of 397 m (1,300 ft) and 171,000 tons carrying 11,000 boxes of unseen goods, is itself unseen most of the time when it is plying the ocean. This leviathan is operated only by a tiny crew of between twelve and 30 mariners, displaced men and women removed for long periods of time from family, friends and community, and from sight of land. These people can never be absolutely certain of what is concealed within those brightly coloured boxes stacked in rows above and below the deck of the ship on which they live and work. And, although out of sight is out of mind, imagined scenarios, such as the detonation of a nuclear device concealed in a shipping box delivered to a major port city or the poisoning of food transported by container, inspire paranoia. Such possibilities were thrown into sharp relief by the use of commercial airliners as weapons against the World Trade Center in New York in 2001. Enormous cargo vessels could do even more damage.

Although the result of an accident in wartime, such a horror was experienced by the community of Halifax, Nova Scotia, as long ago as 1917. In this bizarre incident the city was devastated by an explosion aboard a French munitions carrier, the 97.5-m (320-ft) 3,121-ton general cargo ship SS *Mont-Blanc*, which accidentally collided with a Norwegian ship, SS *Imo*, in the narrow mouth of Halifax harbour and caught fire, detonating its lethal cargo as it drifted into the docks. Although the crew had abandoned ship and reached safety before the explosion, around 2,000 people in the town were killed and more than 9,000 were injured in what remains the world's worst accidental non-nuclear explosion. Every structure within a one-mile radius of the blast was razed while the explosion generated a tsunami in the harbour, wrecking all the vessels moored or docked there and further devastating the shoreline. Although the blast was less than one quarter the force of the atomic bomb dropped

The peaceful waterfront of Halifax, Nova Scotia, shortly before the 1917 munitions ship explosion that devastated the town, killing or injuring more than 11,000 people, still the largest accidental non-nuclear explosion in history.

on Hiroshima, its effect was so terrible that it has remained a stark warning of what an ordinary merchant ship laden with explosives can do to a port city.

In an effort to reduce the genuine risks posed by terror cargoes, the US Bureau of Customs and Border Protection, part of the Department of Homeland Security, launched the Container Security Initiative (CSI) in 2002. The Bureau was formed to enhance security for container cargo shipped to the United States. In 2004 CSI was extended by agreement to countries of the European Union, and by 2006 had expanded to 47 countries including Singapore, Japan, China, South Korea, Malaysia, South Africa and Brazil, demonstrating both worldwide concern and the project's global reach. The main elements of the CSI initiative were the use of intelligence to identify containers that may pose a risk, screening those containers at their port of departure using gamma ray detectors and promoting the use of anti-tamper container locks.

These last devices are produced by many security companies worldwide, such as Navalock, who in 1984 introduced the first all-steel, heavy-duty container locking-bar fitted with a 'tamper-evident seal'. In development are a number of prototype Advanced Container Security Devices (ACSD), similar to an aircraft's black box, which will record a container's journey from when it is sealed to its arrival at the final destination. The ACSD is intended to detect evidence of tampering or of human intervention (e.g. illegal immigrants travelling secretly in containers) throughout the box's voyage and send an early warning to shipping officials or port security in advance of the ship docking. The latter idea is meant to counteract the simple fact that ships typically pop up quite suddenly over the visual and radar horizons when they arrive within a half hour of a port.

Although they are intended to avoid causing additional congestion at ports, such advanced detection systems will come at a cost that has inevitable implications for world trade, particularly during an economic downturn, and it has yet to be proven that they will be effective. Senator Warren Rudman, an original supporter of the CSI in the US Congress, reported to the journal *Congress Daily* in December 2007 that despite major efforts and significant advances the problem of port security remained unsolved. He stated that the 100 major US ports were effectively 'wide open' to potential abuse.[15]

Piracy

It is not only the idea of terror cargoes that plagues the shipping industry today, but also the reality of modern ocean piracy. The history of piracy at sea is long, colourful and highly romanticized. Its popular essence is summed up in Robert Louis Stevenson's novel *Treasure Island*, published in 1883. This coming-of-age story replete with buried treasure, mysterious maps, swift schooners and exotic characters, set among the tropical islands of the Caribbean, established an image of lawless bravura and honour at sea that remains with us today. The tale is set toward the end of the so-called Golden Age of Piracy, which lasted from around 1650 to 1725, during which the lightly patrolled waters of the Indian Ocean, the east coast of colonial America and the Caribbean provided rich pickings for the mainly British men and women who preyed on French and Spanish ships carrying valuable cargoes between European and colonial ports. Notable among these colourful historical figures were Sir Henry Morgan, Captain William Kidd, Ann Bonny and her partner, John Rackham, who first flew the black and white flag known as 'Jolly Roger' with its motif of skull and crossed cutlasses. Today, it is worth noting that these 'free spirits' operated within a culture of seafaring and a system of national rivalry that encouraged their actions and ensured that they went down in the mythology of the sea as iconic figures.

Across the Atlantic, in the Mediterranean Sea, from the late Middle Ages until the early nineteenth century, the Barbary pirates were the scourge of commercial shipping and of coastal communities. These mainly Muslim privateers became notorious not only for seizing ships' cargoes and their crews, but also for capturing into slavery large numbers of Christians from coastal settlements throughout the Mediterranean, the Atlantic coast of Europe and even as far away as Iceland. There, on the tiny island of Heimay in 1627, three Algerian pirate ships, led by a Dutch captain, Jan Janzten, raped, killed or captured most of the island's 242 residents. According to Icelandic legend, one woman captured in this raid, Gudrídur Símonardóttir (aka Tyrkja-Gudda), was taken to Algiers enslaved, sold as a concubine, eventually returned to Iceland under the protection of the Danish king Christian IV, and eventually rehabilitated as a Christian

The mystery and glamour of piracy in literature: Robert Louis Stephenson's *Treasure Island*, illustrated by G. E. Varian in 1918.

in Demark by a young minister, Hallgrímur Pétursson. Hallgrímur returned with her to Iceland, married her, and went on to become one of the country's most famous and beloved poets.

Of the Barbary pirates, one of the most successful was Hayreddin Barbarossa, known popularly in the English-speaking world as Redbeard. One of four sons of a prosperous potter on the island of Lesbos, Hayreddin worked with his brothers in the family business, becoming seamen in order to distribute their father's wares. However, Hayreddin and his brother Oruc found privateering more lucrative, turning their seamanship and naval daring against the Knights of St John, vying for dominance of the Mediterranean. Like many other Barbary Coast and Caribbean pirates, Barbarossa was not simply a lone marauder, but also operated as a privateer under the protection and direction of a political ruler, in his case the Ottoman sultan Suleiman the Magnificent, who was waging cultural, religious and commercial attacks against Christian Europe. Yet Hayreddin was also the fleet admiral of the Turkish Navy. His swashbuckling exploits against his arch enemy, the Genoan admiral Andrea Doria, could have provided scripts for scores of Errol Flynn movies, and he has gone into history as the most successful Ottoman naval hero of all time. Hayreddin and the Ottoman corsairs, as those pirates were also known, captured Algiers from the Spanish, and when Hayreddin declared himself Sultan of Algiers, they made the city the base of their operations. Algiers then became the centre of Mediterranean piracy and remained the major regional slave market for over three hundred years.

The corsairs primarily used the ancient galley-type ship, propelled by enslaved oarsmen, although these formidable vessels were also rigged with lateen sails that enabled them to beat close to the wind. Galleys were long, slender and fast. Their adversaries in square-rigged sailing ships, without the benefit of oars, were frequently becalmed in the light winds of the Mediterranean. They were, there-fore, particularly vulnerable to the manoeuvrable galley, which carried fighting crews of between 50 and 150 men who could quickly board an enemy ship from the galley's single flush deck, since the aim was to capture rather than destroy enemy ships and enslave their crews. With such well-adapted vessels and state backing, the Muslim pri-vateers were probably the most successful maritime outlaws in the history of seafaring until the First and Second Barbary Wars (1801–05, 1815–16), when the United States curtailed their activity. Algiers remained a pirate stronghold until the French took it in 1830, by which time European colonization in the region was imposing its authority over the local Muslim powers.

Today's maritime piracy operates in an even more independent culture than in days of old because it does not need a terrestrial base, such as Algiers. And its working practices correspond closely to the slippery ethics and shady legality of much merchant shipping for which flags of convenience and frequent changes of a ship's identity enable owners to avoid unwanted regulation in a ruthlessly competitive industry. According to William Langewiesche:

> the new pirates . . . have emerged on a post-modern ocean, where identities have been mixed and blurred and the rules of nationality have been subverted. Scornful of boundaries, these ambitious pirates are organized into ephemeral multi-ethnic gangs that communicate by satellite and cell phone and are capable of cynically appraising competing jurisdictions and laws.[16]

Since the 1950s the main guardian of safety at sea has been the International Maritime Organization (IMO), the London-based agency of the United Nations whose mission is to set technical standards and operational practices for the prevention of maritime accidents and to ensure the responsible deployment of ships at sea. IMO 'conventions' are democratically agreed by the organization's 162 sovereign member nations, who then have the right to enforce or not to enforce its laws. The IMO, itself, has no enforcement powers, and as a result, its gold standard regarding the design, maintenance, crewing and behaviour of ships at sea is an ideal, not always realized. Langeweische explains:

> the ocean looks tight in print . . . The problem, as some insiders will admit in private, is that the entire structure is something of a fantasy floating free of the realities at sea. Worse, from the point of view of increasingly disillusioned regulators, the documents that demonstrate compliance are used as a façade behind which groups of companies can do what ever they please.[17]

While referring only to 'companies' above, Langewiesche's point is that lawful shipowners can operate with the same sketchy adherence to IMO regulations as genuine criminals. They disguise their activities beneath a veneer of paperwork that allows them to go about their business uncontrolled in the vastness of the world's oceans and even in the largest ports, which are little more than frontier towns, on the border between apparent civilization and the wild ocean, with relatively ineffective marshals who are responsible for upholding remote and largely irrelevant laws. Thus, the mountains of well-intended regulation, specification and protocols established, agreed and published by the IMO, on behalf of the United Nations, have limited meaning in the face of life at sea.

In his study on the ultra-free enterprise culture of merchant shipping, *The Outlaw Sea*, Langewiesche cites the case of the *Alondra Rainbow*, a 113-m (370-ft) 7,000-ton general cargo ship worth US $10 million and carrying a cargo of aluminium ingots valued at a

further US$10 million. In October 1999 the three-year-old Japanese-owned and Panamanian-registered vessel was en route from the Indonesian port of Kuala Tanjung to Miike in Japan when a group of pirates, armed with guns and knives, pursuing in a speedboat, boarded the slower-moving vessel by the stern. The *Alondra Rainbow* was an honest, well-run ship staffed by two experienced Japanese officers and a crew of fifteen Filipinos, all of whom were subjected to several days of terrifying incarceration, first on board their own ship and later in the hold of the pirates' mother ship, a rusty hulk named *Sanho*. Eventually, they were set adrift in an inflatable lifeboat from which they were rescued ten days later by a passing fishing boat. The pirates, now in possession of the *Alondra Rainbow* and its cargo, transformed the ship's identity, first renaming it *Global Venture*, from which they sold nearly half of its valuable cargo to the operators of

Even very large vessels can quickly disappear into the marine weather or simply vanish within the vastness of the world's oceans – often by accident but sometimes intentionally.

a ship named *Bansan II*, encountered off the coast of Borneo. The receiving ship was itself renamed *Victoria* and eventually sold the remaining aluminium in the Philippines with all the requisite paperwork, forged to demonstrate the vessel's proper registration and legal ownership of the cargo. The *Alondra Rainbow* was repainted, once again renamed, as *Mega Rama*, and the home port displayed on its stern changed to Belize. Following this near-comic pantomime, the ship simply disappeared.[18]

How such a large ship can vanish in an age of radar, satellite surveillance and international regulation is explained simply; its passage across the ocean leaves only a momentary trail, its wake, which quickly disappears as the ship moves over the huge expanse of the ocean's surface. That the oceans of the world cover more than 70 per cent of the planet's surface is a simple but nearly incomprehensible fact for all landlubbers. This is made worse by the ambiguity of the horizon. While a reconnaissance aircraft flying at 3048 m (10,000 ft) can see in excess of 160.9 km (100 miles) in clear weather. From a ship floating on the sea the horizon lies no more

A ship's passage across the ocean leaves only a momentary trail – its wake, which quickly disappears from the huge expanse of the ocean's surface.

than 16.09 km (10 miles) distant – not much in the great expanse of an ocean. Even on that same ship a person on an upper deck can see farther than someone nearer the water line. And the horizon line is not the only limitation of sight; there is only a slightly further horizon for radar, beyond which that technology will not reach. Finally, the weather conceals ships in fog, rain, spray and swelling waves that can tower above even a large vessel's superstructure. Josie Dew described the disappearing horizon from her perch high on the 'monkey deck' above the bridge of the 18,663-ton general cargo ship *Speybank* in the North Atlantic during a voyage in 2005 to New Zealand:

> I remained, hour after hour, hypnotized by watching the dipping and diving horizon rise and fall below and between and over the horizontal

An elevated position for the watch, well above the deck, has always enabled mariners to see further into the distance.

bars of the deck's side railings. Sometimes, when the ship plunged into a particularly deep valley of water, the horizon disappeared altogether.[19]

In such an unstable environment it is perhaps not surprising that, although the highjacked *Alondra Rainbow* sailed off into calm seas, it remained invisible for a full month before an Indian Navy patrol boat, the *Tarabai*, sighted, identified and eventually arrested the captive ship and the pirate crew – Indonesians working under the instruction of a shadowy boss, who may have been Chinese but was never identified. The resulting trial and conviction was a rare demonstration of order being imposed over lawless behaviour at sea. Yet it was not sufficient to convince an Indian Navy veteran, Captain UK Thapa, that it indicated a genuine improvement in the civilization of global shipping. Writing in 2006, he pointed to the intimate link between modern piracy and terrorism:

It now seems that the scourge of piracy and terrorism at sea are increasingly intertwined, as piracy on the high seas is becoming a key tactic of maritime terrorist groups. Unlike the pirates of old whose sole objective was guided by commercial gains, many of today's pirates are maritime terrorists with an ideological bent of mind and broad political and religious agenda[s]. This connection is especially dangerous for energy markets, as most of the oil and gas is shipped through the world's most piracy infested waters. More alarmingly, most of the crews for world shipping are recruited from Indonesia and the Phillipines, whose waters are home to terrorist groups with experience of sea borne operations. 50 per cent of the world's piracy incidents also occur around these waters.[20]

We now live in a world, where there is no clear period of war, no clear period of peace and no clear intervening period between war and peace. The enemy is invisible but omni-present and there are no battle-lines.[21]

Although Captain Thapa's comments refer to relatively recent events at sea, they also resonate with the conditions of the privateers of old, whose activities seem analogous to the current piracy off the coast of Somalia, a country with no effective government and a well-organized class of pirates, whose motives are as complicated and unstated as ever they were in the lawless Caribbean of the seventeenth century. In a country with no meaningful currency, piracy has become the most significant income generator for whole communities, making the pirates themselves rich and feeding the local economy of shopkeepers, farmers, fishermen and services. According to the BBC, in the year preceding November 2008 Somali pirates received over US$150 million in ransoms.[22] This did not include a ransom paid soon after for a Saudi-owned very large crude carrier (VLCC), the 330-m (1,090-ft) 162,252-ton *Sirius Star*, the largest vessel ever highjacked, and its cargo of 2.2 million barrels of crude oil.

In November 2008 the spanking-new Liberian-flagged *Sirius Star* was travelling with its 25 international crew members from Saudi Arabia to the United States via the Cape of Good Hope when it was captured 830 km (520 miles) south-east of Kenya. Like the *Alondra Rainbow*, the *Sirius Star* was riding low in the water because of its full cargo and was therefore easy for the pirates to board from their attack speedboat, which had been launched from an unseen mother ship hiding beyond the horizon. Its location was well outside the area of previous Somali attacks and demonstrated the increasing reach of these well-organized pirate groups, whose activities now cover an area of ocean more than 2.8 million sq. km (1.1 million sq. miles), taking them far beyond the scrutiny of current international anti-hijacking patrols. According to Lieutenant Nate Christensen of the US Navy Fifth Fleet, which is responsible for the protection of shipping in the Persian Gulf, Red Sea, Arabian Sea and coast of East Africa as far south as Kenya:

The hijacking was shocking because it highlighted the vulnerability of even very large ships and pointed to widening ambitions and capabilities among ransom-hungry pirates who have carried out a surge of attacks this year off Somalia. To attack so large a vessel and so far south of Somalia presents a nearly impossible security problem for the anti-piracy naval task force.[23]

After nearly two months in captivity and the payment of an estimated US$3 million ransom, the *Sirius Star* and its crew were released. Its significance, however, was to stimulate a number of new rules and international agreements aimed to facilitate extradition and the prosecution of captured pirates in order to give teeth to the recently reinforced multi-national taskforce stationed in the Indian Ocean to hunt pirates. Recent arrests and the interception of pirates by members of the fourteen navies contributing to the task force establishing a 'safe corridor' for commercial shipping past the Gulf of Aden have inspired the Secretary-General of the IMO, Efthimios Mitropoulos, to believe that the situation may be controllable; but the sheer immensity of the challenge suggests otherwise.

Questions remain as to whether commercial ships should be provided with armed security, as many merchant vessels were in earlier times, although this has significant cost implications for the owners. There is also an issue about how a merchant vessel might be armed. During World War Two, for example, armed 'V' Class tankers, constructed by Harland and Wolff of Belfast, would typically be fitted with an array of weapons. However, by law they would have to be mounted aft, since merchant ships were allowed to fire only while running from an attacker.

And a debate continues about whether the international task force should attack the pirates' land bases as the US Navy did during the Barbary Wars. According to Mitropoulos, this has not been possible in the past because 'the authority was not there', but recently the UN has 'sanctioned any necessary means to arrest and prosecute the pirates'.[24] Thus, the strategies of the Barbary Wars may see a return in the near future. The pirates, themselves, assert their right to fight against the illegal over-fishing of their territorial waters and the pollution of their coastline by mariners of any nations who see the ungoverned state of Somalia as fair and easy game in their own nefarious businesses.

The capture of a ship at sea today may also be the political act of organizations dedicated to environmental protection. Greenpeace, founded in Vancouver, Canada, in 1971, is the best-known non-governmental organization for the protection of natural resources and uses confrontational strategies on land and at sea to promote its opposition to commercial activities such as the dumping of toxic waste in the ocean and industrial whaling conducted by Russian and Japanese fishing fleets. The organization's diesel-assisted schooner, *Rainbow Warrior*, uses low-impact systems for heat and hot water, to dispose of its waste, and to set an example of responsible operation at sea. *Rainbow Warrior*'s many confrontations at sea have been described as 'mind bombs' intended to transform complicated ethical issues into easily consumable media events of the David and Goliath type in order to galvanize public opinion and force change. In 2009 Greenpeace activists, using a tactic similar to Somali pirates, boarded a Hong Kong registered bulk cargo ship, *East Ambition*, as a protest against the ship's cargo of pine kernels, a crop associated with the destruction of rain forests. However, unlike the captors of *Alondra Rainbow*, instead of incarcerating the crew the Greenpeace hijackers chained themselves to specific parts of the ship's equipment, preventing it from landing at the New Zealand port of Tauranga where it was to unload its cargo. Such action has proved an effective means of exposing and preventing so-called climate crime.[25] Greenpeace offshoots include the Sea Shepherd Conservation Society based in the American state of Washington and in Melbourne, Australia. Using the MV *Steve Irwin* as its assault vessel, Sea Shepherd is regarded as employing more aggressive tactics, including scuttling ships at anchor and ramming or boarding vessels under way, to confront whaling, seal hunting and industrial fishing practices such as the use of drift nets. Because of the ethics underpinning such confrontational acts at sea, these environmental crusaders have gained the respect of a wider population denied to most pirate organizations, who appear to be motivated by personal gain, although their activities might also have valid but less eloquently publicized political motives.

Unhappy Endings

Beyond the planned activities of pirates and terrorists, the ocean wilderness carries an even more substantial and tenacious danger to mariners, landlubbers and to the ecology of the planet – accidents. Typically, the weather combines with irresponsible ship handling, with the neglect of vessels by their owners, the corruption of inspectorates and lethal flaws in ship design or construction to create a cocktail of factors that regularly send ships and their crews to ocean graves. And this seems to be a permanent condition of commercial shipping. David Stevenson described the condition of a 24-year-old tanker, *San Felix*, on which he served from 1946–7. After a quarter-century of hard service *San Felix* was worn out. The ship's boilers were faulty, leading to manoeuvrability problems and collisions in crowded ports. Leaky rivets caused pollution incidents in every harbour the ship visited. The vessel's huge refrigerator failed, spoiling most of the supplies for a long voyage. Finally, the boilers became so feeble in their performance that the ship could make only 1¼ knots of headway.

The reason for the parlous state of *San Felix* was that the Company were in two minds about scrapping her. On the one hand she was 24 years old, a venerable age for a tanker. On the other, after losses suffered during the war, tanker tonnage was in great demand, but to give the old lady a really good 'Beat up' would cost a lot of money. So we officers had to keep her staggering on, being patched up as required.[26]

Although immediate post-war shortages of tanker capacity may have justified the prolonged service of the *San Felix* and other old ships like it, they alone cannot justify the ship's continued service into the mid-1950s. Thus, corporate economics is the greatest single determinant of the condition of merchant vessels at sea. The irony of *San Felix* and other decrepit ships is that their crews, nursing them beyond what would seem reasonable limits and despite their obvious dangers, sometimes become fond of them. Stevenson confessed such an attachment:

I left *San Felix* in Thameshaven on 23rd June 1947, twelve months all but five days from joining her. It had been an exciting year, of storms, breakdowns, passengers, and sheer hard work. She had been an intractable old cow, a floating wreck. But she had been a happy ship. This is quite a common paradox. Ask a sailor what his happiest ship was and he will almost always mention some broken down old tramp. I had learned an invaluable lesson for a seaman. To improvise, to make use of my brains and common sense, to make the best use of whatever is available, whether it be men, materials or the elements.[27]

However, when they fail such vessels endanger more than just the crew that has tended them. Their cargoes may remain lost treasures in their holds, may eventually be salvaged, or may pour out and pollute vast areas of sea and coastline, killing wildlife and destroying livelihoods with no regard for national boundaries or for the wealth or poverty of the communities affected. There is nothing new about this phenomenon since the sea has always been a very dangerous place in which to conduct commerce. What has changed is the scale of disasters caused by the wreckage of super-sized vessels in the last 50 years and particularly those carrying toxic cargoes such as crude oil, of which tankers move around 2 billion metric tonnes annually.

The first steamship built as an oil tanker was the Red Star Line's 2,773-ton *Vaderland*, built in 1873 to carry the output of the newly exploited Pennsylvania oilfields. The vessel was never used for its intended purpose, since there were as yet no port facilities for handling bulk storage of oil, but *Vaderland* marked the transition from transporting oil in barrels to its bulk carriage in a ship's hold. Following *Vaderland*, the world's first successful oil tanker was Ludwig Nobel's 56-m (184-ft), *Zoroaster* of 1878. Nobel's influential design isolated the cargo of kerosene, extensively used for lamp oil, in two conjoined metal tanks, keeping combustible fumes away from sources of ignition, such as the engine room. He allowed for expansion and contraction of the liquid cargo, provided ventilation to the oil tanks and fitted the ship with 21 watertight compartments to increase buoyancy.

Nobel built a further three tankers, *Blesk*, *Lumen* and *Lux*, designed by Colonel Henry F. Swan, who divided the ships' holds laterally and longitudinally into numerous compartments, an innovation that prevented free-surface movement of the liquid cargo, which could destabilize and quickly capsize a ship. The technique soon became the industry standard and remains so today. Nobel also introduced in 1903 *Vandal* and *Sarma*, the first two oil tankers to be powered by diesel-electric motors, replacing steam power and consequently reducing the number of crew required to run the vessel. Swan's

further contributions to tanker design included the capability to take on seawater ballast (now recognized as a serious ecological threat) in lieu of cargo to improve stability, cargo filling valves operated from the deck, a modern piping layout, vapour lines, and coffer-dams providing an insulating space between watertight bulkheads for safety.

By the end of World War One the mature tanker form was established and remained relatively unchanged until the 1950s, although the development of specialized vessels continued. One notable example, refuelling ships, made it possible to replenish the tanks of destroyers and other naval warships while they were under way, a significant advantage in submarine-infested waters. Some large submarines, themselves, were employed as tankers to supply the German Wolf Pack U-boats and Allied submarines during World War Two; they became known fondly as 'milk cows'. Meanwhile, the technology of manufacturing tankers changed radically with the refinement

The Nobel Brothers' oil barge *Prokudin-Gorskii*, Russia, 1909.

of mass-production systems. Exponential increases in the demand for petroleum with the expansion of car production, commercial and military aviation and the rapid development of new petroleum-based plastic materials also placed heavy new demands on oil shipping. During World War One relentless U-boat attacks on tankers demanded the rapid construction of new ships of standard design, which were built for the first time using Fordist production methods yielding 3.2 million tons of cargo capacity between 1916 and 1921, 50 per cent more than all existing tonnage at the outbreak of the war.

Hazards aboard a tanker are not restricted to catastrophic failure and enemy attacks in wartime or by privateers in peacetime. The simple tasks required of any crew member can be dangerous. Such was the potential of tank-cleaning aboard a British Liberty tanker in 1940:

The Mate began to organise 'Tank-cleaning' in readiness for the next cargo. A modern tanker has special high-pressure steam cleaning equipment for cleaning her cargo compartments. This makes short work of the disposal of oily sludge formed by corrosion and rust mingling with petroleum. But in 1940 sweat, elbow grease, and a high pressure Mate accomplished what high pressure steam does today . . . The tank was a huge steel box, some thirty feet square by forty feet deep, one of twenty such divisions of the ship's hull. A steel-runged ladder led from the hatch to the bottom of the ship. The hatch itself was about three feet by two. A tanker has no double bottom, save in the engine room. She is built on a system of longitudinal heavy beams, tied together by deep transverse frames and smaller stiffeners. Known as the 'Isherwood System', to all intents and purposes she is a huge box girder. So my tank was a big box, from whose inner surface protruded at intervals, deep frames about two and a half feet wide, on which men could walk . . . Though it was hard to see from the deck, the bottom was illuminated by a dim but sufficient light, rather like that in a cathedral. It was hot, very hot. It also reeked of petrol fumes . . . The smell was powerful, heady. The smell of a hundred filling stations rolled into one. Gradually the fumes got into one's lungs, into one's taste buds even; so that to spit was to spit petrol. To swallow was to swallow petrol . . . A great exhilaration took hold of me. Presently I began to sing. This was the life. How magnificently my voice rang in the tank. Why were they looking at me so curiously? . . . I gagged on the rum, gasping and choking as the fiery liquid ran down my gullet . . . I had passed out in the tank, my lungs full of petroleum vapour.[28]

During World War Two, the construction of such Liberty ships, ungainly but immensely practical, no-frills vessels armed for protection against aircraft and submarine attack, was greatly accelerated, as it had been in the Great War, due to the rate of loss from submarine attacks. Increased production was accomplished first in the US by the innovative use of welding rather than riveting and by the introduction of 'block construction', a method of prefabricating large sections of a vessel in factories adjacent to assembly docks, where they were then fitted together. Block construction was the key innovation of the Liberty ships, designed by the naval architect William Francis Gibbs, reducing construction time from months to as little as five days. This method was pioneered in the assembly of tankers by Daniel Keith Ludwig at his shipyard in Norfolk, Virginia, under the US government's Emergency Shipbuilding Program, and was essential to the mass production of Liberty ships in a group of shipyards headed by Henry J. Kaiser. Among the ships that featured most prominently in the Allied war effort, the T2 tanker, such as the one later bought by Malcom McLean and renamed *Ideal X*, is a notable type. The

16,613-ton T2-SE-A1 model was the most successful variant of this standard-type ship, with 500 completed by 1945. Like the *Ideal X*, many T2 tankers were sold off cheaply and then used commercially after the war, forming the basis of some of the world's greatest commercial fleets, such as those built by McLean and by the Greek shipping magnates Aristotle Onassis and Stavros Niarchos.

Recently completed Victory cargo vessels are seen here lined up at a California shipyard awaiting commission, *c.* 1943.

New technologies and rapidly increased production, however, had their hazards. This was vividly illustrated on 16 January 1943, when the newly completed tanker SS *Schenectady*, the first T2 built by the giant Kaiser Shipbuilding Company, broke in half spectacularly, and with a cracking sound heard over a mile away, in its fitting-out dock within full sight of the citizens of Portland, Oregon. Shocking photos of the broken ship, its bow and stern submerged, were published in the national press and highlighted the potential problems of novel technologies executed on frantic production schedules. They also brought to public attention ten earlier instances of new ships failing because of either bad welding or metal fatigue, or both.

Such incidents have not gone away over the passing decades, and new shipbuilding techniques, such as 'jumbosizing', have created new opportunities for mayhem. The 35,953-ton container ship *Carla*, built in 1972, broke in half during a storm off the Azores while en route from Le Havre to Boston in November 1997. Although the bow sank, the aft section remained afloat and was towed to the Canary Islands with the crew of 34 safely aboard. At the time of the accident the ship's

The newly completed T2 tanker *Schenectady* snapped in half while docked for fitting out. The cause was poor welding.

officers were criticized for overloading the ship and for maintaining full speed in a very heavy sea. However, subsequent research led to a US court ruling that the ship's structure failed dramatically because of poor welding when, in 1984, the vessel was lengthened 14 m by the Hyundai Corporation in South Korea.

As the size of tankers expanded along with the demand for oil in the 1950s, the danger of increasingly huge vessels sinking took on ever-greater importance. The problem was illustrated staggeringly when in March 1978 the Spanish-built, Liberian-flagged, American-owned *Amoco Cadiz*, a very large crude carrier of 334 m (1096 ft) and 109,700 tons, was wrecked en route from the Persian Gulf to the Netherlands, via Britain. Having encountered a heavy storm while passing 5 km (3 miles) off the coast of Brittany at the entrance to the English Channel, the ship's steering gear failed allowing the vessel and its crew of 44 to drift towards the rocky coast, where it ran aground and eventually split in two. *Amoco Cadiz* was carrying 1,604,500 barrels (219,797 tons) of Arabian Light and Iranian Light crude oil, all of which was lost into the sea as the ship disintegrated, resulting in the largest oil spill yet to have happened. The spill quickly formed a 19-km (12-mile) slick described as 'chocolate mousse', a gooey mixture of oil and water, which spread west during the months that followed, eventually coating 320 km (200 miles) of the French shore. The *Amoco Cadiz* accident caused the worst loss of marine life ever recorded from an oil spill and is estimated to have cost more than US$250 million in damage to the tourism and fishing industries. After twelve years of litigation, the French government was finally awarded $120 million from the ship's owners, the American oil giant Amoco. The captain's delay in issuing an SOS and in gaining permission from the ship's owners in Chicago to accept the costly assistance of a German tug, which was in attendance, were cited as contributing factors to the loss of the *Amoco Cadiz*.

In addition to dramatic accidents, invisible threats to the ocean habitat are caused by the simple day-to-day operation of tankers and other large cargo vessels. Prominent among such problems is the movement from one aquatic environment to another of harmful pathogens and sea organisms through the uptake and release of ballast water from ships. Ballast is necessary to maintain the stability and seaworthiness of ships when they are less than fully loaded with cargo, and in the twentieth century water replaced solid ballast, such as sand, since technology made it easier and more economical to fill and empty ballast tanks as ships load and unload their cargoes. Yet this practice also presents a major threat to marine ecology. Shipping transfers between 3 and 5 billion tons of ballast water around the world every year. All ballast water contains

Accidents WILL happen! The very large crude carrier *Amoco Cadiz* breaking up and releasing its cargo of 1.6 million barrels (250,000 m³) of oil near the French coast in 1978.

bacteria and other forms of small marine life that can, in certain conditions, invade and destroy habitats thousands of miles from its home waters. For example, the common North American jellyfish, transferred to the Black Sea, has multiplied to such an extent that it has killed native plankton, thereby contributing to the widespread failure of local fish stocks. Among many additional examples, tiny Red Tide algae transferred to several countries have contaminated popular shellfish, causing severe illnesses to humans who have eaten them.

Beside the controversial practice of loading and unloading ballast water at sea rather than in ports, as recommended by IMO guidelines, no alternative methods of safer ballasting have been agreed. Options include mechanical filtration, sterilization using ozone or ultraviolet light, or controversial chemical biocidal treatments that pose environmental and human-health risks. Any or all of these would also add cost, however, and it is the shipping companies that would ultimately decide what they could afford. Ultimately, research and development groups tend to work in isolation from one another and from naval architects, shipping companies and national governments, a situation ameliorated somewhat by the IMO through conferences, publications and new conventions.[29]

Despite all its disadvantages, transportation by ship remains more fuel-efficient than air or overland transport, and therefore it continues to be the least carbon-emitting method of carrying goods around the world. However, questions are being directed increasingly to the viability of shipping such a high percentage of the world's materials, manufactured goods and waste products to distant ports. The world's 50,000 merchant vessels currently emit 800 million tonnes of CO_2 per year, and the IMO estimates that current carbon pollution from commercial shipping is now 1.1 billion tonnes, three times previous estimates. CO_2 from merchant ships now contributes

nearly 4.5 per cent of global emissions and is expected to rise to 6 per cent in the next decade.[30] In response, one European wine producer has begun to ship their products from France to the Irish Republic and the UK on a restored classic sailing vessel. Such an example, however small, eliminates fuel costs, emits no toxins and also adds a Green cachet to products aimed at a discerning and socially responsible consumer. While concerns over global warming are galvanizing debate and strong opinions, the rising cost of oil

A German Navy Bottsand-class oil recovery ship awaits the next spillage, 2007.

rather than an ecological conscience may be the key factor in changing patterns of transportation and reducing dependency on transport overall in the years to come. Meanwhile, researchers and campaigners alarmed by the effects of anthropogenic global warming are turning to the issue of globalization as the crucial factor creating the problem.

Anti-globalists favour local production and consumption patterns. Some political economists conclude that rising fuel costs over the longer term will make global shipping more expensive and therefore less desirable in relation to local production and consumption, which would reduce harmful emissions considerably. Others contend that globalization is such an entrenched phenomenon in the twenty-first-century economy that any rise and fall in fuel price changes would have relatively little impact on overall emissions from sea shipping or other forms of cargo movement and that technological 'fixes' are the best option.[31] Anti-capitalist critics exhort the people of developed and developing nations to reduce or eliminate their consumption of everything imported, from exotic and unseasonal food to petrol for their cars. One popular response to such a view is the annual 'Buy Nothing Day', which highlights the environmental and ethical consequences of globalized consumption. This event began in the United States in the early 1990s and has now spread to many developed countries. Thus, the heavy reliance of international commerce on ocean cargo shipping can no longer go unquestioned as a natural right or as a good thing while the disastrous effects of environmental breakdown loom in the near future.

Other initiatives to address the increasing global concern over the ecological dangers of modern shipping include gatherings such as the International Symposium on Ship Design and Construction convened in Tokyo by the Royal Institute of Naval Architects, the Japan Society of Marine Engineering and the Japan Institute of

Navigation in 2009. The aim of this symposium was to bring together practitioners and theorists from fields including design, construction and manufacturing to establish a blueprint for an environmentally sound modern ship that would reduce the consumption of fossil fuels and reduce significantly CO_2, NOX and SO_2 emissions, as well as minimising the effects of ballast water discharge. Although cargo vessels are the major source of concern today because of their size and numbers, cruise liners and military ships also suffer many of the same defects and figure prominently in such dialogues. Wide-ranging subjects for interdisciplinary discussions include non-ballast ships, ship recycling, high-performance operational methods, hull design, energy-saving machinery, and methods of propulsion including solar, hydrogen fuel cell, wave, and wind – yes, a modern sailing ship.[32]

As surely as shipping remains the conduit for 90 per cent of the world's materials, food and manufactured goods, the factors of inadequate communication, human error, irresponsible or greedy management, technical failure, design flaws and uncontrollable weather will contribute to accidents – spectacularly huge or apparently insignificant – but many resulting in pollution, financial ruin, prolonged litigation, political argument and death. Well-intentioned regulation will, inevitably, continue to expand in an effort to control the uncontrollable, while enforcement will surely remain patchy. In a climate of global economic retreat, when the self-regulated shipping industry saw its cargo rates drop by 90 per cent in the last four months of 2008, economic and political pundits will speculate on the direction of commercial shipping. Meanwhile, stern warnings have been issued by the Baltic Exchange chairman, Michael Drayton, that the challenges of financial stringencies, bankruptcies and contract disputes will strain the ethics of the industry, which must uphold established standards of behaviour if it wishes to retain its singular regulatory independence.[33] Given the historical freedom of enterprise at sea, it would be reasonable to expect the forces of chaos to dominate the culture of ocean commerce in the years to come.

5 Port

Nature's Golden Doors

Departing New York harbour aboard the *Queen Mary 2* on its maiden Eastbound voyage from New York in January 2004, the art historian Suzanne Fagence-Cooper observed:

> the NYPD were giving us a memorable send-off, with speed boats and helicopters circling the liner. The sun was setting and the Manhattan skyline looked like the backdrop to a filmset; in all the skyscrapers, New Yorkers were enjoying the spectacle of this enormous ship easing her way along the Hudson river – we could see the flashbulbs of their cameras lighting up the apartment blocks. As we came alongside the Statue of Liberty, we were treated to a fireworks display, and we saw the QE2 steaming beside us. Both ships were crossing the Atlantic side by side for the first and last time.[1]

Once at sea even such conspicuous vessels are lost to the terrestrial world and to the everyday life of the landlubber. Only during their departure or when they appear over the horizon and enter a port of call do they become real to those on land. In this sense the port is the one place on earth where ships are familiar to the entire population, where they are viewed close up at their docks, where

Bird's-eye view of New York Harbor c. 1880, showing Brooklyn Bridge and the busy docks of Manhattan, Brooklyn and New Jersey.

their arrivals and departures are awaited, watched or celebrated, and where their presence generates immediate activity, local revenue and a clear sense among the population of connection with other distant ports and with the high seas.

The scene became a cliché of illustrated magazines and cinema newsreels during the first half of the twentieth century. A massive liner towers over the pier. The ship's railings are crowded with waving passengers who throw brightly coloured streamers to their friends and family members standing in groups on the quayside below, each holding their end of the ribbon to maintain contact until the great vessel pulls slowly away from the dock. On deck the ship's band plays a stirring tune. Horns bellow. Powerful engines churn. Tears gather and stream over smiling faces. As the ship disappears from sight, and as its wake vanishes, the deflated crowd disperses from the quayside leaving the litter of departure discarded over the utilitarian

The Cunard liner *Lusitania* arrives in New York following its maiden voyage from England in 1907.

backdrop of wooden sheds, asphalt paving, lowered gangways, idle cranes and a vacant rectangle of calm water where the ship had stood moments before – as if an important building had been suddenly removed from the fabric of the city. Temporarily idle, the pier awaits its next guest.

While the great piers and docks of the steamship era were an essential element of the port city, many of the major ports became great primarily because of the favourable geography of their harbours, formed in networks of deep-water estuaries, bays and rivers, the precise placement of their docks determined by channel depths, tidal flows and sheltered headlands, among other maritime factors. The natural advantages of New York's harbour led to that city becoming the major port of the United States in the nineteenth century and one of the most important international shipping destinations of the twentieth. The harbour's location, spaciousness and navigable channels provided ideal conditions for the growth of New York City as a commercial centre linking (particularly after the construction of the Erie Canal) the American mid-west with the cities of the eastern seaboard and the major ports of Europe.

Similarly, the development of the port city of Southampton, on the English Channel, was influenced by its maritime geography. The city grew on a peninsula between two rivers that converge in an estuary, formed at the end of the last Ice Age, with a bed of soft silt that makes dredging relatively easy. The city's extensive western docks were built on land reclaimed from the dredging of the main channel, Southampton Water, keeping its depth sufficient to accommodate increasingly large vessels of all types, some of them among the biggest afloat today. Furthermore, the location of the Isle of Wight, south of the city, generates an unusually long period of high tide, facilitating the passage of very large ships in and out of the port. As a result, Southampton became a major embarkation point

for the Royal Navy from the eighteenth century. It was the harbour from which the Pilgrims sailed to America on the *Mayflower* in 1620 and it was also the home port of RMS *Titanic*, aboard which many so-called Sotonians perished. In the 1930s, linked by fast train services with London, Southampton was home to Cunard's Blue Riband liner, *Queen Mary*, joined after 1945 by its sister ship, *Queen Elizabeth*. In 1968 the Southampton Container Terminal began operation, eventually becoming one of the largest cargo ports in Europe.

To any ocean-going traveller, the first sight of a port as it appears over the horizon must be compelling, regardless of the complex personal feelings it may inspire in the circumstances of that particular voyage. Millions of immigrants to the United States, passing sculptor

Immigrants queuing in the reception hall of the Ellis Island terminal building in 1904.

Frédéric-Auguste Bartholdi's statue of *Liberty Enlightening the People* as they entered New York harbour, saw that monumental image as the symbol of all the hope and the prospect of freedom towards which they had struggled across thousands of miles of ocean, often in tremendous discomfort. The dramatic skyline of the city, beyond the statue, stood for the economic possibilities many immigrants sought in the New World.

Yet for over twelve million passengers landing at the government terminal on Ellis Island, the main east coast port of entry between 1892 and 1954, the dreams could quickly be tarnished by harsh treatment, hospitalization or even repatriation (at the expense of the shipping line) for the unlucky 2 per cent – the grim prospect that earned Ellis Island the nickname 'Heartbreak Island'. Such a scenario was vividly portrayed in the story of Italo-American immigration told by Emanuele Crialese in his 2007 feature film, *The Golden Door* (*Nuovomondo*). And a similar real-life story was reported by Edward Steiner, who in 1914 witnessed the interview of an elderly Russian Jew and his son in the court of Ellis Island. The immigration officer conducting the interview told the translator:

Ask them whether they are willing to be separated; the father to go back and the son to remain here? They look at each other; no emotion yet visible, the question came too suddenly. Then something in the background of their feelings move, and the father, used to self-denial through his life, says quietly, without pathos and yet tragically, 'Of course.' And the son says, after casting his eyes to the ground, ashamed to look his father in the face, 'Of course.' And, this one shall be taken and the other left, for this was their judgment day.[2]

The terrible grandeur of the main terminal buildings served as an appropriate backdrop for such experiences. Architects Edward

Lippincott Tilton and William Alciphron Boring designed the permanent Ellis Island Immigrant Station after winning a competition in 1897 with a design for which they received a gold medal at the 1900 Paris Exposition and several other prestigious architectural awards. Tilton and Boring had worked for the firm of McKim, Mead and White before forming their own partnership, and their design for the Ellis Island building demonstrates the influence of the Beaux-Arts formality and impressive ornamentation employed in public buildings by McKim, Mead and White during the last quarter of the nineteenth century.

Like the many grand ocean liners that transported immigrants in their steerage class, the terminal's monumental exterior and epic reception hall drew attention away from the less than welcoming character and detailing of its working spaces – the massive frosted

Architects Tilton & Boring designed the permanent Ellis Island Immigrant Station after winning a competition in 1897, a design for which they received a gold medal at the 1900 Paris Exposition.

glass windows that let in light but obscured views of the New York skyline, the crowded sleeping accommodation, labyrinthine passageways and stair halls, and the austere hospital quarters, where many immigrants spent long periods of time before admittance to the United States. The personal dramas of individuals arriving at the immigration station became part of American folklore, described in novels and films such as Mario Puzo's bestseller, *The Godfather*, and Francis Ford Coppola's *Godfather* film trilogy in which the young Vito Andolini is held in the Ellis Island hospital and registered with the subsequently infamous name of Corleone, derived from his home town in Sicily. For those landing at Ellis Island, the class in which they travelled aboard ship determined their treatment at the port. According to an article published in *Harper's Weekly* in 1893:

The grandeur of the reception hall in the Ellis Island terminal building is enhanced by the spectacular vaulted ceiling tiled by the Catalan engineer Raphael Gustavino.

For the saloon [cabin] passenger our doors still swing wide open. He may come and go freely save for the inquisitive custom-house examiner and the boisterous and importunate dock cabman. But the voyager in the steerage finds his course strewn thick with obstacles. For him the New World speedily becomes a mighty interrogation point.[3]

And it was not only class of travel that impeded some would-be entrants to the United States. After World War One, American fears of Bolshevism, Anarchism and Communism became fervent and prompted severe tightening of immigration restrictions. Any applicant suspected of belonging to any radical political persuasion was detained as a prisoner at Ellis Island until their case had been reviewed and decided. The Czech actor and dramatist Jiří 'George' Voskovec, who was held at Ellis Island under the Internal Security Act in 1951, observed that

the Russians have long made heavy propaganda use of Ellis Island. They call it a concentration camp, which, of course, is outrageous. No one mistreats us here. Our jailers – nearly all of them, anyway – are very kindly people, who go to extraordinary lengths, within the system, for which they don't pretend to be responsible, to make our stay here as little like a nightmare as they can. There is a movie here every Tuesday and Thursday night; the children get milk six times a day and go to school three hours a day. We are kept warm and fed generously – nothing like the Colony, I assure you, but more than enough. And, as people are always pointing out to us, it doesn't cost us anything. But I will tell you, it is hard to not be depressed at the realization that within the American government, which has rightly been honored so long as the guardian of individual freedom and human dignity, there is one small agency that can seize a man and bring him to this place.[4]

And so, within the splendour of the vast Beaux-Arts terminal building, and with the inspiring skyline of New York City so close at hand, the eager and well-intentioned newcomer could be subjected to a Kafkaesque detention for an indefinite period. Unfortunately, the twists and turns of US political attitudes, particularly during the Red Scare of the McCarthy Era and the second Bush presidency, confirm that such injustices are recurrent and have recently been resurgent.

That port cities like New York are typically considered to be beautiful is a product of their situation by water, often enhanced by a topography or architecture providing extensive views of bay, estuary or river. One of the most lauded ports is Rio de Janiero, its natural harbour located on the south-western shore of Brazil's Guanabara Bay, named as one of the Seven Natural Wonders of the World. Surrounding the bay's deep blue waters is a cluster of mountainous rocky outcroppings dominated by the Sugar Loaf Mountain and Corcovado Mountain, which provides a natural pedestal for the monumental statue of *Christ the Redeemer*, the symbol of Rio. According to a former merchant seaman, David Stevenson, Rio

is one of the most beautiful natural harbours in the world. It looks as if a huge landlocked bay has, in the distant past, been the crater of an extinct volcano. The rocks and nearby hills are basaltic in composition. The approach to the harbour is made through a channel between two islands and once the ship is through the gap, a wonderful vista opens out before your eyes. On the port hand the sweep of Copacabana Beach with its magnificent hotels and homes is quite literally, the 'String of Pearls'. By the time the vessel has reached her anchorage in Quarantine, Sugar Loaf Mountain has been passed and the whole of the inner bay lies in breathtaking loveliness. Ships of all nations crowd the harbour. Beyond, like some fantastical theatre background, rise the serrated black peaks of the distant mountains.[5]

Such a spectacular setting for an arrival by ship, combined with the additional attractions of endless white beaches, the famous annual Carnival and the tradition of samba music, have made Rio a popular destination of cruise liners for over 100 years. Heat, rhythm and the city's liberal cosmopolitan society have famously raised the libido of pleasure-seeking visitors for generations. Rio was also the capital of Brazil until 1960, and thus a centre of political power, a magnet for wealth and a destination for emigrant ships such as the ostentatious Italian liner *Conte Grande*, and many lesser ships coming from Europe or Africa bringing cargoes of new settlers and cheap labour along with the pleasure-seeking rich and famous. Like many other ports, Rio is also well known for its high crime rate. The city's culture of theft and violence is exaggerated by Brazil's

Emigrants gathered on the dock at Queenstown (Cobh), Ireland, waiting to board a steamship for New York. Published in *Harper's Weekly*, 1874.

extremes of wealth and deprivation, with impoverished and flimsy *favelas* (shanty towns) standing immediately adjacent to the most elegant and wealthy neighbourhoods of the city. Thus, for naive tourists, the sumptuousity of a gorgeous port city can become the bait for a perilous encounter with criminality.

Bad News

This dark side of port culture has been a recurrent theme in twentieth-century literature, highlighting the tension existing in many such towns between wiley residents and wide-eyed transients, between powerful shipping companies and organized labour, between water-front gangs, petty criminals, saboteurs and law enforcement – in short, the conflict between order and chaos. Every port city is on the frontier, the last outpost of civilization before the tremendous, ungovernable expanse of the sea. From them, ships steam off into invisibility, become detached from the stability and protection of

The smallest pieces of harbour equipment may be the most important to shipping. This buoy, anchored in Portsmouth Harbour on the English Channel, marks the boundary of the shipping channel.

A major functional element of every port is the lighthouse. This example in the port of Copenhagen sits on a jetty that provides a prominent public outlook over the harbour.

land, subject to the mayhem of the weather, to the foibles of the captain or crew, and to the technical reliability of the vessel, itself. Such a position lends the port city a distinctive character bred of anxiety, ambition and daring that infects the local population, those who work on ships and ordinary passengers, who place themselves temporarily at the mercy of the port and then of the vessel. As Albert Camus wrote, 'What gives value to travel is fear.'[6]

The relation between the denizens of a port city and the mariner – whether of the navy, merchant marine, a maritime outlaw or a civilian traveller – is traditionally edgy, a walk on the wild side, often romantic or sexually exploitative, as in the archetypical sailors' brothel. Thus, the physical fabric and amenity of the town have been as important to a seafarer in personal terms as were the harbour and docks in serving the practical navigational demands of the merchant vessels or military ships moored there.

Sydney Harbour Control Tower, opened in 1974, incorporates radio communications, vessel surveillance and 'ShIPS', an internet-based system of tracking vessels' movements, cargo handling and fuelling.

The Breton Port of Brest is located at the western most point in France. The town is built on a dramatic hillside to the north of a large protected bay, the Rade de Brest, and is bisected by the Penfeld River, which empties into the bay. Its position and geography provide ideal conditions for shipping, and enable the port to accommodate vessels of any size or type, including the current flagship of the French naval fleet, the nuclear-powered aircraft carrier *Charles de Gaulle*, which was built in Brest and completed in 1994. As a major port on the wild North Atlantic, Brest amply demonstrates those qualities that came to be associated with port cities and that mariners traditionally expected at the end of a voyage:

Smaller features of the dock-scape, such as this mooring bollard, serve specific functions while also contributing to the special maritime character of all ports.

Whether they descend from the heavens or ascend from some realm where they have consorted with sirens and other more fabulous monsters, these sailors, when ashore, inhabit solid buildings of stone – barracks, arsenals, or palaces – in strong contrast to the fluid, nervous, almost feminine irritability of the restless ocean (don't sailors sing in their shanties of the consolation of the waves?); they live by jetties loaded with chains, bollards, buoys, and other maritime paraphernalia to which, even when at the extremist ends of the earth, they know themselves to be anchored. To match the nobility of their stature, they are provided with arsenals, forts, convict-prisons converted to modern use, all architecturally magnificent.

Brest is a hard and solid town, constructed of grey granite hewn from Breton quarries. This rock-like quality anchors the port, giving the sailor a sense of security, for it provides him with an advantageous launching-point when outward bound and a haven of rest after the perpetually boisterous billows.[7]

In addition to the security it may offer the weary mariner, a town like Brest will also offer pleasures and opportunities for mayhem that cannot be easily achieved in the communal space of a ship or within its rigidly organized crew structure, at least not while at sea. In his novel *Querelle of Brest*, Jean Genet explores the criminal underside of the port to disclose how sex and crime combine to form a cocktail of fantastic potency when located within the collision between the ultimate freedom of the sea and the peculiar organization of a military and commercial port city, with its medieval castle and fortifying walls, its bent police and exceptional moral codes. The anti-hero, George Querelle, is a thief and multiple-murderer, whose crimes are the expression of a curious lust for life satisfied only through extreme experience and action. Just as the ship is his vehicle of adventure, escape and redemption, the centre of his activities

in the port is the brothel known as La Feria, the most notorious whorehouse in the port, 'decorated with purple and gold, whither repair to seek their solace sailors from overseas, lads of the Merchant and Coastal Navies, and men from the docks . . . When night falls, La Feria further fires the imagination, for it has all the excitement of a dazzling crime.'[8]

Historically, it has seemed somehow inevitable that the sexual tension built up among sailors after a long sea voyage would explode into various sorts of activity when they reached a port. Drink figures prominently in the lore of such places, and the sailors' quarter of any port will typically house many bars whose proprietors know how to handle a brawl. Before the development of cheap commercial air travel, most of the world's drug traffic was carried by ship, and sailors returning to the ports of the West from the Orient were

Until recent times the sexual segregation of seamen and their spartan, dutiful lives at sea have justified wild behaviour in port.

prominent among smugglers. Visiting a luxurious Paris opium den during the 1930s, the photographer Brassaï described the routine delivery of such a package, posted by a sailor from the port. 'Did it come from Smyrna, from Istanbul, Egypt, Iran, Hong Kong? Merely from Marseilles. The mailman left and there was an outburst of joy. The stuff had arrived!'[9] In the ports, themselves, the sailors' quarter became neighbourhoods known for their opium dens, and indeed Genet's Querelle serviced such establishments as part of his enterprise. Sailors were also the most prominent patrons of the portside brothels, such as La Feria. Picasso referred to such a place in his first Cubist painting, *Les Demoiselles d'Avignon* of 1907, which depicts in its fractured geometry an image of prostitutes working in the Rue d'Avignon, at the centre of Marseille's red light district, the sailors' quarter.

Beyond the seamy, glamorous criminality of the port, its local population engaged in legitimate trades that, nevertheless, could be seen to exploit the many transients passing through – tourists and commercial travellers who stayed overnight in its hotels, who ate in its restaurants, drank at its bars, patronized its shops, or changed currency while waiting to board a ship. Founded in the sixteenth century, the port of Veracruz on Mexico's Gulf coast is built around a natural harbour. It served as the main port of Mexico during the period of Spanish rule and in the twenty-first century remains the country's most important east-coast shipping centre, with freight handling now the city's most lucrative industry. Yet as a tourist resort, Veracruz is also a destination for cruise ships, and in the days before mass aviation it was the busiest staging point for travel by ship from Mexico to Europe.

It was against this background that Katherine Ann Porter described the atmosphere of the city as passengers gathered to meet a ship for departure in the autumn of 1931. 'The port town of Veracruz is a little purgatory between land and sea for the traveler, but the people who live there . . . carry on their lives of alternate violence and lethargy with a pleasurable contempt for outside opinion.'[10] Yet Verecruzanos were not unique in their attitudes, since any port city may earn the contempt of travellers who are themselves suffering from anxiety and tension before a long ocean passage. The problem particular to port life and culture is the relation of the city's denizens and port officials to the constant flow of strangers through their home town. David Stevenson reported on the corrupt practices of Latin American ports in the 1940s:

> The port authority launch comes ponderously alongside, and the first man up the gangway is the port health officer. He is followed by at least two of his minions, carrying his briefcase, and perhaps his umbrella. He is greeted by the chief officer, if not the master. Though this is done with ill grace, it must be done, for these petty officials have it in their power to delay and fine the ship, more or less at their whim. A sad state of affairs. Each of these officials has to be 'squared'. That is, given a gift of some kind. Usually duty free cigarettes or spirits. Even the customs officers expect this. Only after this visit has been made can the ship proceed to her berth. Sometimes a ship will wait as long as five hours for the official visit to be made. But she can not do a thing about it. I call this holding a ship or company to ransom.[11]

While the local practices or rituals of ports may adversely affect the operators of cargo ships, the exploitation of emigrants in the age of mass steamship migration was much worse. Edward Steiner recalled that, after his own harsh experience of transatlantic emigration, he had studied such practices alongside the newer immigrants:

Many a time since, I have visited every harbour from which emigrants go to the New World. I have travelled with them voluntarily from their homes into the steerage, as I then travelled from necessity, and I found no bad men until we came to the places where we were merchandise – the stuff to be exploited.[12]

Here he is referring to a variety of corrupt business people associated with the emigrant trade, from the agents of certain steamship lines to the owners of rooming houses near the docks. In her description of Veracruz, Porter similarly denounced the sharp business attitudes of the ordinary shopkeeper, bar owner, hotelier and restaurant owner toward the unwary traveller en route to a ship in the harbour:

The travelers wish only to be carried away from the place, and the Verecruzanos wish only to see the last of them; but not until every possible toll, fee, extortion, and bribe due to the town and its citizens has been extracted. It is in fact to the passing eye a typical port town, cynical by nature, shameless by experience, hardened to showing its seamiest side to strangers: ten to one this stranger passing through is a sheep bleating for their shears, and one in ten is a scoundrel it would be a pity not to outwit. In any case, there is only so much money to be got out of each one, and the time is always short.[13]

She also makes it clear that travellers are little better, as the worst of them insult, abuse and rob the port's merchants, while even the best-intentioned relate to port-dwellers with ill-concealed condescension before crossing the gangplank and swanning off to sea.

Yet it was not only the avariciousness and unmannerly behaviour of port culture that disturbed some observers, but also the sheer ferocity of activity that surrounded the arrival and departure of a

ship. The greatest commercial ports of the late nineteenth century generated a terrific assault of noise, fumes, uncontrolled hubbub and dangers, both physical and moral, that could overwhelm the senses of a refined Victorian traveller. The novelist J.-K. Huysmans imagined, with some disgust, the sensations of a hyper-sensitive man like himself arriving on the cross-channel steamship at the Port of London. He imagined the city as 'fog-bound, colossal, enormous, smelling of hot iron and soot' wrapping in a thick cloak of smoke and mist a forest of masts and cranes amidst an endless string of piers crowded with heaps of cargoes, handled by swarms of down-trodden dock workers. Nearby, screaming, steaming trains raced by 'while along every avenue and every street, buried in an eternal

Noisy, crowded, smoky and dangerous, Buenos Aires in 1900 was typical of the world's major port cities in the age of iron, coal and steam.

twilight and disfigured by the monstrous, gaudy infamies of advertising, streams of vehicles rolled by between marching columns of men, all silent, all intent on business'.[14]

Despite causing such revulsion, ports of the steam age did have a louche appeal for some observers, such as Genet. And with the arrival in the twentieth century of a generation of young machine-obsessed avant-garde artists came a new admiration for such turbulent environments. The Italian Futurist architect Antonio Sant'Elia enthused about them in his 1914 *Manifesto of Futurist Architecture*, extolling a taste for huge machinery, for mobility and for practicality while rejecting the traditional monumentality of cathedrals and palaces. Instead, he enthused over 'big hotels, railway stations, immense roads, colossal ports . . . We must invent and rebuild the Futurist city: it must be like an immense, tumultuous, lively, noble work site, dynamic in all its parts.'[15]

The mad enthusiasm of Sant'Elia was motivated by exactly the aspects of ports that had so disconcerted Huysmans: their mechanistic and dynamic appearance, their speed and heroic scale, their commercial imperative, and their constant state of flux. The Futurists valued these physical attributes, which belonged to the engineering of the quayside, more than the erotic social dynamics of the port that Genet so admired, which were absorbed from the culture of the ship and then embedded in the crevices of the town.

The simple fact was that until very recent times sailors have been characterized as lusty fellows who, when in port, were driven by their sexual desires and an insatiable appetite for reckless adventure. A reputation for having a girl in every port gained respect among fellow mariners. In the days before women joined ships' crews (except for the famously voracious women pirates of the Caribbean), sailors belonged to a club of men who understood the rigours and privations of the ocean life and the exceptional pleasures of shore leave. Only seagoing men shared such knowledge, and their appearance reflected it. The sailor's traditional striped jersey and snug-fitting bell-bottom trousers showed the young mariner's physique off to its best advantage, and a cap raked at a jaunty angle topped out the uniform with a cocky gesture. They looked what they were, men on the make, out for a good time, perhaps with a bit of trouble thrown in. Even a light-hearted Broadway musical, such as Jerome Robbins's and Leonard Bernstein's *On The Town* (1944), the story of three amorous sailors on 24-hour shore leave in Manhattan during World War Two, employs such a stereotype for its main plot device. Wherever they went such men carried the scent of brine and the romance of the ship.

Early in the twentieth century the Russian Constructivist artist, Vladimir Tatlin produced a series of Cubist-inspired drawings and paintings of such young men while himself a sea cadet between 1909 and 1911, when he sailed to ports in Libya, Turkey and Greece. In a self-portrait dated 1912, Tatlin wears the striped jersey, blue denim collar and flat-topped cap of a Russian sailor; his open expression and clear blue eyes add to a robust, healthy countenance, which gives the impression of a young man bursting with life and up for anything. In the background are two full-length figures, also wearing the sailor's uniform that is easily recognizable even in silhouette, both of them in attitudes suggesting readiness for action, the tassels of their caps fluttering in the breeze.

That same generation of sailors were the heroes of the aborted 1905 mutiny aboard the 12,500-ton, 115-m (377-ft) Russian Imperial Navy battleship *Potemkin*, when moored in Odessa harbour on the Ukrainian coast of the Black Sea, where a workers' uprising had broken out in support of the mutineers. The distinctive harbour steps provided the setting for the best-known sequence in Sergei Eisenstein's epic silent film, *Battleship Potemkin*, shot partly in

Odessa in 1925. Although the actual violence had happened in the narrow streets of the old town, the grand flight of steps leading down from the town to the harbour provided a spectacular cinematic backdrop for Eisenstein's montage in which Czarist troops fire on the people of the city, who are gathering to send supplies and greetings out to the anchored ship, the act that prompted the mutineers to fire on government headquarters in the town. The arrival of that ship in the port of Odessa was the catalyst for an event with enormous repercussions leading up to the Revolution of 1917.

Historically, the arrival of any ship in a port brought information, as well as passengers and cargo. In the early days of trans-oceanic travel, ships were the major sources of news from distant places, making the port an information hub in the age before electronic communication or even before the mail. This phenomenon was illustrated in 1848 by the arrival of a steamship in Boston harbour:

When the *Ocean Monarch*, James Murdoch commanding, was overdue in September 1848, an arriving steamship approached Boston pier to encounter over three thousand people, collected along the waterfront and crowding the wharves. The steamer's captain stood on the bridge with his brass speaking trumpet in hand. Before the first lines were hauled to their bollards, he shouted down the news, 'The *Ocean Monarch* was burned off Orm's Head. Four hundred passengers burned or drowned . . . Complete wreck and complete loss.[16]

Maritime Architecture

Venice, one of the greatest maritime powers of the Middle Ages, has also long been considered one of the world's most beautiful ports of call, a pilgrimage site for artists and an inevitable destination for tourists who appreciate painting, sculpture and architecture as well as the city's culinary attractions, cultural events and relaxed pace. The eighteenth-century painter Canaletto famously depicted the canals and lagoon of Venice bathed in a golden light; and in particular he portrayed a festival, *The Bacino di San Marco on Ascension Day* (c. 1733–4). This painting shows the *Bucintoro*, a ceremonial vessel used annually to celebrate the city's principal feast-day, moored in front of the Doge's Palace and awaiting the start of a maritime procession through the lagoon to the Adriatic Sea, where the doge would deliver into the water a blessed ring to reaffirm the 'marriage' between Venice and the sea.

This large galley, built in 1728 at the Arsenale and encrusted with gilded decoration by the sculptor Antonio Corradini, was the last of a series of palatial ships built for the doges that were used for over 600 years to celebrate the *Sposalizio del Mare*. This ship was 50 m (165 ft) long with two decks, the lower one seating its 168 oarsmen and the upper deck a large reception hall for the doge and his party. Following the fall of Venice to Napoleon, this ship survived in altered form under successive foreign rulers until it was finally scrapped in 1824. In Canaletto's view of the ceremony and in similar paintings by Luca Carlevarijs (1710) and Francesco Guardi (1780) the boats of the procession and the *Bucintoro* are seen in relation to the background ensemble of magnificent buildings, harmoniously scaled and sympathetically ornamented to form a seamless composition of structures on water and land, all contributing to the ritual and culture of the Venetian port.

Since the decline of both the city's trade and its naval importance, the Venetian economy has come to rely almost exclusively on tourism, much of which is brought by cruise liners that navigate the ecologically sensitive lagoon and the major canals of the city centre to give passengers on arrival and departure an architectural tour from an unrivalled, elevated vantage point. With the recent

dramatic increase in the overall size of new ships visiting the port, the proportional relationship between the vessel and the cityscape has radically altered to create an almost surreal juxtaposition of the two. No more the grand vessel set against the backdrop of an even grander urban architecture. Now, the sleek, international, hotel-like cruise liners tower above the palaces and churches of the Giudecca Canal, which by contrast seem to resemble the miniature buildings and squares of a model city, a jewel-like toy town.

Even the tall Venetian bell-towers are dwarfed by ships such as the *Grand Princess*, of 109,000 tons, with a length of 290.2 m (952 ft) and a beam of 35.4 m (116 ft). The ship draws 7.9 m (26 ft) of water and stands thirteen decks tall. It carries a crew of over 1,150 and nearly 3,000 passengers, who swarm into the city for a quick glimpse of the medieval, Renaissance and Baroque splendours on offer there, providing a living for the city's important service industries. They also provide a living for the many charlatans selling 'knock-off' Gucci bags

One of more than 500 massive cruise ships that call in Venice each year, P&O's *Grand Princess* looms over the city's historic architecture.

and Pucci scarves in the streets, when the police are not looking, and the many skilled pickpockets who haunt the *vaporetto* stops and other crowded places in the city. *Grand Princess*, like other ocean-going leviathans that visit Venice, looms over the city like a horizontal skyscraper, which then quietly removes itself from the town fabric after an overnight stay, somewhat in the absurd comic manner of an *Archigram* fantasy from the 1960s.

The most impressive architecture of many other port cities is more overtly connected with the business of shipping than are the palaces and churches of Venice, however much the city's maritime economy made them possible. Genet referred to the 'architecturally magnificent' forts, arsenals and jetties of the port in Brest, built in the austere local granite. In Liverpool, too, the city's most important and recognized masonry buildings were constructed in the service of shipping. Among the major centres of art and tourism in Liverpool at present is the converted Albert Dock, designed by two civil engineers, Philip Hardwick and Jesse Hartley, and built between 1841 and 1846; it is now a Grade I Listed Building.

The Albert Dock complex was original in several ways, beginning with its materials. It was the world's first fireproof warehouse, built of granite, sandstone, brick and cast iron, with no structural woodwork. The combination of docks and warehouses, which were also designed to accommodate offices in an enclosed, purpose-designed building complex, was also new, if not a 'first', and had several advantages. The most significant was to enable the stevedores to unload the cargoes from sailing ships directly into the warehouses. Direct loading and unloading greatly speeded up this laborious process and also earned the docks a reputation for security, reducing the rate of theft and damage for the high-value cargoes, such as brandy, cotton, china, ivory and silk, that were then attracted to this state-of-the-art facility. Furthermore, perishable goods such as

tobacco, hemp, tea and sugar kept fresh longer as a result of the building's good ventilation through large, regularly spaced windows that also provided plentiful natural light. The dock was also soon fitted with the newly invented Armstrong hydraulic crane system to facilitate cargo handling. The complex was expanded during its early years to include houses for the harbour master, his assistant and the warehouse master; and a cooperage was added to provide the many thousands of barrels that were the primary cargo containers of the nineteenth century.

Although the docks were enlarged considerably during their first fifty years, they had been designed for sailing ships, and with their narrow entrance they could not accommodate the increasingly large merchant steamships of the late nineteenth century. Furthermore, the absence of a quay, a design innovation that had made the quick and efficient direct loading of sailing ships possible, actually slowed down the loading and unloading of the new and larger steamships, which could be filled and emptied more efficiently onto

Liverpool's Albert Dock, once a cutting-edge cargo facility, is now a heroic survivor of the age of sail, transformed into an upmarket harbourside arts and leisure complex.

a quay; consequently, the use of the Albert Dock declined and the buildings were eventually closed.

The dock's Palladian-inspired colonnade, with its cast-iron Doric columns and distinctive shallow arches, supports the four upper storeys of brick-walled warehousing, its austerity tempered by the contrapuntal rhythms of columns and arches below, with loading doors and windows above. The warm brickwork and sandstone of the upper walls enliven the structure over its cool granite foundations, creating an appearance and ambience that lent itself well to conversion in the 1980s to a chic, high-end leisure and arts complex, home of the Tate Liverpool art gallery, the Merseyside Maritime Museum, two boutique hotels, loft-style apartments, shops and many bars and restaurants, as well as a marina for pleasure boats. Similar lavish conversions of the late twentieth century can be found in the docklands of many leading nineteenth-century port cities including London, Boston and New York. Yet their significance here is their specialized relationships with the technically evolving merchant ships that bore cargoes to them.

In old port cities, where cargo has moved out to new container terminals, architects and developers stretch their aesthetic horizon, as here in Rotterdam's Lloydkwartier.

During the Edwardian era, when the port of Liverpool was the home of the world's most important passenger line and the city was extremely wealthy thanks to shipbuilding and other maritime enterprises, the Cunard company constructed its new headquarters opposite the Pier Head, adjacent to the Albert Dock, and between the two other most significant buildings on the city's waterfront, the Royal Liver Building (1908) and the Port of Liverpool Building (1903). The Cunard headquarters was designed in 1914 by William Edward Willink and Philip Coldwell Thicknesse in collaboration with Arthur J. Davis who, with his partner Charles Mewès, had recently overseen the hotel-like interiors of the Cunard liner *Aquitania*, which entered service in 1914 and is often cited as the most elegant passenger ship of its day.[17] Similarly, it would be difficult to find a more palatial corporate headquarters than Cunard's at the time of its completion in 1917.

The building contained the head offices of the company, which then dominated the North Atlantic passenger trade, and served as the

The boundary between ship and wharfside architecture may blur, as in the case of the 175-room Amstel Botel, a hotel/barge which easily re-located from a central Amsterdam canal to the recently redeveloped NDSM shipyard, a new tourist mecca.

line's main Liverpool passenger terminal until the firm moved its operations to Southampton in the 1960s. The main hall of marble and mosaic was illuminated by a coved ceiling of coloured glass supported by an Ionic colonnade. A classical theme continued throughout the building in combination with nautical motifs and images of the company's best-known pre-World War One ships. Thus, the elaborate portside architecture embodied Cunard's historic pride and current status as industry leader. It also helped to promote that image among the wealthy travellers who passed through the terminal to reach their ship, since this route was for cabin class only. As the starting point of the voyage, the stylish architecture of the terminal was simply extended into the ship, creating a sense of continuity for those passengers boarding a speck of iron about to be launched onto the Atlantic Ocean, perhaps in the midst of a winter storm. Together with the earlier structures along the Pier Head, the Cunard Building also contributed to the visual image of Liverpool as the pre-eminent shipping city of the day on the eve of its decline.

A pilot boat guides the mine-hunter HMS *Shoreham* past lighthouse and breakwater at the mouth of its cosy home port. Smaller harbours often possess an unpretentious maritime character distinct from great port cities.

In addition to warehouses, terminals and corporate headquarters that characterize individual ports around the world, several other building types or structures have made significant contributions to the maritime character of port cities. These include lighthouses, breakwaters, wharves and customs houses, all directly connected with navigation and the ship. In the English Channel port of Shoreham, the modern concrete breakwater provides a sheltered and welcoming entrance for ships arriving at the small commercial and naval harbour, where a medium-sized mine hunter, fishing trawlers, tankers and bulk carriers negotiate a snug lock to reach their docks. The harbour mouth appears to have been invented by Beatrix Potter, with the toy-like Kingston Buci lighthouse, built of French limestone in 1846, and a single line of tiny terraced houses, all standing to attention for the incoming and outgoing ships.

On a significantly grander scale, the Nova Duana (Customs House), sited at the very centre of Barcelona's old port, where Columbus arrived in 1493 after his first American voyage, dominates the city's original harbour with its elaborate Neo-baroque ornamentation.

Dominating Barcelona's old harbour, this grandiose Customs House makes an eye-popping declaration of Catalan economic power based on its historic manufacturing, financial and shipping enterprises.

The building was designed by the prolific Catalan architect Enric Sagnier, with Pere García Faria, and was completed in 1902. Sagnier mixed Gothic, Baroque and *modernista* motifs in lush designs for many apartment houses in the new Eixample area of the city and for important public buildings such as the Customs House, encrusted with sculpture and the coats of arms of Barcelona, Catalonia and Spain, testifying to the importance of the port in Iberian maritime trade. The building was conceived as an eye-popping declaration of Catalan economic power, based on its manufacturing, financial and shipping enterprises. Intense civic and cultural pride was thus invested in the port – still Spain's most important – in the twenty-first century and represented through the grandiosity of the port's architecture, then and now.

Today, the port of Barcelona is one of the busiest in the Mediterranean. Although the city was not favoured with a great natural harbour, centuries of diligent effort have created a major international

The modern Barcelona Logistics Port is now one of the most important cargo terminals in southern Europe.

shipping facility from an unpromising river mouth and delta. Following the death of Generalissimo Francisco Franco in 1975 and the adoption of a new Spanish constitution in 1978, the Autonomous Community of Catalonia flourished economically, and Barcelona in particular developed a reputation for innovation, style and hospitality. It enjoyed the largest late twentieth-century increase in tourism of any Mediterranean city, with the Olympics of 1992 sparking a major redevelopment of the waterfront and beaches. With the huge influx of visitors to the Games, the port augmented the hotel capacity of the city by accommodating eleven of the world's largest cruise ships to provide rooms for the occasion. After such a visible demonstration of its capabilities, the cruise port continued to grow and prosper, up to the onset of economic recession in 2008. A great advantage was the proximity of the cruise terminals to the city centre – it is possible to walk to the central waterfront

A visual conversation between Barcelona's Montjuic Cemetery, the nearby container port and harbour creates a satisfying nexus of timeliness, eternity, motion, stasis and the materiality of this world in relation to what may lie beyond.

district and La Rambla, the geographical spine of old Barcelona, in around 30 minutes from the main Muella de Adosado terminal.

The commercial port grew alongside the tourist facilities, with the arrangements for container traffic achieving a degree of efficiency that led to the port of Barcelona becoming one of the most important cargo terminals in southern Europe. The port's free-trade zone, Zona Franca, dates back to 1916, when it was conceived as a customs-free area for freight in transit. From then on the commercial ambition of the port expanded alongside the transport infrastructure of the road and rail networks and nearby airport, with an advanced, state-of-the-art 'Logistics Park' for containerized freight. The park's design included office space and housing near enough to the town centre to make it a viable neighbourhood, unlike similar developments on the far-flung outskirts of much larger port cities around the world.

The spacious and rational layout of this container port is clearly visible from the Montjuïc Hill, which looms over it and provides expansive views from a number of the city's major sports and cultural amenities and from Barcelona's main cemetery. Built in terraces up the south-eastern slope of the hill, the cemetery itself is highly visible from the harbour and from the many passenger planes approaching the nearby airport – an ever-present reminder of human mortality. Designed by Leandro Albareda, the cemetery today bears a curious resemblance to the nearby shipping port.

That peculiar likeness is evident in the formal structure of the sarcophagi, containing in glass-fronted, box-shaped niches the remains of Barcelona's great civic leaders, merchants and entrepreneurs who built the textile factories, iron works and the ships that imported tobacco and other high-value cargoes from the remaining Spanish colonies of Latin America and from the Caribbean. These containers of the distinguished departed are arranged in horizontal monoliths, flanking spacious avenues, each structure accommodating hundreds of tombs, rectilinear boxes built into the wall, stacked five or six storeys high, reminiscent of the stately *manzanas*, or apartment blocks, of the Eixample and foreshadowing the stacked formations of metal boxes that now stand in the container port at the foot of the hill, themselves suggestive of a Minimalist art installation by Donald Judd or Carl Andre.

The verticality of the cemetery's crosses and funerary monuments is echoed in the tall cranes that loom up like Meccano giraffes over the stacked containers of the logistics port and which lift the boxes, carry them and gracefully deposit them into the vast ships moored at the quays. The conversation between Barcelona's middle-class apartment blocks, Montjuïc Cemetery, the container port and the ships docked there creates a satisfying nexus of formal syncopations, timeliness and eternity, motion and stasis, and the materiality of this world in relation to what may lie beyond.

Barcelona's current engagement with global commerce and its integration with Europe have developed within highly charged national and regional political debates concerning cultural identity, Catalan political autonomy within Spain, and the importance of the Catalan language in relation to Castilian Spanish. This port city is a locus of contrast between its prominence on the world stage and the microscopic communities living within its richly diverse urban fabric, its high international reputation for architecture and design and its medieval heart, its extroverted world view represented by its tourist and cargo ports and the introverted protectionism towards its traditional local culture. Above all, it is a city whose character is saturated with the charismatic presence of the ship.

Nowheresville

Along with monster vessels, the modern container port ranks among the largest man-made features of the world's coastal landscapes, and its startlingly mechanistic appearance has attracted fierce hostility, especially in beauty spots such as the Islands of the Bahamas. During the summer of 2008 in the Bahamian city of Nassau fish merchants and restaurant owners at the picturesque Arawak Cay fumed over a government initiative to construct a new container port in their midst, a plan that quickly became a political football. Former prime minister Perry Christie blasted the proposal, which he said would 'destroy the whole concept of the use of Arawak Cay as a beautiful gateway to Nassau. Under their plan, the first and last site tourists will see is an industrial centre.'[18] Yet the intentions of those who plan and build new ports have little to do with aesthetics or habitat and everything to do with efficiency and the economy of scale.

Thus, one of the clearest features of container ports is their tendency to gigantism, a characteristic demonstrated amply to Josie Dew when the general cargo ship on which she was travelling as a passenger stopped to load freight at Le Havre in 2006. Dew and a fellow traveller took the opportunity to leave the ship for a walk and a look around the city; but they didn't get far:

> Walking through the port of Le Havre is not quite like going for a pleasant saunter in the countryside. It is interminably vast and spectacularly dicey in so far as weaving a path among the furious fleets of gargantuan straddle-carriers and container-loaded articulated trucks is concerned. As we didn't fancy getting mown down among the many bulldozing death traps, we darted in zig-zagging ground-hugging SAS style across the enemy ground of the docks until we

reached the relative safety of the outer fenced-in perimeters of the prisoner-of-port camp.[19]

The Port of New York Authority led the way in growth and mechanization during the 1950s as passenger numbers dropped and cargo handling rose exponentially. With ever larger ships, existing Manhattan and Brooklyn cargo and passenger docks quickly became obsolete, while a vast tract of undeveloped marshland near the town of Elizabeth, New Jersey, offered the opportunity for a purpose-designed terminal, which was to become one of the largest container facilities in the United States covering over 2.4 sq. km (600 acres) by the turn of the millennium. The Port Authority dredged a deep channel from what had been a narrow creek and formed two main slips in the shallow waters of Newark Bay, using the 9.94 million cu. m (13 million cu. yards) of dredged material to fill land for the new terminal that began operation in 1956, the same year that Malcom McLean launched the *Ideal X*.

With the construction of both a new rail link and the New Jersey Turnpike (Interstate 95) in the mid-1950s, and the Port Authority's expansion of Newark Airport next door, the Port Elizabeth terminal was ideally situated and serviced to provide an intermodal hub for freight entering and leaving the north-eastern United States. In addition to the container ship, itself, the final element of this highly complex system of cargo handling was computerization, which was introduced by firms such as McLean's Sea-Land Shipping when they moved into their new administrative building at Port Elizabeth. Their bulky and powerful IBM 360 computer system made it possible to track the arrivals and departures of all Sea-Land's ships and their rapidly expanding tonnage of containers, to provide efficient delivery while yet again reducing labour, this time on the clerical side of their operation.[20]

With the construction of such ports throughout the world by the 1980s, the days of the romantic port city were truly over, and an era of efficient, gigantic satellite cargo ports emerged. Echoing the removal of shops and markets from city centres to out-of-town malls, the new ports developed as entities independent of local communities, relying exclusively on nearby transport links – roads, airports and train lines – to support their shipping activities. They did not spawn a culture of their own, beyond the routine labour of a diminishing number of increasingly skilled dock workers and the clerical officers who became specialists in logistics, employing sophisticated digital tracking systems to monitor their service. New ports are not the sites of bars and brothels (although there is some-times an all-night café or diner), yet they have developed a mystique and a provocative imagery that has appeared increasingly over the years in literature and film.

Whatever interpretations observers may place upon the mecha-nized port, these are sites of industry comparable to the great auto-mobile plants of Detroit in its heyday from the 1920s through the 1950s. Just as the coming of the Model T Ford demanded the continuous expansion of the Albert Kahn-designed River Rouge factory for its mass production, the development of the container ship created a need in the world's cargo ports for much larger berths with bigger 'aprons' or quays to accommodate increasingly large ship-to-shore gantry cranes as well as greater space around the docks to store stacked containers and to manoeuvre the new con-tainer-handling equipment essential to the port's functioning. These machines, such as those that 'terrorized' Josie Dew in Le Havre, in-cluded straddle carriers and other massive articulated vehicles for delivering and collecting containers. Although the container port has not yet found its own Charles Sheeler to translate its audacious geometries into art, its representations in the media have become increasingly dramatic and poetic, adding to the container port's mythology as its history lengthens.

The plot line of the popular American television series *Dexter*, based on the novels of Jeff Lindsay, revolves around a vigilante serial killer's quest to execute the man who had savagely murdered his mother inside a shipping container while he and his young brother looked on. The children of the story were then left for two days in the blood-soaked container, sited in the Port of Miami, with their mother's corpse and the dismembered remains of other victims, until police finally rescued them. The terrible interior quality of the windowless shipping box evokes the eternal darkness of a coffin, just as the stacks of containers in the port of Barcelona echo the stacked tombs in the cemetery opposite. The setting of a shipping container appears repeatedly in the Lindsay novels, with the two brothers meeting years later in a storage box similar to the one in which they were held prisoner as children. During another episode, Dexter discovers a container full of illegal immigrants, half-starved and dehydrated by their long-term incarceration while in transit by ship from the Orient to North America. Here, the container is depicted as a site of human trafficking equal in its horror to the slave ships of the eighteenth and early nineteenth centuries, while the port is portrayed as an amoral no-man's land where any act of brutality can be executed unseen and unreported, despite the elaborate and sophisticated digital tracking and monitoring systems employed by shipping companies.

In purely aesthetic terms, container ports like those of Southampton and Singapore can be seen to have contributed a new type of monumentality to the man-made landscape. Like motorways and modern suspension bridges, the new ports have developed a familiar set of heroic forms that realise the abstract aspirations of the Italian Futurists. They closely resemble the fantastic, large-scale drawings of massively engineered cities created by Antonio Sant'Elia, conceived shortly before he was killed in the mechanical horror of World War One. The modern container port also answers his call for a city that would be in constant movement, like a gigantic machine. In this respect, all new ports exceed the modernity of highways and bridges, whose infrastructures are static, even as they are traversed by millions of fast-moving vehicles. In the port, the infrastructure, itself, is active. The constant coming and going of giant ships delivering and collecting freight set the tone of the port. Giraffe-like cranes are continually in motion, lifting, carrying, placing their cargoes in the ships that will then convey them over the surface of the world's oceans to other ports where robotic creatures of the same lineage – Hyundai of Korea, Associated Hoists of India, Foshan Nanguiwang Cranes of China – will lift and carry them again.

The London-based television company Channel 4 adopted the kinetic image of the container port for one of its celebrated continuity films. *Dock* (aka *Dockyard*) was filmed on location in 2006 at the port of Felixstowe, one of Britain's busiest cargo ports, and then extensively edited using computer animation in post-production. A camera pans slowly across a dense grouping of rubber-tyred cranes (RGTs) as they, themselves, appear to weave around one another, their upper portions gradually forming into an image of the number 4, which then quickly disperses. Such a surrealistic juxtaposition of elements, derived from the practical geometry of a modern container port, conveys the spooky, enigmatic quality of the real port into a cinematic context through the creative use of CGI software.

While the Channel 4 continuity film depicts the port as a magical garden of steel and asphalt, the waterfront garden of the Park Poblenou and the Mar Bella Beach along Barcelona's revitalized waterfront commemorate the maritime history of the district in a lyrical landscape now devoted to leisure and sport, as well as to the

contemplation of nature and to the area's deep association with shipbuilding and the living shipping activity of the nearby harbour. Designed by architects Manuel Ruisánchez and Xavier Vendrell and completed in 1992 to coincide with the Olympic Games, the parkland stretches over an area of pine groves, beaches and sand dunes and incorporates a diverse array of sculptures, some contributed by leading international artists, and others consisting of found objects relating to the railway history of this former industrial neighbourhood. The most prominent installations are parts of ships – bow section, stern, anchor – big chunks of rusting metal recognizable as the remnants of large vessels long ago broken up but not entirely vanished. These are set into the dunes to be seen, touched, used as temporary shelter from the scorching summer sun, but mostly as tangible reminders of the source of Barcelona's past wealth and traditional identity, which live on in the modern working port a few kilometres along the coast.

Big chunks of rusty metal salvaged from long-gone ships can be found decorating redeveloped waterside areas of many port cities. This stern section rests in a new park on Barcelona's Mar Bella Beach.

On the Beach

The true graveyards of ships today, however, are not found in chic waterfront parklands of the developed world, but rather along the underdeveloped beaches of India, Pakistan and Bangladesh, where ships are driven aground at the end of their lives to meet their breakers. These are not ports, in the conventional sense, but they are the last landing places for many of the world's ships. It is in such locations that the meeting place of land and sea has become a most bizarre and controversial site, particularly in light of concern over environmental pollution and exploitation of labour, a concern that has found a voice over the past 30 years. The work of investigative journalists, lone environmental campaigners and organizations such as Greenpeace have exposed the nature of a necessary but problematic industry that has migrated from developed nations, who once built, operated and scrapped the world's ships, first to emerging economies such as Turkey and China and more recently to deeply impoverished areas of the world in neighbourhoods where nationhood has only the most superficial of meanings and regulation barely exists. This, today, is where the story of the ship ends, and it is worth discussing, by way of conclusion.

The subject of ship breaking has long had an emotional edge, reflected in pictorial imagery as far back as 1838, when J.M.W. Turner painted the famous *Fighting Temeraire, Tugged to her Last Berth to be Broken Up*. A once-glorious sailing warrior is shown being towed ignominiously by new-fangled steam tugs to a breaker's dock at John Beaton's wharf at Rotherhithe on the River Thames in London. If ships have a powerful animistic character, connected with their size and appearance as well as their history of service, then we, like Turner, respond to their demise as to that of a well-known personage, with sadness and respect. Yet the reasons for high emotions regarding the disposal of ships have become more complex in the past two hundred years as the sites of ship breaking have moved and evolved. *Temeraire* was scrapped near where it was built and its timbers were largely recycled in England, some of them finding their way into choir benches for a local parish church. Oak from the Royal Navy training ships *Impregnable* and *Hindostan*, both scrapped on the Thames, were famously employed in the rebuilding of the London department store Liberty's in 1922. Shopkeepers and publicans, in particular, prized ships' figureheads, and some were displayed proudly by ship-breakers themselves. And in more recent times such ship-breakers have ensured that every salvageable element of a retired ship was found a new use.

The US Navy took the reverse approach with the hugely symbolic reuse of steel from the collapsed New York World Trade Center in the construction of a new 24,900-ton 209-m (684-ft) battleship, the USS *New York*, launched in 2007. This was a state-of-the-art amphibious transport dock featuring stealth geometry and their first ship designed entirely using CAD technology. Such vessels carry troops, landing craft and helicopters into war zones and incorporate both well decks and a flight deck to launch a variety of airborne and seaborne landing vehicles. New Orleans-based Northrop Grumman Ship Systems recycled 7.5 tons of steel from the ruins of the Trade Center, melted down and cast to form the ship's stem bar, the leading edge of the bow, a piece of metal that evoked from the shipyard workers a respect normally associated with religious relics.

During most of the twentieth century ship breaking continued in the major maritime nations who built and operated the ships. As noted above, Britain's role was long established. In the United States, too, many companies were involved in ship breaking. Notable among them, International Shipbreaking of Brownsville, Texas, was founded in the 1930s to dismantle obsolete vessels and is now the largest and most technically advanced among a small number of American ship-breaking companies remaining in business. With a site totalling 174,014.0 sq. m (43 acres), it is able to dismantle and recycle material from ships up to 304.8 m (1,000 ft) long and 42.6 m (140 ft) in width. Nevertheless, the company has had a chequered history that reflects the changes in approach and attitude to this thorny maritime activity.

International Shipbreaking's Texas port had the advantage of easy access to railways connecting it with Mexican and southern United States mills, which were major customers for scrap steel. Its location near the Mexican border also provided cheap immigrant labour to carry out the dirty and dangerous jobs associated with dismantling large vessels. Under such conditions, International Ship-breaking and other similar businesses around the country operated profitably for decades until the 1980s, when increasing regulation made proper scrapping of ships uneconomic. Such companies re-mained solvent mainly because of US environmental legislation passed in 1994 requiring that government-owned ships be scrapped in American ports.

However, in 1996 the industry was rocked by a series of inves-tigative reports, published in the *Baltimore Sun*, about ship-breaking practices revealed first in the local area then fanning out across the country and throughout the industry. In addition to their exposé of very poor working conditions, the articles by Will Englund and John Carroll reported the scandalously casual treatment of many deadly pollutants released by the scrapping process, citing major safety violations in Maryland, Virginia, Delaware, North Carolina, Rhode Island and California. As a result of such adverse publicity and falling scrap metal prices, the remnants of the American ship-breaking industry were nearly ruined when in 2001 Congress ordered its reserve fleet, consisting largely of World War Two and later-vintage merchant vessels such as the container ship *American Racer*, to be scrapped by 2006 using environmentally sound methods and, in cooperation with the unions, ensuring the workers' safety. To this end, the government put more than $41 million into the project, enabling firms such as International Shipbreaking to invest in the latest recycling technology and protective equipment for its workers, whose jobs were now better regulated. The result was to make the process of breaking naval vessels far more expensive than their scrap value. Thus, such a responsible but non-commercial approach still applied only to government-owned ships, while the privately owned merchant fleet went its own way.

Not all countries have taken such an ethical stand, even in regard to state-owned vessels. In 2004 the French Navy's 43-year-old former lead ship, the 265-m (870-ft) 22,000-ton aircraft carrier *Clemenceau*, built and based in the port of Brest, was scheduled to be scrapped by an Indian ship-breaking company on the infamous Gujurati beach known as Alang. Although this plan contravened the 1989 Basel Convention, intended to ensure the proper disposal of ships, including their toxic contents, *Clemenceau* set sail from France laden with built-in pollutants such as lead, mercury, asbestos and polychlorinated biphenyls. En route, the ship was boarded by activists from the organization Greenpeace. It was a highly-publicized event that embarrassed the French president, Jacques Chirac, and forced him to recall the vessel ignominiously to its home port of Brest, where it sat for two years before sailing to the Teesside Environmental Reclamation and Recycling Centre in the English port of Hartlepool, where the ship was scheduled to be dismantled responsibly. The *Clemenceau* episode displayed to the world how inconsistent and thoroughly capricious is the process of disposing of the world's superannuated shipping tonnage, including famous ships with heroic histories owned by the governments of major naval powers.

The proposed final destination of the *Clemenceau*, Alang beach, had been under the scrutiny of environmentalists since 1997, when resporters from the *Baltimore Sun* visited the site in response to US Navy pressure to repeal the export ban on their ships, thereby allowing them to be scrapped in such ports abroad. Although this never came about, there remained the larger issue of US merchant vessels, which were free to be scrapped anywhere their owners liked. The breakers at Alang compete fiercely for this trade, tending to the destruction of nearly half the world's ships scrapped annually – that is, around 300 of the approximately 700 vessels broken up each year. And many are brought there illegally. In 1999 the Environmental News Service in Bombay reported that Greenpeace and Indian trade unions had charged the huge Anglo-Dutch shipping company P&O Nedlloyd with sending a toxic ship, *Cardigan Bay*, to Alang for breaking after changing its name to *Marion 2* and re-flagging it to avoid identification, thereby violating an Indian Supreme Court ruling banning such hazardous ships from importation.[21] Yet many slip through the legal net. The breaking methods are crude but effective. The process begins with beaching the ship, a dramatic art described by the investigative reporter William Langewiesche, who was on the beach one winter dawn to witness the 'death' of a 157-m (515-ft) general cargo ship, *Pioneer 1*:

A high tide had raised the ocean's level by thirty feet, bringing the waterline a quarter mile inland and nearly to the top of the beach . . . The *Pioneer* came looming out of the darkness, thrashing the ocean's surface with its single screw, raising a large white bow wake as it rushed toward the beach. I could make out the figures of men peering forward from the bridge and the bow. Now the sound of the bow wave, like that of a waterfall, drowned the drumming of the engine. A group of workers who had been standing nearby scattered to safety . . . The

Pioneer kept coming. It was caught by an inshore current that carried it briefly to the side. Then the keel hit the bottom, and the ship drove hard onto the flooded beach, carried by its weight, slowing under full forward power until the rudder no longer functioned and the hull veered out of control and slid to a halt not a hundred yards from where we stood. Anchors the size of cars rattled down the sides and splashed into the shallows. The engine stopped, the lights switched off in succession from bow to stern, and abruptly the *Pioneer* lay dark and still.[22]

Once such a ship is firmly anchored in place by men using small mechanical winches, it joins a fleet of other hulks arranged in a row where the sea meets land. When business is good there could be as many as 200 vessels in various states of demolition, 'submitting to the hands of forty thousand impoverished Indian workers',[23] stripping out the reusable electrics and plumbing, panelling and carpets, emptying oil and hydraulic fluids, and then slicing through the steel of superstructure and hull to deliver manageable pieces of metal to trucks that haul the now unrecognizable scrap away for conversion into reinforcing rods used by the south Asian building industry.[24] Like similar industrial beaches in Pakistan and Bangladesh, Alang is the fiery, smoke-belching hell at the end of a production and consumption cycle that forms the modern world of maritime commerce. It has been estimated that a worker dies there every day of the year, although there is no way accurately to count the human cost of such poisonous labour in an industry that does not keep records and in a country where the air of the cities can be seen as well as smelt and where rivers run with the colours used by local textile factories, dulled by its mixture with human effluent.

The process of ship-breaking reveals the internal immensity of the ship, whatever its type or purpose, seen at last only as form and space stripped of its purpose and, as such, more abstractly poetic than a functional warship, cargo vessel or passenger liner. As Langewiesche argues, such a port as Alang dramatically reflects the economically driven, ungovernable nature of seafaring today and the amoral condition of the ocean, itself. Yet it also exhibits the spatial grandeur of the modern ship and reveals the raw heroism of the people who build, sail, service and destroy them.

The last port. Ship-breaking reveals the internal immensity of a vessel, whatever its type or purpose, seen at last only as form and space.

References

Introduction

1 Le Corbusier, *Towards a New Architecture* (London, 1970), p. 86.
2 Ibid., p. 93.
3 Theorists such as Paul Virilio, writing about speed in relation to modern life, David Pascoe in his study of aircraft, and Mitchell Schwartzer on the motorist's view of the world.
4 Siegfried Giedion, *Mechanization Takes Command* (London, 1975), pp. 10–11.

1 Voyager

1 Gabriel García Marquez, *The Story of a Shipwrecked Sailor,* as told to GGM by Luis Alejandro Velasco (London, 1986), pp. 4–5.
2 Josie Dew, *Saddled at Sea: A 15,000 Mile Journey to New Zealand by Russian Freighter* (London, 2006), pp. 211–12.
3 Gaston Bachelard, *The Poetics of Space* (Boston, MA, 1994), pp. 38–46.
4 Charles Dickens, *American Notes* (London, 1842), chap. 20
5 Stephen Fox, *The Ocean Railway* (London, 2003), pp. 98–9.
6 Dew, *Saddled at Sea*, pp. 62–3.
7 Ibid., pp. 59–60.
8 Henry David Thoreau, *Walden and 'Civil Disobedience'* (New York, 1980), p. 37.
9 Ibid., p. 93.
10 Evelyn Waugh, *Brideshead Revisited* (New York, 1960), pp. 228–9.
11 Ibid., p. 233.
12 Ibid., p. 239.
13 Nicholas Fogg, *The Voyages of the 'Great Britain': Life at Sea in the World's First Liner* (London and Adelaide, 2002), p. 18.
14 Ibid., p. 31.
15 *The Boston Daily Atlas*, 7 June 1852. http://www.bruzelius.info/Nautica/News/

BDA/BDA(1852-06-07).html [accessed 12 August 2009].

16 Despite the United States' prohibition on the importation of African slaves in 1808, pirate ships continued to smuggle slaves into the Southern states until the start of the Civil War in 1861. The fast luxury yacht *Wanderer* and the schooner *Clotilde* were the last two such smuggler ships caught slaving in 1858 and 1859 respectively.

17 Stephen Fox, *The Ocean Railway* (London, 2003), pp. 175–7.

18 Edward A. Steiner; *From Alien to Citizen: The Story of My Life in America* (Grand Rapids, MI, 1914), pp. 37–8.

19 Ibid., p. 181.

20 John A. Butler, *Atlantic Kingdom: America's Contest with Cunard in the Age of Sail and Steam* (Washington, DC, 2001), p. 59.

21 Warren S. Tryon, *My Native Land: Life in America, 1790–1870* (Chicago, 1961), p. 182.

22 David Stevenson, *Ship and Shore: Life in the Merchant Navy* (Whitby, 2001), pp. 137–8.

23 Michel Foucault, 'Des Espace Autres' [Of Other Spaces], *Architecture/Mouvement Continuité* (October 1984), based on a lecture given by Foucault in March 1967. Translated from the French by Jay Miskowiec (http://www.foucault.info/ [accessed 7 July 2008].

24 Ibid.

25 Jack Fritscher, *Titanic* (San Francisco, 1999), pp. 18–19.

26 Lorraine Coons and Alexander Varias, *Tourist Third Cabin: Steamship Travel in the Interwar Years* (New York, 2003), pp. 75–6.

27 Ibid., pp. 66–76.

28 Ibid., p. 79.

29 James Steele, *Queen Mary* (London, 1995), p. 96.

30 Gregory Votolato, *Transport Design: A Travel History* (London, 2007), p. 123.

31 Katherine Anne Porter, *Ship of Fools* (New York, 1962), p. 33.

32 Stevenson, *Ship and Shore*, pp. 139–40.

33 Dew, *Saddled at Sea*, p. 36.

34 Jules Verne, *A Floating City* (Amsterdam, 2002), p. 20.

35 D. Howarth and S. Howarth, *The Story of P&O* (London, 1994), pp. 60–61.

36 Fogg, *The Voyages of the 'Great Britain'*, p. 119.

37 Charlie Connelly, *Attention All Shipping: A Journey round the Shipping Forecast* (London, 2004), pp. 93–4.

38 Fox, *The Ocean Railway*, pp. 218–19.

39 Fogg, *The Voyages of the 'Great Britain'*, pp. 151–2.

40 Russell Lynes, *The Tastemakers* (New York, 1954), p. 89.

41 Anne Wealleans, *Designing Liners: A History of Interior Design Afloat* (London, 2006), p. 21.

42 Ken Baynes and Francis Pugh, *The Art of the Engineer* (Guildford, Surrey, 1981), pp. 159–69.

43 Wealleans, *Designing Liners*, p. 36.

44 Le Corbusier, *Towards a New Architecture* (London, 1982), pp 92–4.

45 Ibid.

46 Wealleans, *Designing Liners*, p. 82. See also Howarth and Howarth, *The Story of P&O*, pp. 130–35 and Victoria and Albert Museum, *The Panelled Rooms: I. The Bromley Room* (London, 1922).

47 Votolato, *Transport Design*, p. 115.

48 Gordon R. Ghareeb, 'A Woman's Touch: The Seagoing Interiors of Dorothy Marckwald', http://home.pacbell.net/steamer/marckwald.html [accessed 20 August 2009].

49 Ibid.

50 Geoffrey Salmon, 'Canberra', *Design* (September 1961), pp. 67–8.

51 Corin Hughes-Stanton et al. 'Queen Elizabeth 2', *Design* (April 1969), pp. 36–76.

52 'Prora Holiday Resort', http://www.johndclare.net/Nazi_Germany3_Prora.htm [accessed 14 September 2009].

53 'The "Strength through Joy" Cruise Ship', http://urban-archolo-gy.blogspot.com/2009/03/strength-through-joy-cruise-ships.html [accessed 14 September 2009].

54 Vittorio Garroni Carbonara, 'Futuristic Cruise Liners', Conference speech presented at *Seatrade Asia Pacific Cruise Convention* (Singapore, December 1996): http://www.cybercruises.com/garronispeech.htm [accessed 27 August 2009].

55 Ibid.

56 Ibid.

57 E. B. White, quoted in Alexis Gregory, *The Golden Age of Travel, 1880–1939* (London, 1998), p. 176.

58 Votolato, *Transport Design*, p. 148.

59 Coons and Varias, *Tourist Third Cabin*, p. 48.

60 Suzanne Fagence-Cooper to the author, 26 October 2009.

61 Ibid.

62 Suzanne Fagence-Cooper, 'Lecturing Cruise Style', *Research Matters* (Buckingham Chilterns University College, Spring 2004).

2 Myth and Image

1 Genesis 16:13–16

2 Roland Barthes, *Mythologies* (London, 1980), p. 74.

3 Ibid.

4 Arthur Rimbaud, *The Drunken Boat* (1871): http://www.mag4.net/Rimbaud/poesies/Boat.html [accessed 10 January 2009].

5 Jules Verne, *Twenty Thousand Leagues Under the Sea* (London, 1992), pp. 262–3.

6 Herman Melville, *Moby-Dick* (New York, 1962), p. 79.

7 Katherine Anne Porter, *Ship of Fools* (New York, 1962), p. 30.

8 David Hornsby, *Ocean Ships* (Shepperton, Middlesex), pp. 18, 24.

9 J.-K. Huysmans, *Against the Grain* (New York, 1969), pp. 18–19.

10 Barthes, *Mythologies*, p. 159.

11 Raymond Loewy, 'White Star Line Advertisement', *National Geographic Magazine*, LII/5 (May 1928).

12 Lorraine Coons and Alexander Varias, *Tourist Third Cabin: Steamship Travel in the Interwar Years* (New York, 2003), pp. 143–4.

13 Ibid., p. 177.

14 Claire O'Mahony, *Brunel and the Art of Invention* (Bristol, 2006), p. 29.

15 Begg was a watercolour painter, illustrator and sculptor who contributed to the *Illustrated London News* between 1896 and 1913. S. Begg, *Illustrated London News* (25 March 1905), pp. 424–5.

16 Gerald Murphy quoted in Calvin Tomkins, *Living Well Is the Best Revenge* (New York, 1971), p. 139.

17 Christos Joachimides and Norman Rosenthal, *American Art in the Twentieth Century: Painting and Sculpture, 1913–1933*, exh. cat., Berlin and London (1993), p. 52.

18 Ibid., p. 55.

19 David Harrison, 'Unveiled: The Clean Queen of the Sea', *The Telegraph* (13 March 2005): http://www.telegraph.co.uk/news/html [accessed 1 September 2009].

20 Peter Cook, *Experimental Architecture* (New York, 1970), pp. 71–4.

21 Sir Alan Peacock, *The Enigmatic Sailor* (Caithness, 2003), pp. 113–14.

22 Ibid., p. 12.

3 Conflict

1 'In 1991, Congress repealed the law prohibiting women serving on combat aircraft in the Air Force and Navy. In 1993, Congress repealed the law barring women from Navy combat ships.' David F. Burrelli, *CRS Issue Brief, 92008*: 'Women in the Armed Forces', Foreign Affairs and National Defense Division (updated 12 December 1996): http://www.fas.org/man/crs/92-008.htm [accessed 24 January 2009].

2 http://www.globalsecurity.org/military/systems/ship/cv-design.htm [accessed 12 February 2009].

3 Jim Prender, 'Sister Ship to Nimitz', *Carrier* (Public Broadcasting System, 2008): http://www.pbs.org/weta/carrier [accessed 25 August 2009].

4 Sir Alan Peacock, *The Enigmatic Sailor* (Caithness, 2003), p. 67.

5 Reyner Banham, *Megastructure: Urban Futures of the Recent Past* (London, 1976), p. 2.

6 Gregory Votolato, *Transport Design: A Travel History* (London, 2007), p. 161.

7 John Hammond Moore, 'The Short, Eventful Life of Eugene B. Ely', *United States Naval Institute Proceedings* (Annapolis, MD, 1981), pp. 58–63.

8 Norman Friedman, *US Aircraft Carriers: An Illustrated Design History* (Annapolis, MD, 1983), p. 243.

9 C. H. Barnes, *Shorts Aircraft since 1900* (London, 1989), pp. 92, 110.

10 http://www.globalsecurity.org/index.html [accessed 26 August 2009].

11 Friedman, *US Aircraft Carriers*, p. 271.

12 Cdr Michael Bosworth, Scott Black and John Meyer, 'Well Deck Deployable Naval Combatants', *Naval Engineers Journal*, published online 18 March 2009 [accessed 26 August 2009].

13 Robert Hughes, *Barcelona* (New York, 1993), pp. 264–71.

14 Ibid.

15 James S. Reyburn, *Electric Boat Corporation* (Charleston, SC, 2006), pp. 4–18.

16 D. Howarth and S. Howarth, *The Story of P&O* (London, 1994), p. 15.

17 Ibid., p. 16.

18 W. Karig, quoted in RADM Jerry Holland, USN (Retd), 'Nimitz', *The Submariner, Undersea Warfare: The Official Magazine of the US Submarine Force*, 18 (Spring 2003): http://www.navy.mil/navydata/cno/n87/usw/issue_18/ [accessed 27 February 2009].

19 Ibid.

20 Frederick Simpich, 'Chemists Make a New World', *National Geographic Magazine*, LXXVII/5 (November 1939), p. 608.

21 Hans Goebeler, *Steel Boat, Iron Hearts: A U-boat Crewman's Life Aboard U-505* (London, 2005), p. 28.

22 David Stevenson, *Ship and Shore: Life in the Merchant Navy* (Whitby, 2001), p. 84.

23 Ibid., pp. 130–31.

24 Ibid., p. 132.

25 Able Seaman Charles Andrews DMC, unpublished ship's log, *HMS Safari*, 1942.

26 Votolato, *Transport Design*, pp. 124–5.

27 Goebeler, *Steel Boats, Iron Hearts*, p. 20.

28 Ibid., p. 165.

29 Raymond Loewy, *Industrial Design* (London and Boston, MA, 1971), pp. 163, 202.

30 Votolato, *Transport Design*, pp. 124–5.

31 Allan C. Fisher, 'You and the Obedient Atom', *National Geographic Magazine*, CXIV/3 (September, 1958), p. 344.

4 Cargo

1 'Boom and Bust at Sea', *The Economist* (18 August 2005). See also *International Shipping: Lifeblood of World Trade*, International Chamber of Shipping promotional film, made to explain the importance of shipping to the health of the world economy, and to convey the message that shipping is safe, clean and comprehensively regulated. The film also stresses the vital need for global

regulation for a global industry. ics@marisec.org.

2 Bernie Woodall, 'US Port Traffic Casts Shadow on Energy Demand', Reuters UK Business and Finance, Thursday, 29 January 2009, 1:00 pm GMT: http://uk.reuters.com/ [accessed 31 January 2009].

3 'Shipping Rates Hit Zero as Trade Sinks', www.thefinancialdaily.com 15 January 2009 [accessed 31 January 2009].

4 *Examelia* is rated at 5,590 tons or 4,981 tons depending on source http://www.theshipslist.com/ships/lines/americanexport.htm [accessed 31 January 2009].

5 Arthur Donovan and Joseph Bonney, *The Box that Changed the World* (East Windsor, NJ, 2006), p. 4.

6 'Seatrain', *Time* (17 October 1932): http://www.time.com/time/magazine/article/0,9171,744603,00.html [accessed 1 February 2009].

7 uboat.net, 'Allied Ships Hit By Uboats': http://uboat.net/allies/merchants/ships/2252.html [accessed 26 August 2009].

8 Michael W. Pocock and MaritimeQuest: http://www.maritimequest.com/daily_event_archive/2005/nov/02_zaandam.htm [accessed 9 February 2009].

9 David Stevenson, *Ship and Shore: Life in the Merchant Navy* (Whitby, 2001), p. 55.

10 Donovan and Bonney, *The Box that Changed the World*, p. 39.

11 Ibid., p. 42.

12 Brian Lavery, *Ship* (London, 2005), p. 360.

13 Donovan and Bonney, *The Box that Changed the World*, pp. 111–12.

14 Bram Stoker, *Dracula* (London, 1897), chap. 7: http://onlinebooks.library.upenn.edu/webbin/gutbook/lookup?num=345 [accessed 1 February 2009].

15 'US Container Security: Feasible or Fantasy?', *Port Strategy*, online edition (6 February 2009): http://www.portstrategy.com/archive101/2008/january-february2 [accessed 6 February 2009].

16 William Langewiesche, *The Outlaw Sea* (New York, 2004), p. 45.

17 Ibid., p. 33.

18 Ibid., pp. 70–81.

19 Josie Dew, *Saddled at Sea* (London, 2006), p. 62.

20 Capt. UK Thapa, *Maritime Terrorism and Lessons for India*, 'Naval Despatch', December 2006, p. 9: http://indiannavy.nic.in/NavDespatch06/Chapter%201.pdf [accessed 15 February 2009].

21 Ibid., p. 11.

22 BBC News Channel, 17:57 GMT, Friday, 21 November 2008: http://news.bbc.co.uk/1/hi/world/africa/7742761.stm [accessed 17 February 2009].

23 'Pirates take "super tanker" towards Somalia', CNN, 17 November 2008: http://edition.cnn.com/2008/WORLD/africa/11/17/kenya.tanker.pirates/index.html?eref=rss_world [accessed 18 February 2009].

24 Efthimios Mitropoulos, interviewed by Gavin Essler, *Hardtalk*, BBC News, 18 February 2009: http://news.bbc.co.uk/1/hi/programmes/hardtalk/7897100.stm [accessed 19 February 2009].

25 http://themaritimeblog.com/1255/greenpeace-hijacks-bulk-cargo-ship [accessed 10 November 2009].

26 Stevenson, *Ship and Shore*, p. 145.

27 Ibid., p. 150.

28 Ibid., pp. 8–10.

29 International Maritime Organization, *Go-Ballast Partnerships* (London, 2000–9): http://globallast.imo.org/index.asp [accessed 25 February 2009].

30 'Tall Ships Make a Comeback as Oil Price Hits Exports', *The Times*, 23 July 2008, http://www.timesonline.co.uk/tol/news/environment/article4380921.ece [accessed 15 November 2009].

31 J. Samuel Barkin 'The Counterintuitive Relationship between Globalization and Climate Change', *Global Environmental Politics*, III/3 (August 2003), pp. 8–13.

32 Royal Institution of Naval Architects, *International Symposium On Ship Design and Construction 2009: The Environmentally Friendly Ship* (London, 2009): http://www.rina.org.uk/ISSDC2009 [accessed 10 November 2009].

33 Michelle Wiese Bockmann, 'Baltic Chief: We Must Uphold Self-regulation Standards', *Lloyd's List*, 10 February 2006: http://www.lloydslist.com/ll/home/blogView.htm;jsessionid [accessed 19 February 2009].

5 Port

1 Suzanne Fagence-Cooper, 'Lecturing Cruise Style', *Research Matters* (Buckingham Chilterns University College, Spring 2004).

2 Edward A. Steiner, cited in 'Immigration: The Living Mosaic of People, Culture and Hope', *Thinkquest*: http://library.thinkquest.org/20619/Past.html [accessed 2 September 2009].

3 'The Detained Immigrant', *Harper's Weekly* (26 August 1893): http://www.fortunecity.com/littleitaly/amalfi/100/deten93.htm [accessed 2 September 2009].

4 George Voskovec, cited in 'Immigration', *Thinkquest*: http://library.thinkquest.org/20619/index.html [accessed 20 October 2009].

5 David Stevenson, *Ship and Shore: Life in the Merchant Navy* (Whitby, 2001), p. 148.

6 Albert Camus, *Notebooks, 1935–1942* (New York, 1963), vol. I, p. 14.

7 Jean Genet, *Querelle of Brest* (London, 1984), p. 8.

8 Ibid., p. 27.

9 Brassaï, *The Secret Paris of the 1930s* (London, 1976), n.p.

10 Katherine Ann Porter, *Ship of Fools* (New York, 1963), p. 5.

11 Stevenson, *Ship and Shore*, p. 149.

12 Edward A. Steiner, *From Alien to Citizen: The Story of My Life in America* (New York, 1914), p. 30.

13 Porter, *Ship of Fools* p. 16.

14 J.-K. Huysmans, *Against the Grain* (London and Toronto, 1969), p. 121.

15 Antonio Sant' Elia and Filippo Tommaso Marinetti, *Futurist Architecture* [1914], in U. Conrads, *Programmes and Manifestoes on Twentieth Century Architecture* (London, 1970), pp. 35–6.

16 John A. Butler, *Atlantic Kingdom: America's Contest with Cunard in the Age of Sail and Steam* (Washington, DC, 2001), pp. 163–4.

17 Anne Wealleans, *Designing Liners: A History of Interior Design Afloat* (London, 2006), pp. 66–7.

18 'Arawak Cay Vendors Protest Port Move', *ReEarth, Environmental Issues in the Islands of the Bahamas*: http://reearth.org/?p=509 (2 June 2008) [accessed 6 September 2009].

19 Josie Dew, *Saddled at Sea: A 15,000 Mile Journey to New Zealand by Russian Freighter* (London, 2006), p. 43.

20 Arthur Donovan and Joseph Bonney, *The Box that Changed the World* (East Windsor, NJ, 2006), pp. 84–5.

21 Frederick Noronha, 'Indian Unions, Greenpeace: Toxic Ship Sneaked In', *Environmental News Service* (Bombay, 20 March 1999): http://www.ban.org/BAN_NEWS/indian_unions.html [accessed 10 November 2009] .

22 William Langewiesche, *The Outlaw Sea* (New York, 2004), pp. 198–200.

23 Ibid., p. 201.

24 Ibid., p. 224.

Select Bibliography

Andrews, Charles, DMC, unpublished ship's log, *HMS Safari*, 1942

Bachelard, Gaston, *The Poetics of Space* (Boston, MA, 1994)

Banham, Reyner, *Megastructure: Urban Futures of the Recent Past* (London, 1976)

Barkin, J. Samuel, 'The Counterintuitive Relationship between Globalization and Climate Change', *Global Environmental Politics*, III/3 (August 2003)

Barnes, C. H., *Shorts Aircraft since 1900* (London, 1989)

Barthes, Roland, *Mythologies* (London, 1980)

Baynes, Ken, and Francis Pugh, *The Art of the Engineer* (Guildford, Surrey, 1981)

'Boom and Bust at Sea', *The Economist*, print edition (London, 18 August 2005)

Bosworth, Cdr Michael, Scott Black and John Meyer, 'Well Deck Deployable Naval Combatants', *Naval Engineers Journal,* CVI/1, published 18 March 2009 [accessed 26 August 2009]

Brassaï, *The Secret Paris of the 1930s* (London, 1976)

Butler, John A., *Atlantic Kingdom: America's Contest with Cunard in the Age of Sail and Steam* (Washington, DC, 2001)

Camus, Albert, *Notebooks, 1935–1942* (New York, 1963), vol. I

Connelly, Charlie, *Attention All Shipping: A Journey round the Shipping Forecast* (London, 2004)

Cook, Peter, *Experimental Architecture* (New York, 1970)

Coons, Lorraine, and Alexander Varias, *Tourist Third Cabin: Steamship Travel in the Interwar Years* (New York, 2003)

'The Detained Immigrant', *Harper's Weekly* (26 August 1893)

Dew, Josie, *Saddled at Sea: A 15,000 Mile Journey to New Zealand by Russian Freighter* (London, 2006)

Dickens, Charles, *American Notes* (London, 1842)

Donovan, Arthur, and Joseph Bonney, *The Box that Changed the World* (East Windsor, NJ, 2006)

Fagence-Cooper, Suzanne, 'Lecturing Cruise Style', *Research Matters* (Buckingham Chilterns University College, Spring 2004)

Fisher, Allan C., 'You and the Obedient Atom', *National Geographic Magazine*,

CXIV/3 (September, 1958)

Fogg, Nicholas, *The Voyages of the Great Britain: Life at Sea in the World's First Liner* (London and Adelaide, 2002)

Foucault, Michel, 'Des Espace Autres' *Architecture /Mouvement/ Continuité* (October 1984)

Fox, Stephen, *The Ocean Railway* (London, 2003)

Friedman, Norman, *US Aircraft Carriers: An Illustrated Design History* (Annapolis, MD, 1983)

Fritscher, Jack, *Titanic* (San Francisco, 1999)

Genet, Jean, *Querelle of Brest* (London, 1984)

Giedion, Siegfried, *Mechanization Takes Command* (London, 1975)

Goebeler, Hans, *Steel Boat, Iron Hearts: A U-boat Crewman's Life Aboard U-505* (London, 2005)

Harrison, David, 'Unveiled: The Clean Queen of the Sea', *The Telegraph* (London, 13 March 2005)

Hornsby, David, *Ocean Ships* (Shepperton, 1998)

Howarth, D., and S. Howarth, *The Story of P&O* (London, 1994)

Hughes, Robert, *Barcelona* (New York, 1993)

Hughes-Stanton, Corin,, et al., 'Queen Elizabeth 2', *Design* (April 1969)

Huysmans, J.-K., *Against the Grain* (London and Toronto, 1969)

Joachimides, Christos and Norman Rosenthal, *American Art in the Twentieth Century: Painting and Sculpture, 1913–1993*, exh. cat., Berlin and London (1993)

Langewiesche, William, *The Outlaw Sea* (New York, 2004)

Lavery, Brian, *Ship* (London, 2005)

Le Corbusier, *Towards a New Architecture* (London, 1982)

Levinson, M., *The Box: How the Shipping Container Made the World Smaller and the World Economy Bigger* (Princeton, NJ, 2006)

Loewy, Raymond, *Industrial Design* (London and Boston, MA, 1971)

Lynes, Russell, *The Tastemakers* (New York, 1954)

Márquez, Gabriel García, *The Story of a Shipwrecked Sailor, as Told to GGM by Luis Alejandro Velasco* (London, 1986)

Melville, Herman, *Moby-Dick* (New York, 1962)

Moore, John Hammond, 'The Short, Eventful Life of Eugene B. Ely', *United States Naval Institute Proceedings* (Annapolis, MD, January 1981)

O'Mahony, Claire, *Brunel and the Art of Invention* (Bristol, 2006)

Peacock, Sir Alan, *The Enigmatic Sailor* (Caithness, 2003)

Porter, Katherine Anne, *Ship of Fools* (New York, 1962)

Reyburn, James S., *Electric Boat Corporation* (Charleston, SC, 2006)

Rimbaud, Arthur, *The Drunken Boat* (1871)

Salmon, Geoffrey, 'Canberra', *Design* (September 1961)

Sant' Elia, Antonio, and Filippo Tommaso Marinetti, 'Futurist Architecture', 1914, in U. Conrads, *Programmes and Manifestoes on Twentieth Century Architecture* (London, 1970)

'Seatrain', *Time* (17 October 1932)

Simpich, Frederick, 'Chemists Make a New World', *National Geographic Magazine,* LXXVI/5 (November, 1939)

Steele, James, *Queen Mary* (London, 1995)

Steiner, Edward A., *From Alien to Citizen: The Story of My Life in America* (Grand Rapids MI, 1914)

Stevenson, *David, Ship and Shore: Life in the Merchant Navy* (Whitby, 2001)

Stoker, Bram, *Dracula* (London, 1897)

Suzanne Fagence-Cooper, letter to the author (26 October 2009)

'Tall Ships Make a Comeback as Oil Price Hits Exports', *The Times* (London, 23 July 2008)

Thoreau, Henry David, *Walden and 'Civil Disobedience'* (New York, 1980)

Tomkins, Calvin, *Living Well is the Best Revenge* (New York, 1971)

Tryon, Warren S., *My Native Land: Life in America 1790–1870* (Chicago, 1961)

Verne, Jules, *A Floating City* (Amsterdam, 2002)

Verne, Jules, *Propeller Island* (London, 1965)

Verne, Jules, *Twenty Thousand Leagues Under the Sea* (London, 1992)

Victoria & Albert Museum, *The Panelled Rooms: I. The Bromley Room* (London, 1922)

Votolato, Gregory, *Transport Design: A Travel History* (London, 2007)

Waugh, Evelyn, *Brideshead Revisited* (New York, 1960)

Wealleans, Anne, *Designing Liners: A History of Interior Design Afloat* (London, 2006)

Acknowledgements

When I was invited to write a book titled *Ship* for Reaktion's Objekt series, I was intrigued but wondered what I could add to the vast literature on that subject. I had researched ships and boats for my recently published *Transport Design: A Travel History* (Reaktion, 2007) and therefore had some idea of the themes and issues surrounding the ship, those that interested me and that I hoped would interest readers approaching the subject from a variety of disciplines, perspectives and levels of knowledge. With the encouragement of my publisher, I began to think that I could make connections between history, technology, literature, society and art that were often absent from specialist literature. And so I would first like to thank Vivian Constantinopoulos for entrusting me with this endlessly rich subject.

I realised the benefit of having spent many hours of my youth 'messing around in boats', a relatively idle pastime that, nevertheless, put me frequently within sight of big ferries, frighteningly bigger cargo vessels and the occasional destroyer, flat-top or submarine. Mercifully, these were nearly always seen from a safe distance, as they hogged the shipping channel and I hugged the shore. Sometimes, however, I was close enough to feel their enormous power when crossing a sickeningly large wake in my tiny racing sloop. Thanks for that go to my brother, Arthur, for the gift of sailing. In later years my connection with the sea diminished to the occasional voyage on a Baltic, Mediterranean or English Channel ferry and a couple of North Atlantic crossings, as ships became for me exotic objects, hardly ever seen when living, as I did, away from the coast.

Yet the opportunity to write about the greatest moving objects ever built was irresistible, and the notion that they are hard to see added a necessary challenge and suggested including a chapter on ports, where ships are most often visible to the general population. During many visits over the years to ports and harbours around the world, certain individuals have guided me expertly through these diverse and amazing places. Among them, I owe particular thanks to Xavier Garriga and Jose Maria Abadal for their tireless efforts to familiarize me with the Barcelona waterfront and its historic connection with the city, and to Rodrigo Boufleur for an intensive introduction to the Brazilian port of Santos. My gratitude also goes to Dr Russ Ricci for accompanying me on various explorations of New York City's maritime history and for his acute observations along the way. That mysterious relationship between the ship and the shore, which developed as a major theme in this book, was clarified for me in conversation and correspondence with Noeline Thompson-Bee. Peter Cornish also added significantly to my appreciation of harbour geography and its importance in this work.

Many colleagues contributed useful advice and information that found its way into the previous pages. Suzanne Fagence-Cooper was a mine of information on contemporary liner travel. Professor Anne Massey, who has written and lectured extensively on historic ocean liner design, liberally offered ideas, information and inspiration throughout this project. Professor Arthur Donovan lent his experience, encouragement and contacts at the beginning of my research. For opening up an entirely new way of understanding shipping routes and for his insight into the port city, I thank Professor John Andrews. John's colleague, Dr Ivana Wingham, gave me the opportunity to test my work in progress by contributing to *The Mobility of the Line Conference* at Brighton University in 2009. Similarly, Professor Priscila Lena Farias invited me to present a keynote lecture at the *P&D Design, 8th Brazilian Congress on Design, Research & Development* in 2008, a talk based on research for this book. Claire I. O'Mahony, who organised the conference *Modern Voyages: Sea Travel Since Brunel* at Bristol University in 2006, introduced me to the brilliant restoration and interpretation of SS *Great Britain* and to a group of ship scholars including Bruce Peter and Professor Tim Unwin, whose conference papers and writings informed this work. All the above experiences broadened my knowledge and understanding of the ship as an element of the global transport fabric and as a designed object in its own right.

Among the many friends, relatives, students and academics who contributed to a rich stream of sources that fed the pool of material from which I constructed this story of the ship, Stella Whalley, Barbara Sokolski, Greer Crawley and Dolores Barchi were notable for their interest and generosity. Inscrutable technical aspects of the modern submarine were carefully explained to me by James Shaw, formerly of Electric Boat Corporation. My son, Max Votolato, shed light on the role of Toyota in the development of the culture and economy of the Port of Los Angeles. Ed Ritchie piloted the light plane from which I shot aerial photographs to illustrate this book.

For a relative landlubber like myself, visits to historic ships and museums have provided valuable opportunities for direct observation of some of the world's greatest surviving historic vessels and their terrestrial infrastructure. Such visits also enabled me to consult those people most familiar with the objects, themselves, in terms of their curation, conservation and interpretation. Among the most important of these sites and museums were the Ellis Island Immigration Museum, USS Intrepid Sea Air and Space Museum and the New York Yacht Club in Manhattan, SS *Queen Mary* and the Soviet submarine *Scorpion* in Long Beach, California, USS *Nautilus* in Groton, Connecticut, HMS *Belfast*, the clipper ship *Cutty Sark* and the National Maritime Museum in London, the SS *Great Britain* in Bristol, Merseyside Maritime Museum in Liverpool's Albert Dock and Museu Maritim de Barcelona.

Towards the completion of the project, Robert Williams at Reaktion Books demonstrated his editorial wisdom through much helpful advice; Danuta Votolato provided generous technical support whenever I needed it.

Photo Acknowledgements

The author and publishers wish to express their thanks to the below sources of illustrative material and/or permission to reproduce it:

Jose Maria Abadal; p. 271; Courtesy of John Andrews: pp. 162, 163; Photo courtesy Jim Bar: p. 243; Deutsche Marine: p. 226; Marta Gutowska: p. 95; Courtesy of Laurence Lowry: p. 58; Library of Congress, Washington, DC: pp. 12, 14, 21, 26, 27, 29, 34, 41, 45, 46, 48, 55, 71, 75, 80, 93, 99, 104, 117, 137, 144, 145, 147, 148, 151, 160, 171, 173, 174, 181, 184, 185, 201, 204, 218, 230, 232, 234, 246, 250, 261; © Estate of Gerald Murphy / DACS, London / VAGA, New York 2010: p. 109; National Oceanic and Atmospheric Administration, Washington, DC: p. 224; Stock xchng: pp. 66, 257, 67 (David Buswell), 70 (Gregory Runyan), 87 (Alvaro Campo), 88 (Bjarte Kvinge Tvedt), 128 (Martin Boulanger), 146 (Antonio Jiménez Alonso), 178, 191, 194 centre (Athewma Athewma), 190 (Chutiporn Chaitachawong), 194 top (Christian Ferrari), 198 (Carsten Lenz), 209 (Bruce Tuffin), 210 (Stefano Barni), 241 (Ian Beeby), 242, 279 (John Nyberg), 244 (Pasqualantoio Pingue), 255 (Attila Butjas), 258 (Roger Waleson), 262 (Jelle Wiedema); Jeff Tabaco: p. 121; US Coast Guard, Washington, DC: p. 222; US National Archives, Washington DC: p. 221; US Navy, Washington, DC: pp. 84, 124, 129, 132, 135, 139, 142; Virtual Steve: p. 33; Gregory Votolato: pp. 6, 16, 22, 32, 39, 42, 78, 85, 86, 91, 94 top and bottom, 100, 105, 141, 165, 167, 236, 237, 240, 259, 260, 263; Courtesy Max Votolato: pp. 196, 197, 208.

Index